The House-Tree-Person Technique
————Revised Manual————

John N. Buck

Published by

WESTERN PSYCHOLOGICAL SERVICES
Publishers and Distributors
12031 Wilshire Boulevard
Los Angeles, California 90025

The House-Tree-Person Technique: Revised Manual
Library of Congress Catalog Card Number: 65-28468
Standard Book Number: 87424-301-7

Eighth Printing .... October 1987

DEDICATION

This book, embodying many years of clinical and experimental study, is dedicated to my wife, Fan, without whose limitless patience, constructive criticism, and never-failing encouragement the House—Tree—Person projective technique would never have been developed.

ACKNOWLEDGMENTS

In this revision of the original H—T—P Manual, the author has been aided greatly by the contributions of Dr. Emanuel F. Hammer, Mr. Isaac Jolles, Miss Selma Landisberg, and Dr. V. J. Bieliauskas. Grateful acknowledgment is made for suggestions offered by Mrs. William N. Whitehead, Miss Hannah Davis, Mrs. Audrey Mailer, Miss Patricia Nigg, Mr. John F. Hurley, Mr. Bernard Meiselman, Mr. Allen Cohen, and the late Mr. Daniel Hutton.

The author expresses his deep indebtedness to Dr. Fred C. Thorne, Editor of the *Journal of Clinical Psychology* for permission to draw freely upon the original H—T—P Manual material and upon various articles on the H—T—P Technique published in that Journal. Gratitude is expressed also for the editorial assistance of Dr. Morse P. Manson.

TABLE OF CONTENTS

TABLES

FIGURES

Chapter 1   Description

The House—Tree—Person (or H—T—P) is a technique designed to aid the clinician in obtaining information concerning an individual's sensitivity, maturity, flexibility, efficiency, degree of personality integration, and interaction with the environment, specifically and generally.

The H—T—P is a two-phased, four-step clinical approach to a meaningful analysis of the total personality within its milieu.

In *Phase One*, the first step in testing is non-verbal, creative and almost completely unstructured; the medium of expression is relatively primitive: the freehand. pencil drawing of a House, a Tree, and a Person.

The second step is verbal, apperceptive, and more formally structured: in it the subject (hereinafter referred to as S) is given an opportunity to describe, define, and interpret his drawn objects and their respective environments, and to associate concerning them.

In *Phase Two,* the first step again involves the freehand drawing of a House, a Tree, and a Person, but with crayons.

The second step provides the S with the opportunity (albeit in more limited fashion than in step two of *Phase One*) to describe, define and interpret his chromatic drawings of a House, a Tree, and a Person, and to associate concerning them and their respective environments.

The present form of the H—T—P technique has evolved over more than twenty-five years of study and clinical application. In 1938, freehand pencil drawings of House, Tree, and Person were sought only because it had been discovered that withdrawn Ss tended to respond more freely to interrogation while actively engaged in drawing these objects, and it was found clinically useful to take advantage of this "pencil release" factor to facilitate verbalizations on the S's part.

The objects of House, Tree, and Person were chosen because they (1) were familiar items or concepts even to very young children; (2) were more willingly accepted for drawing by Ss of all ages and types than were

1

other suggested objects; and (3) appeared to stimulate more frank and free verbalization than did other items.

It was soon discovered that although Houses, Trees, and Persons could be drawn in an almost infinite variety of ways, a quantitative scoring system could be (and was) devised to elicit useful information concerning the level of an S's intellectual function. And not long thereafter it was found that more valuable information concerning the non-intellective aspects of the personality could be derived from intensive qualitative analysis of the drawings. Finally it became evident that, with a carefully designed post-drawing interrogation system, more accurate interpretation of the graphic productions could be made and additional analytic material (verbal) could be brought out.

The author feels strongly that the H–T–P may be employed usefully in individual examinations to provide the clinical psychologist, psychiatrist, or other qualified examiner with diagnostically and prognostically significant data concerning Ss which otherwise might take much more time to acquire. H–T–P re-examinations made during the course of an individual's progress while under treatment provide a valuable check upon the validity of changes occurring during therapy.

The H–T–P may be used in therapeusis. Free association can be facilitated by presenting first one and then another of the drawings to an S with the comment: "Certain people might see this as _____. What does it suggest to you?" Ultimately the S may be presented with increasingly deeper interpretations of his drawings, comments and associations related thereto to help him gain insight.

The H–T–P has been used to good advantage in other ways: (1) group testing, as a screening device (by itself or in a battery of tests) to identify the maladjusted; (2) to evaluate an S's adjustment prior to entrance into a school or specialized training program; (3) to appraise personality integration and adjustments prior to employment; (4) as a research tool to identify personality factors common to Ss of a given group.

THEORETICAL POSTULATES

Postulate 1: *The H–T–P is a projective device.*

Conventionally it is argued that a clinical procedure to qualify as a *projective device* must present an S with a stimulus so ambiguous or unstructured, in fact or in effect, that the meaning which the S assigns to the stimulus must emanate from the S himself. The best known projective techniques are the Rorschach with its relatively unstructured ink blots and the Thematic Apperception Test (TAT) with its comparatively ambiguous story-evoking pictures.

At first it might be thought that the stimuli presented in the H–T–P in the drawing steps of the two phases (the only constant stimulus is the printed word *House,* or *Tree,* or *Person* at the top of the respective drawing page) are too unambiguous and too well-structured for the H—T—P to qualify as a projective device. More careful examination, however, reveals that H—T—P structuring is slight and H—T—P stimuli are highly ambiguous.

An S is told to draw a House, a Tree, and a Person, *but* he is *not* told which House, Tree, or Person to draw, and he is *not* restricted or directed as to the type, size, age, condition, or method of presentation of his House; the species, size, age, condition, or method of presentation of his Tree; the sex, age, race, size, apparel, state of health, action or inaction, or method of presentation of his Person. Even very young children have seen many houses and trees and have become emotionally involved with a number of persons, and these experiences are the precursors of H—T—P projection. The S, then, must construct a single (or composite) picture of a House, a Tree, and a Person from among the many of each he has seen and with which he has become emotionally involved.

In the second step of each phase (Post-Drawing Interrogation) the only constant stimulus is the drawing of the House, the Tree, and the Person which the S has produced. These graphic productions (themselves projections) tend to stimulate verbal projection.

Postulate II: The H—T—P measures intellectual function in a situation deliberately designed to activate non-intellective aspects of the personality which enhance or diminish efficiency of intellectual function.

In the non-verbal steps, the specific problem is the reproduction, in two-dimensional form, of a memory image, (or, as is frequently the case, a combination of memory images) in three-dimensional form, first with a pencil and then with crayons.

The S's level of intellectual function is appraised from: (1) elemental information (details); (2) size and spatial relationships (proportion and perspective); (3) concept formation (as evidenced by the organization and quality of the completed wholes); and (4) vocabulary.

Postulate III: Each drawn whole — the House, the Tree, and the Person — is regarded as a psychological self-portrait of the S as well as the drawing of a specific (or composite) House, Tree, and Person, respectively.

By *self-portrait* is meant far more than body-projection *per se.*

Postulate IV: Each drawing arouses strong conscious, subconscious, and unconscious associations.

The House, a dwelling place (and as such usually it is the site of the S's most intimate interpersonal relationships), tends to arouse associations concerning home and those living in the home with him. The Tree, an inanimate living (or once-living) thing, stimulates associations concerning the S's life-role and ability to derive satisfactions in and from his environment in general. The Person, a living (or once-living) human being, arouses associations of interpersonal relationships, specific and general. In each instance, the past, present, and future (psychologically and chronologically) all may be involved.

On a continuum of association-arousal levels ranging from conscious to unconscious, the Person lies farthest to the left, the Tree farthest to the right, and the House somewhere in between.

Postulate V: Any emotion exhibited by the S while drawing or being questioned concerning his drawings is presumed to represent an emotional reaction to the relationships, situations, needs or presses. or other dynamics which the S feels are directly or symbolically represented or suggested by one or more of his drawings or a part thereof.

Postulate VI: No detail or combination of details in the H—T—P has a single fixed or absolute meaning.

It has been observed convincingly that the meaning (or meanings) assigned by an S' to a given detail or combination of details, or the method of its presentation often is completely different from the usually accepted symbolic meaning (or meanings).

Qualitative signs in the H—T—P are regarded as signposts only; never as having fixed invariable diagnostic significance. Obviously, however, the greater the number of diagnostic signposts pointing toward a specific maladjustment (and the greater the magnitude of their deviation from the average), the greater is the likelihood that the suggested maladjustment is, in fact, present.

Postulate VII: An S may indicate that a given detail or combination of details, or his method of its presentation, is of special significance to him in two ways:

Positively by:

(a) overtly exhibiting emotion before, during, or after drawing a detail or combination of details, or while commenting upon the detail or combination of details while drawing or during the Post-Drawing Interrogation;

(b) presenting a detail or combination of details in a sequential order that deviates from the average;

(c) exhibiting unusual concern over the presentation of a detail or detail combination, as by: (1) erasing excessively — particularly when the erasure is not followed by improvement in form, or (2) returning to the detail or combination of details one or more times during the drawing of the given or some subsequent whole, or (3) using excessive time in drawing the detail or combination of details;

(d) presenting the detail or combination of details in a deviant or frankly bizarre manner;

(e) perseverating in the presentation of a given detail;

(f) making a frank comment (spontaneous or induced) concerning a whole drawing or any part thereof.

Negatively by:

(a) omitting one or more "essential" details;

(b) presenting incompletely a detail or combination of details;

(c) commenting evasively, or refusing to comment about a whole or any part thereof in the Post-Drawing Interrogation.

Postulate VIII: Accurate interpretation of a detail or a combination of details can be made only after its relationship to the configuration has been established.

Postulate IX: Interpretation of an S's H—T—P productions must be made with great care and caution and with as complete a knowledge of the S and his milieu (past and present) as can be obtained.

Blind analyses of H—T—P protocols can and have been made with great accuracy, and blind analysis is of value in studies of the validity of projective techniques. But the author feels strongly that blind analysis should not be used in clinical practice. The competent examiner will not permit himself to become "history bound", so to speak, and he will wish to know as much as he can about the presumptively traumatic experiences the S has had: of particular interest will be those experiences which have not produced the traumatic scarring that might have been expected.

Postulate X: The S's reaction to color and his use of color in the H—T—P chromatic phase furnish evidence of the S's tolerance of, control of, and reaction to additional emotion-arousing stimuli at a time when he may be extremely vulnerable to such stimuli.

Postulate XI: Comparison of the quantitative and qualitative analyses of the achromatic and the chromatic sets of H—T—P drawings provides insight into the degree of permanence of the S's present demonstrated functioning level of intelligence and the permanence and magnitude of his attitudes, emotional reactions, and other manifested behavior.

If the S is only mildly maladjusted, his chromatic drawings ordinarily will differ but little from his achromatic drawings quantitatively and qualitatively, and neither set will be more than mildly pathoformic. But if the S is severely maladjusted, many of the pathoformic characteristics revealed in the achromatic drawings will be repeated (often in exaggerated form) in the chromatic drawings, and other signs of maladjustment often will appear for the first time.

Postulate XII: H—T—P achromatic and chromatic drawings are highly sensitive to and speedily reflect the presence of psychopathological factors in an S's personality.

It has been found that evidence of the presence of disruptive and destructive elements within the personality appear in the H—T—P drawings early in the development of a pattern of maladjustment and are often of greater magnitude than the clinical picture would suggest. It has been found, also, that pathological signs persist in the H—T—P drawings for a time (occasionally for a long time) after the S apparently fully recovers.

Postulate XIII: The achromatic-chromatic H−T−P is a longitudinal study in miniature of an S since it demands that he perform essentially the same graphic and verbal tasks at two different time periods.

True, chronologically the time lapse is slight, but psychologically it can prove to be great. The concept of "psychological time" is used to account for the marked change which frequently occurs in an S as a result of drawing his achromatic House, Tree, and Person and being questioned at length concerning them. A change of this magnitude ordinarily would occur only after the passage of far more objective time.

Chapter 2   Standardization Studies

When it was recognized that the H–T–P might serve as a measure of intelligence, it was decided to construct a system of quantitative scoring, which would be more objective than mere analysis by inspection.

It was not difficult to devise a simple point score system, which differentiated accurately between relatively gross classification levels of intelligence; but this system was found to have the same flaws as those like it, based upon the premise that the sum of a given number of points constituted an adequate evaluation of intelligence level; further, it tended to produce only a relatively sterile figure of constricted meaning, i.e., to permit much worthy of specific note to go to waste. For example, it made no provision for scoring that which was not drawn or for providing differential score weights for what was or was not drawn. Accordingly, it was decided to attempt to establish tentative norms for adult intelligence (an adult arbitrarily was defined as one 15 years or older).

Subjects. Because it was impossible to secure an adequate random sample from the general adult population, it was decided to use a restricted but carefully selected sample of 120 adults at six intelligence levels (imbecile, moron, borderline, dull average, average, and above average); later a group of 20 superior Ss was added who, as far as could be ascertained, had no marked personality flaws which might cause them to produce "abnormal" drawings. The number of Ss at each intelligence level arbitrarily was set at 20.

Ss in the imbecile level through the average level were white residents of Virginia, patients or employees of the Lynchburg State Colony, Colony, Virginia. They were placed in intelligence level groups in accordance with the complete clinical picture presented by each, following careful psychological examinations and short periods of observation. The ulti-

7

mate criterion for inclusion in a level of intellectual function was the clinically demonstrated level of intellectual function of the S and not a score on one or more standard intelligence tests.

Ss of the above average group were college students of the Universities of Nebraska and Virginia: all in active collegiate standing, all but two having completed successfully two years or more of college work; one was a graduate student.

All Ss of the superior group were graduate students of the Medical School of the University of Virginia in active college standing. Table 1 shows the composition of the standardization Ss' groups by intellectual level, sex, educational achievement, and life age.

Table 1

Characteristics of Standardization Groups

Intellectual Level	M	F	Mean Educational Achievement	Range life Age		
				Minimum	Mean	Maximum
Imbecile	5	15	Low 2nd Grade	13:6*	20:1	29:0
Moron	4	16	4th Grade	16:0	20:9	38:11
Borderline	9	11	8th Grade	18:7	27:1	45:0
Dull Average. . . .	11	9	2 years High School . .	18:0	25:6	39:11
Average	11	9	3 years High School . .	18:11	25:6	48:4
Above Average . .	11	9	3 years College.	17:7	21:1	31:11
Superior.	19	1	6 years College.	20:0	22:6	26:0

* This S, a girl, was the only one of the 140 whose life age was less than 14 years, 11 months. She was included because her clinical picture and psychometric examinations, made two years apart, supported the conclusion that she had attained her intellectual majority.

Methods. The 100 sets of drawings produced by the Ss of less than above average intelligence were obtained by the individual examination method. The following technique was adhered to rigidly:

An S was given an ordinary lead pencil (Grade No. 2) with an eraser on the end; next a sheet of white paper (8½'' x 14'') folded (as a four page folder — each page 7'' x 8½'') so that the second page was uppermost (the horizontal axis of the page, 8½'', was the greater) with the printed word "House" at the top of the page was placed before the S.

The examiner said to the S: "I want you to draw me as good a House as you can. You may draw any kind of House you like; you may take as long as you wish; you may erase as much as you like; it won't count against you. Just do the best you can."

As soon as the S began to draw, a stopwatch was started: the S was not told he was to be timed, but no attempt was made to conceal the stopwatch. If the S asked for a ruler, or any drawing aid, he was told his drawing must be a freehand production.

After the S completed his House, the examiner turned the drawing form so page three was presented to the S with the vertical axis (8½") the greater, with the word "Tree" printed at the top of the page.

The examiner then said: "Now, I want you to draw me as good a Tree as you can." If the S asked what kind of Tree he should draw, he was told he might make any kind he chose.

After the S indicated he was finished with his Tree, the examiner refolded the form sheet so page four was presented to the S, with the page's vertical axis (8½") the greater, with the word "Person" printed at the top of the page. The S was told to draw as good a Person as he could, the whole Person, not only head and shoulders. For the few persons of limited intelligence who did not know the meaning of the word, "Person," the examiner amended the instructions by saying:

"Draw me as good a man, woman, or child as you can, but be sure to make all of it — not just the head and shoulders."

After the S completed his Person, the examiner recorded the time used by the S for all three drawings, and asked the S to designate the sex and approximate age of the Person he had produced; to tell the kind of Tree (*evergreen* or *deciduous**) he had drawn; to state whether his House was a one or a two-story affair, and whether it was frame or brick construction.

The drawings of the group of college students were obtained by the group-test method.

The students of the above average group were told by their Professor (and those of the superior group were told by the Psychologist who conducted the examination) that they would be expected to make as good a freehand drawing of a House, a Tree and a Person as they could; that they should draw as rapidly as they could without sacrificing the calibre of their drawings. They were informed they might erase as much as they wished without incurring a penalty. They were instructed to write (on the line or lines furnished for that purpose in the upper right-hand corner of

* If "deciduous" was not understood, "leaf-dropping" was used.

each page) the same information concerning the House, the Tree, and the Person (but to give the information for each item as that particular item was completed) that was sought, in inverse order and following the completion of all three drawings from the Ss examined individually. The students were directed to notify the Professor (or the Psychologist) as soon as they completed their drawings so he might tell them the time they had used, and they could record it at the bottom of page four.

The main differences between the individual and the group method were: (1) under the latter the students knew they were to be timed (but they were specifically instructed not to permit speed to lower the calibre of their drawings); (2) the students were asked to give information concerning each drawing as soon as each individual drawing was completed, rather than to give it (as in the individual examination method) in three, two, one order, and after all three drawings were finished; and (3) the students were presented with a triple problem at once, rather than a three-step problem presented one item at a time. Actually, however, the problem basically was little different, for the pages (in turn) were clearly headed, "House," "Tree," and "Person," and the information sought for each item was indicated on the line or lines provided for its recording on each page.

In any event, what might have proven an insurmountable instructional handicap for morons did not prove so for the college students, as was clearly evidenced by the results. The drawings which the students made (under the group test method) conformed in all major points to drawings obtained (after the study was almost completed) from a number of Ss known to be of above average or superior intelligence and without major personality flaws who were examined individually.

The 140 sets of drawings obtained were subjected to minute and careful analysis in an attempt to identify and list as many as possible of the items which might by their presence or absence serve to differentiate Ss on the basis of intelligence. As a result of this analysis it was found that items of detail, proportion, and perspective appeared best to differentiate between the Ss at the various levels. This is not surprising as it has been shown in studies by Goodenough (6) and Anastasi and Foley (1,2,3,4,5) that very young children present in their drawings only a few details, show little recognition of proportion and perspective; that as a child matures he shows first an increasing awareness and expression of the proportional relationship of the details, and then their spatial relationship. Concomitant with this increased recognition of proportion and perspective, the detail depiction of the growing child becomes more accurate and extensive.

Definitions.

A *DETAIL* is construed to be any discrete, identifiable part of the whole: for example, the roof of the House, the branch of a Tree, the arm of a Person.

By *PROPORTION* is meant: (1) the size (that is height, width, or area) of one *DETAIL* in relation to the size of another *DETAIL* (or complex of *DETAILS*): for instance, the size of a window in relation to the size of a door in the same wall of a House; the width of a branch in relation to the width of the trunk of a Tree; the length of an arm in relation to the length of the trunk of a Person; or (2) the ratio of height to width in a given *DETAIL*: to illustrate, the ratio of height to width in the wall of a House; the ratio of length to width in a two-dimensional branch of a Tree; the ratio of the width to the length of the nose of a Person.

PERSPECTIVE refers: (1) to the placement or presentation of one or more *DETAILS* in a given whole; as the location of a door in the wall of a House; a broken branch dangling from a Tree; the arm with elbow flexed in a Person; (2) to the *PRESENTATION* of a given whole: as both ends and the side of a House shown simultaneously; a Tree drawn flat upon the ground; a Person in absolute profile; or (3) to the *PLACEMENT* of a given whole: as a House drawn in the upper left-hand corner of the page, a Tree with its top cut off by the drawing form page's upper margin; a Person with the feet cut off by the page's lower edge.

From a strictly literal viewpoint any line drawn by a lead pencil must be regarded as having two (if not three) dimensions. For the purpose of this discussion a line is assumed to have but one dimension, length. A one-dimensional trunk of a Tree, for example, would be a trunk represented by a single vertical line.

After the items of detail, proportion, and perspective which best differentiated between the various intellectual levels had been identified, they were first assigned numbers: items for the House were numbered 100 through 134; items for the Tree, 200 through 217; items for the Person 300 through 333.

Next the items were grossly segregated as "good" or "flaw." A "good" item arbitrarily was defined as an item of detail, proportion, or perspective which had been used by at least 50% of the Ss in one of the standardization groups from the borderline level of intelligence upward through the superior level and by less than 50% of the Ss of any group below the borderline level; a "flaw" item arbitrarily was considered to be an item presented by at least 50% or more of the Ss of any group of less than borderline intelligence and by less than 50% of the Ss of all groups from the borderline level upward.

Last of all, each item was assigned a *FACTOR SYMBOL* consisting of a letter and a number on the following basis: the letter *D* was employed for those items of detail, proportion, or perspective used by at least 50% of the Ss of one of the "flaw" groups and by less than 50% of the Ss of each higher group. The letter *A* was assigned to those items used by at least 50% of the Ss of one of the levels borderline through average and by less than 50% of the Ss of any lower level, and the letter *S* to those items employed by 50% or more of the above average or superior groups and by less than 50% of the Ss of each lower level of intelligence. Each item also was assigned a number showing the relative quality value of the group designated by the letter. Table 2 presents the factor symbols used and the intelligence levels each represents.

Table 2

Factor Symbols Used With Intelligence Levels

Category	Intelligence Level	Factor Symbol
"Flaw" --	Very Inferior	D3
	Imbecile . . . . --	D2
	Moron	D1
	Borderline	A1
	Dull Average	A2
"Good" --	Average	A3
	Above Average	S1
	Superior	S2

It was necessary to add at the lower end of the "flaw" group the symbol *D3* to denote certain flaw characteristics which were very inferior, but were produced by less than 50% of the Ss in the imbecile class.

To illustrate factor symbol assignment with two specific items: (1) it was found that 5% of the Ss in the above average group, 10% of those in the average group, 35% in the dull average group, 45% in the borderline group, and 65% in the moron group drew Trees which had only one-dimensional branches. Since this type of branch depiction was employed by less than 50% of Ss of borderline or higher intelligence, this particular item immimmediately was assigned the letter *D* because it automatically fell within the arbitrarily defined "flaw" group. It was then assigned the number 1 since the moron group was highest in which at least 50% of the Ss drew only one-dimensional branches for their Trees. This item finally was assigned the factor rating *D1*; (2) it was found that 15% of the Ss in the imbecile group, 30% of those in the moron group, 30% in the borderline group, 60% in the dull average group, 65% in the average group, 95% in the above average and the superior groups drew Houses with two or more windows. This item, therefore, first was assigned a factor letter of *A*, since it was not produced by as much as 50% of the Ss of any group below the borderline and automatically fell in the "good" group, and since the lowest group in which at least 50% or more of the Ss produced more than two windows for the House was the dull average, the number 2 was added and the factor symbol *A2* was derived.

The intention was to develop a quantitative scoring system which would have valid *qualitative* value; a system which would produce a score which would not be expressed immediately and without careful analysis by a single figure, but instead would provide several measures, whose relationships would have diagnostic value and indicate to some extent whether the scores obtained by an S represented his customary level of function or some diminution of function which might or might not be irreversible.

QUALITATIVE STANDARDIZATION STUDIES

Once the quantitative system of scoring the drawings had been set up as described in the preceding section, it was decided to attempt to identify and evaluate those items which in most instances did not appear to differentiate intelligence levels *per se*, but which might serve to differentiate between drawings produced by persons who did not exhibit major personality maladjustments and those produced by persons who were maladjusted, psychopathic, psychoneurotic, prepsychotic, or psychotic, i.e., to replace the former system of "qualitative analysis by inspection" with a more formalized and more objective approach.

It was recognized it would be impossible to set up as precise a study as that which resulted in the identification of factors differentiating intelligence levels only, because the attempt now was to identify as many as possible of the so-called non-intellective factors which enter into the makeup of the total personality, many of which would be produced by only two or three Ss. It could not be specified, for example, that 50% of the Ss of a given type must present a specific sign for it to have differential meaning.

Subjects. The final criterion for S inclusion was the total clinical picture presented by the individual S. In the spring of 1945 at the University of Virginia Hospital a study was started of the drawings of adults, all presenting marked or definite personality maladjustments. This specific study was continued at the Lynchburg State Colony in 1945 and 1946.

All drawings obtained were by use of the individual examination method.

Table 3 shows numbers and types of the 150 Ss included in the preliminary study. Fifty-two Ss were seen at the University of Virginia

Hospital and 98 at the Lynchburg State Colony or the Colony's Mental Hygiene Clinics in other cities.

The S population although not a well-balanced one did serve, however, to indicate definitely that the H—T—P productions of Ss with personality disorders differ in many respects from drawings produced by Ss who were not maladjusted. It was later possible to analyze drawings of more than 500 other persons exhibiting definite personality maladjustment; to identify other differential factors and to confirm (or occasionally reject) factors discovered in the preliminary study and to make more specific their interpretation.

Table 3

Standardization Groups by Gross Classification

	N
Adult maladjustment	10
Epilepsy with personality maladjustment*	29
Psychopathic personality **	22
Psychoneurosis	53
Pre psychotic state	3
Mental deficiency with psychosis	6
Psychosis:	
(a) organic	11
(b) functional	16
Total	150

* Paranoid and/or neurotic components predominated.
** This "catch-all" classification included psychopathic-like behavior; there were few classical "constitutional psychopaths."

Method. It was found that items which served best to differentiate between the drawings of those definitely maladjusted and those not maladjusted might be designated by these general headings: details, proportion, perspective, time, comments (spontaneous and induced), associations, line quality, self-criticism, attitude, drive, and concept. These general headings, in turn, were broken down into many subheads to provide for a more minute and specific analysis.

It had been hoped, at first, that it might prove possible to assign a factor letter and number to each characteristic as it was identified, as had been done in the quantitative scoring system. It was proposed to accord a rating of *P1* to those factors which appeared to represent a first degree *(pathoformic)* deviation from the average; *P2* to items which seemed to indicate a more serious *(pathological)* deviation; and *P3* to those so grossly and manifestly deviant that they might be regarded as almost, if not actually, *pathognomonic*. It was soon discovered, however, that this could not be done, for few items were found to have persistent weight and meaning. These non-intellective items could be evaluated adequately only when their relationships to the total configuration presented by the individual S was considered. For example: the assignment of a *P2* classification on the basis of its apparent implication in Case A obviously would be completely inappropriate in Case B. Case A might draw his Person slowly, with painstaking care. He might draw his Person's hands in first one position, then another (showing much anxiety), then finally place them out of sight in the Person's coat pockets. Case B might draw his Person quickly and without plan, vacillating until the hands were reached, he might then draw the hands once as visible, then hastily erase them and redraw them as in the coat pockets. Each S would indicate that presentation of the hands troubled him, but the degree of "trouble" patently was different.

It was found not only that an item in a given configuration might have a meaning totally different to that assigned to it in another configuration, but also that it might have more than one meaning in a given constellation.

For example, consider the chimney of a House (conventionally regarded as a male sex symbol). Subject A might, like many Ss, show that a chimney was simply a chimney with no special significance, by: (a) drawing it quickly and easily in the customary sequence of detail presentation; (b) not returning to it later in the drawing; (c) showing none of the signs which might indicate he was preoccupied with the symbol or that it aroused conflict within him. Subject B might show definite concern while drawing the chimney, but in the P—D—I reveal he recently had constructed a house in which the erection of the chimney had occasioned much worry and trouble to him. Subject C might exhibit strong signs of conflict while drawing the chimney and later it might be learned he was badly maladjusted sexually. Subject D might show strong signs of conflict while drawing the chimney, and on the P—D—I indicate he associated the chimney with the fireplace which opened into it from the living-room, which was to him a source of discontent and dissatisfaction. Subject E might evidence strong signs of conflict while drawing the chimney and later state that at one time he regarded the chimney as a phallus; at another time he associated it with the furnace in the basement, another time he viewed it as the largest single item of a House in which he had been very unhappy.

Chapter Bibliography

1. ANASTASI, A. and FOLEY, J. P., Jr. A survey of the literature on artistic behavior in the abnormal; I. Historical and theoretical background. *J. gen. Psychol.*, 1941, 25, 111 – 142.

2. _____. A survey of the literature on artistic behavior in the abnormal: II. Approaches and inter-relationships. *Ann. N.Y. Acad. Sci.*, 1941, 42, pp 106.

3. _____. A survey of the literature on artistic behavior in the abnormal: III. Spontaneous productions. *Psychol. Monog.*, 1940, 52, No. 6, pp. 71.

4. _____. A survey of the literature on artistic behavior in the abnormal: IV. Experimental Investigations. *J. gen. Psychol.*, 1941, 25, 187 – 237.

5. _____. An analysis of spontaneous artistic productions by the abnormal. *J. gen. Psychol.*, 1943, 28, 297 – 313.

6. GOODENOUGH, FLORENCE L. *Measurement of Intelligence by Drawings*. Yonkers-on-Hudson: World Book Company, 1926.

Chapter 3   Administration

Materials needed:

The examiner will need the following test materials and other items:

(1)   Two H—T—P Drawing Forms* (white paper, each page 7'' x 8½'' in size, with space provided on the first page for the subject's name, date of examination, etc., with *House* printed at top of second page; *Tree* printed at top of third page; and *Person* printed at top of fourth page,

(2)   The four-page H—T—P Scoring Folder.

(3)   The four-page H—T—P Post-Drawing Interrogation Folder * * (for use after administering the achromatic drawing step) and the shorter H—T—P Post-Drawing Interrogation Form for use after the chromatic drawings have been obtained.

(4)   Several lead pencils of grade No. 2 with erasers (use of grade No. 2 is imperative; it has been found to reflect more delicately than other grades the subject's motor control and quality of lines, and to aid in making accurate qualitative evaluation of shading used).

---

* All H—T—P materials may be obtained from:
Western Psychological Services
12031 Wilshire Blvd.
Los Angeles, Calif., 90025

** If an S is under 15 years of age, it is recommended that Jolles' Children's Revision of the Post-Drawing Interrogation be used.

(5)   A set of wax crayons of not less than 8 colors: red, green, blue, yellow, brown, black, purple and orange.

(6)   A stopwatch.

(7)   The H—T—P Manual.

Phase One, Step One: Achromatic Drawings

The examiner first will present the S with the drawing form sheet folded so only page 2 is visible with the word *HOUSE* at the top of the page from the S's view. Note: for the drawing of the House the horizontal axis of the drawing form page is greater than the vertical axis; the reverse is true for the other two drawing pages.

The examiner says to the S: "Take one of these pencils, please. I want you to draw me as good a picture of a house as you can. You may draw any kind of house you wish, it's entirely up to you. You may erase as much as you like, it will not be counted against you. And you may take as long as you wish, Just draw me as good a house as you can.'

If the S protests, as middle-aged or elderly adults frequently do, that he is not an artist, or that when he went to school they did not teach drawing as they do now, etc., the examiner assures the S the H—T—P is not a test of artistic ability; that he is not interested in the drawing ability of the S. If the S asks for a ruler, or attempts to make use of any object as a ruler, the examiner tells him his drawings must be *freehand*.

The examiner will then, in turn, ask the S to draw as good a Tree and as good a Person as he can, presenting the appropriate page of the drawing form to the S in each instance and using care to see that the printed word is at the page's top from the S's view.

After the S has been presented with the drawing form and instructed to draw a House, the examiner starts his stopwatch and begins to use the first page of the H—T—P Scoring Folder. On it he records for each drawing: (1) time between finishing instructions to the S and when the S begins to draw (*initial latency period*); (2) the name and number of the details of the House in the order each is drawn, being careful to be as minute and specific as possible; (3) any pause occurring once the S begins to draw, taking care to relate the pause to the detail sequence (*intra-whole pauses*); (4) all spontaneous comments by the S and relating each to the detail sequence; (5) any emotion exhibited by the S, orienting the emotion to the detail sequence; and (6) total time used by the S for his drawing.

The examiner repeats timing and recording as above for the drawings of Tree and Person.

To record most simply the detail sequence, spontaneous comments, etc., the examiner may use the system illustrated below. This example is taken from the case of K.N. (q.v.), the first illustrative case in the Appendix.

HOUSE

1. Roof.
2. Window, with panes, in roof.
3. Porch roof (main wall) — "I can take tools and make a much nicer one," (laughs with embarrassment).
4. Porch pillars.
5. Door.
6. Window, upper right, with panes.
7. Window, lower left, with panes.
8. Window, upper center, with panes.
9. Windows (left and right) flanking door, with panes.
10. Window, upper left, with panes.
11. Window, upper center, with panes.
12. Roof material.
13. Side porch roof and pillar.
14. "That's about all you need to do besides build the garage."
15. Foundation.
16. Latency 18 seconds.
17. "A couple of trees."
18. Tree to left; then tree to right.
19. Driveway from side porch.
20. Walkway from front porch.
21. "Say one here." --a shrub.   Time 5:13

If there had been an initial latency it would have been recorded as item No. 1 and the first detail drawn would have been recorded as No. 2, etc.

The relationship of the spontaneous comments and/or the emotional expressions to the drawn items is determined by the position of the spontaneous comments and/or the emotional manifestations in the recorded material. For example, if the spontaneous comment or emotion was recorded *before* the detail but within the same numbered item, it was made while the S was beginning to draw the detail in question. If the comment or emotion were recorded in the same numbered item with the detail *but following the detail,* it was made after the S began to draw the detail in question and before he completed it. If the spontaneous comment or emotion was assigned an item number of its own, it occurred after the preceding detail had been completed and before the subsequent detail was undertaken. The words *right* and *left* in the recording refer to the page's right and left sides.

To record these various items properly, the examiner must, of course, have a clear view of the drawing being produced by the S. Occasionally this proves impossible because the S (in some instances overly suspicious and in other instances over-anxious, etc.) persists in concealing the drawing sheet. In such circumstances, it probably is best not to antagonize the S by insisting that he allow the examiner to see the drawing as it develops.

Phase One, Step Two: Post-Drawing-Achromatic-Interrogation

After the S has completed his drawings in pencil of the House, the Tree, and Person, the examiner proceeds to give the S an opportunity to define, describe, and interpret the objects drawn and their respective environments, and to associate concerning them. The examiner will wish to make use of the clinically observed fact that the act of drawing the House, the Tree, and the Person often arouses strong emotional reactions; and after an S completes his drawings, frequently it is possible for him to verbalize materials which hitherto he has found inexpressible. Obviously the less withdrawn and hostile, the more intelligent and cooperative an S is, the more productive will be Step Two.

There are 60 primary questions on the Post-Drawing Interrogation Folder. Those pertaining to the achromatic House have the letter *H* preceding the question's number; those dealing with the Tree a *T*; and those about the Person a *P*. In addition, each question is followed by one or more letters to indicate *A* for *Association, P* for *Pressure,* and R for *Reality-Testing.*

The word *pressure* is used in this connection in a broad sense to mean any factor within or without an S's personality with sufficient positive or negative valence to influence the S's behavior.

Any given question at times will involve one or more associations, the expression of strong pressure or pressures from within or without the personality, or reality-testing or any combination thereof. The questions purposely are spiraled to make difficult the establishment of an "answer set" and to make it almost impossible for an S to remember what he has said previously concerning a specific whole. The questions vary in content from direct and concrete to highly indirect and abstract.

The P—D—I is not intended to be a rigidly structured procedure. The examiner is expected always to conduct further interrogations which seem to him to be fruitful. He will wish to determine as completely as possible what the constant stimulus words, *House, Tree,* and *Person* and the drawings of these objects have meant to the S.

After giving the completed achromatic drawings a cursory inspection, the examiner turns the drawing form so the drawing of the Person is before the S with the word *Person* at the top of the page from the S's point of view. The examiner says in effect, "Now sit back and relax while I ask you a few questions about what you have just drawn."

He then asks:

P1. *Is that a man or a woman (or boy or girl)?*   (R)   If the sex of the drawn Person is obvious, the question should be rephrased to: "Is that a boy or a man?" or "Is that a girl or a woman?" In the drawings of mental defectives and the deeply disturbed, it may be difficult to determine the Person's sex in the absence of the S's statement.

P2. *How old is he?* (R)   The gender of the pronoun, of course, is to be altered for this and subsequent questions if the Person is said to be a female.

P3. *Who is he?* (A)

P4. *Is he a relative, a friend, or what?*   (A)   If the answer to P3 indicated the drawn Person was the S himself, this question need not be asked.

P5. *Whom were you thinking about while you were drawing?*   (A) This question should always be asked.

P6. *What is he doing? (and where is he doing it?)* (R & P) If the response is, "Oh he's just standing there," the examiner will want to know where "there" is: for example, indoors (and if so, in what room) or out-of-doors; for whom the Person is waiting, if anyone; what the Person has been doing and plans to do. If the Person is walking or in other motion (as, for example, riding), the examiner seeks to know not only where the Person is going and what he is going to do when he gets there, but where he has been and what he has been doing.

If the S should say in reply to this question "How should I know what he's doing? It's only a drawing." the examiner continues with, "Of course, it's only a drawing but it is a picture of someone. How about making up a story about him? What do you think he might be doing? What does he seem to be doing there?"

P7. *What is he thinking about?* (A & P) At this point frank projection frequently begins.   The examiner will do his best to obtain a frank answer to this question and determine, if possible, what connotations this particular topic has for the S.

P8. *How does he feel?* (P) *Why?* (P) The supplementary question, "Why?" should always be asked unless, in the examiner's opinion, rapport is so poor that the challenge of the question might engender resistance which would interfere seriously with further verbalization. If the S has shown himself to be reluctant to answer questions, the "Why?" should be reserved for a subsequent session.

After the examiner has recorded the S's reply to P8, he refolds the drawing form and presents the drawing of the Tree to the S with the word *Tree* at the top of the page from the S's view. The examiner asks:

T1. *What kind of Tree is that?* (R) If the S cannot identify the Tree as a specific type (for example, maple or cedar) the examiner asks whether the tree is evergreen or deciduous. For S's of limited vocabulary, this may be rephrased: "Is it the sort of tree that stays green the year 'round, or does it drop its leaves?"

T2. *Where is that Tree actually located?* (A) If the S states the Tree is located in a woods or in a forest, the examiner will try to determine what connotation the word *woods* or *forest* has for the S.

T3. *About how old is that Tree?* (R & P)

T4. *Is that Tree alive?* (R & P)

Question T5 has two parts: if the S says the Tree is alive, Part I is used, as follows:

T5. (a) *What is there about that Tree that gives you the impression that it is alive?* (R & A)

(b) *Is any part of the Tree dead?* (P) *What part?* (P)

(c) *What do you think caused it to die?* (P)

(d) *How long has it been dead?* (P)

Part II is used if the S says in answer to T4 that the Tree (the whole Tree) is dead:

(a) *What do you think caused it to die?* (P)

(b) *How long has it been dead?* (P)

T6. *Which does that Tree look more like to you: a man or a woman?* (A & R) For Ss whose rigid, concrete thinking prevents them from grasping the question's meaning or from abstracting masculine or feminine components from the Tree, the examiner continues with: "Oh, I know that Trees do not have sex as people do, but you've probably seen rugged, powerful, robust trees that made you think of a man, and I suspect you've seen other trees that looked either as graceful and trim as a young woman or as large, protective, and motherly as an older woman. Which does *this* Tree make you think of, a man or a woman?" If this still does not produce a statement of possible gender, the examiner asks: "Well, does any *part* of this Tree make you think of a man or a woman?"

T7. *What is there about it that gives you that impression?* (R & A) If additional questioning had to be used to get an answer to T6, T7 may have been answered before reached, and then it need not be asked.

T8. *If that were a Person instead of a Tree, which way would the*

Person be facing? (P)

T9. *Is that Tree by itself, or is it in a group of Trees?* (P) If the emotional tone of an S's reply suggests deep feelings of isolation, the examiner asks: "Do you think it would like to be in a group?"

T10. *As you look at that Tree, do you get the impression that it is above you, below you, or about on a level with you?* (R) If the S replies that he sees the Tree as "down" on the drawing form in front of him, the examiner continues with: "But as you look at that Tree you have just drawn does it appear to be above you, as if it were on a hill, or below you, as if it were down in a hollow or valley?"

T11. *What is the weather like in this picture?* (time of day and year; sky; temperature) (P & R) If the S's description of the weather exactly duplicates the weather pertaining outdoors at time of examination, S's reply may be influenced solely by that weather. The examiner must not accept that presumption, however; instead, he must question the S further. If specific suggestions need to be made to the S, the examiner should check for acceptance as possibly following the line of least resistance.

T12. *Is there any wind blowing in this picture?* (R & P)

T13. *Show me in what direction it is blowing?* (R)

T14. *What sort of wind is it?* (P & R)   If the S describes what seems to the examiner to be an unpleasant wind (as fierce, searing hot or ice cold) the examiner always tries to determine what emotional connotation such a wind has for the S. The examiner might continue with: "How would you feel about such a wind?"

After he has recorded the answer to question T14, the examiner turns to the S's drawing of a House and presents it to the S with the word *House* at the top of the page from the S's view. The examiner asks:

H1. *How many stories does that House have?* (R) If the S does not understand what is meant by "story" the examiner usually can clarify by substituting "floor" for "story," accompanying his substitution by suitable hand gestures to indicate the varying levels of a house. The examiner also may rephrase the question to: "Does that House have an upstairs?"

H2. *What is that House made of?* (R & A)

H3. *Is that your own House?* (A) *Whose House is it?* (A) The second question under H3 is asked only if the first question is answered in the negative.

H4. *Whose House were you thinking about while you were drawing?* (A)

H5. *Would you like to own that House yourself?* (P & A) *Why?* (P & A) The examiner tries to determine: (a) why the S would or would not wish to own this House; (b) what differences there may be between the drawn House and the house now occupied or owned by the S as to size, status, etc., (c) the likelihood of the S's ever owning such a home and the intensity of his desire to own it; (d) his emotional reactions to the House (as a possible source of conflict).

H6. *If you did own that House and you could do whatever you liked with it:*

(a) *Which room would you take for your own?* (P) *Why?* (P) The examiner will wish always to compare the location of the desired room with the location of the room the S occupies in his present abode and, if there is a difference, to attempt to ascertain the reason therefor.

(b) *Whom would you like to have live in that House with you?* (P) *Why?* (P) The S exhibiting rigid, concrete thinking may find it impossible to accept this question until it is explained that he must imagine the House is his; and no one else has anything to do with it. All the examiner is interested in learning is whom this S would wish to live in the House with him.

H7. *As you look at that House, does it seem to be close by or far away?* (R) The examiner attempts to learn whether the ''distance'' expressed by the S is psychological, geographic, or both.

H8. *As you look at that House, do you get the impression that it is above you, below you, or about on a level with you?* (R) Any additional questioning should follow the form suggested for T10.

H9. *What does that House make you think of, or remind you of?* (A)

With this question the interrogation tends to become more abstract and general in character. For the first time relatively free association is sought.

H10. *What else?* (A)

H11. *Is that a happy, friendly sort of House?* (A&P) For Ss whose thinking is rigid and concrete, the examiner might continue with: ''Haven't you ever gone into a house where you felt very much at ease and at home? Is this House that kind of house, or is it the sort of house that seems to have something very unhappy or unpleasant about it?''

H12. *What is there about it that gives you that impression?* (A&P) The examiner will wish to ascertain why the particular aspect mentioned by the S conveys that impression.

H13. *Are most Houses that way?* (P&A) *Why do you think so?* (P&A)

H14. *What is the weather like in this picture? (Time of day and year; sky; temperature)?* (P&R)

After he has recorded the S's answers to H14, the examiner turns the drawing form so only the drawn Tree is visible to the S with the word *Tree* at the top of the page from the S's view.

Note: since the S has last seen his drawing of a Tree, at least 14 questions have been asked concerning the drawing of a House.

T15. *What does that Tree make you think of, or remind you of?* (A)

T16. *What else?* (A)

T17. *Is it a healthy Tree?* (R & P)

Note: at least 25 questions have been asked since the S was re-requested to define the state of health of his Tree.

T18. *What is there about it that gives you that impression?* (R & P)

It has been found that this somewhat devious way of asking: "Why do you say that?" is advantageous, because it implies that the factor influencing the reply lies within the Tree rather than in the S himself; and it implies that the answer is of relatively little importance. Projection almost certainly is compelled, since there is little one can abstract from the drawing of the Tree to justify an affirmative or negative answer to T17. For example, no matter how frail or dilapidated the Tree may appear, at the same time it can be healthy.

T19. *Is it a strong Tree?* (R & P) *Health* and *strength* are two different things.

T20. *What is there about it that gives you that impression?* (R & P)

If the S finds the questions T17 through T20 difficult to answer definitively, or if there is a good deal of ambiguity shown by the S in this series, the examiner will do well to ask the S to draw (unless already done) his concept of the root structure of his Tree. Of course, the examiner does not score an induced root structure quantitatively.

After the examiner records the S's answer to T20, he folds the drawing form page so only the drawn Person is visible to the S, with the word *Person* at the top of the page from the S's view.

P9. *What does that Person make you think of, or remind you of?* (A)

P10. *What else?* (A)

P11. *Is that Person well?* (P & R)

P12. *What is there about him that gives you that impression?* (P & R) To justify his answer to P11, an S almost is compelled to project, since it is difficult in most cases to provide supportive argumentation by reference to aspects of the drawn Person alone.

P13. *Is that Person happy?* (P & R)

P14. *What is there about him that gives you that impression?* (P & R) The examiner must not accept without further questioning an answer such as: "Certainly he is, because he has a smile on his face." In such an instance the examiner continues with: "What is he smiling about?" It is imperative to attempt to establish the depth of the feeling and the degree to which it may be presumed to be a relatively customary state.

P15. *Are most people that way?* (P & R) *Why?* (P & A)

P16. *Do you think you would like that Person?* (A & P) *Why?*

(A & P) This question is asked even when the S indicates he has drawn a picture of himself.

P17. *What is the weather like in this picture? (Time of day and year; sky; temperature)?* (P & R) It has been found that Ss are least likely to draw details indicative of the condition of the weather in drawings of Persons. It is all the more important, therefore, to afford the S the opportunity to express verbally his impression of the weather pertaining in his drawing of the Person. While extremes of weather (very hot, very cold, etc.) suggest unpleasantness, the examiner never assumes such an interpretation is correct, for a description of extremes *may* indicate merely that the S is responsive, even pleasantly responsive, to varied and intense stimuli. Further questioning always is indicated to determine emotional connotations of the S's response.

P18. *Whom does that Person remind you of?* (A) *Why?* (A & P)

P19. *What does that Person need most?* (P & A) *Why?* (P & A)

In many instances this question produces replies restricted to what appear to be relatively superficial things, as clothing, "spending" money, etc. The examiner must not assume superficiality in such instances. The supplementary question: "Why?" usually will produce further information sufficient to indicate the quality level and intensity of the expressed need. If the S states the drawn Person most needs security, happiness, etc., further questioning definitely is indicated to learn what constitutes *security* or *happiness* for the S and why he finds it so essential.

After recording the S's answers to P19, the examiner folds the drawing form so only the drawn Tree is visible to the S with the word *Tree* at the top of the page from the S's view.

T21. *Whom does that Tree remind you of?* (A) *Why?* (A & P)

Concrete thinkers may experience great difficulty seeing the Tree as anything but the pencil drawing of a Tree, in which case the examiner might continue with: "Oh, I know it doesn't look like much of anything but a Tree, but isn't there something about the way it stands or looks that reminds you of some person you know?"

T22. *What does that Tree need most?* (P & A) *Why?* (P & A)

As in P19, the supplementary "Why?" always must be asked unless the S is too resistant.

After he has recorded the S's answers to T22, the examiner presents the S with his drawing of the House, with the word *House* at the top of the page from the S's view.

H15. *Whom does that House make you think of?* (A) *Why?* (A & P)

H16. *What does that House need most?** (P & A) *Why?* (P & A)

---

* Occasionally an S remarks, partly in self-criticism and partly in jest (in answer to P19, T22, or H16): "Someone who can really draw!"

As in P19 and T22, whenever possible the supplementary question "Why?" must be asked.

At this point the examiner interrupts the interrogative procedure and asks the S to draw a sun and a groundline in each drawing in which the S did not produce them spontaneously.

That done, the examiner presents the S with his drawing of a Person, with the word *Person* at the page's top from the standpoint of the S.

Then, if the S has drawn anything in addition to his House (except the sun and groundline), the examiner asks:

H17. *If this were a person instead of a tree (or a shrub, or a windmill, or any other object not a part of the House itself) who might it be?* (A) Of course, if the item in question were a person, the question would be simplified to: "Who might this person be?"

After he has recorded the S's answer or answers to H17, the examiner presents the S with his drawing of a Tree.

T23. *If this were a person instead of a bird (or another tree, or anything else not a part of the originally drawn Tree), who might it be?* (A)

If there has been unusual branch structure depiction, e.g., (1) only two or three large branches are shown (and no branch-to-branch, or branch-to-twig presentation), or (2) one branch is quite different from the other branches, the examiner should ask *who* the branch (or branches) might be if it, or they, were a person or persons.

As in H17, if the additional item were a person, the question would be amended to: "Who might this person be?"

After he has written the S's answer or answers to T23, the examiner presents the S with the drawing form so folded that only the drawing of the Person is visible.

P20. *What kind of clothing does this Person have on?* (R) In a number of instances, it will be found the Person appears to have no clothing (although no sexual organs are drawn) but is regarded by the S as fully clothed.

If the S says the Person is nude, the examiner always asks whether or not the Person is comfortable, and why he or she is undressed.

After the examiner has asked P20 and recorded the S's answers thereto, he presents the S with the drawing of the House and asks the S to tell which room lies behind each window or door of the House; the use of each room ordinarily; the person customarily occupying each room. The S also is asked to identify by location, use, and occupant, the room or rooms on the side or sides of the House not shown in the drawing. All this may be accomplished most easily with Ss of average or higher intelligence, by following the suggestion of Dr. Robert Hughes of Atlanta that the S be requested to draw a floor plan for each floor of his House. This has the advantage of affording the S the opportunity to distort reality further and express by his distortion his attitude toward the room's occupant or occupants and its uses.

To conclude the achromatic P—D—I, the examiner asks questions needed to ascertain the possible significance to the S of unusual or bizarre details; the absence of essential details; and any unusual proportional, spatial, or positional relationships of the drawn wholes or the parts thereof.

For example, the examiner will wish to question the S concerning the possible significance of unusual details such as broken window panes, holes in the roof, fallen chimney, etc., for the House; the presence of scars, broken or dead branches, or shadows cast by the Tree. It has been found, for example, that scars on the Tree's trunk and broken or damaged branches, almost invariably represent "felt scars" left by psychic traumata sustained in the S's past. It should be noted, however, that only those events which the S found "scarring" will be so symbolized (if, in fact, they are symbolized at all), and these will not necessarily be the events which to the objective observer might seem most likely to have left permanent "scars".

If a shadow is shown as cast by the House, the Tree, or the Person, the examiner asks on what surface the shadow is cast, as water, ground, snow, ice, etc.

The examiner should do his best to have the S explain his reasons for unusual positional relationships such as the House drawn as tilted, the Tree drawn as leaning to one side or with trunk twisted, or the Person drawn as if falling.

Attempts always should be made to determine the S's reasons for presenting hands and arms or feet and legs of his Person in an unusual position. If the Person is, for example, in "absolute profile" (with only one side showing and no suggestion of the other side), the examiner should ask the S to tell: (1) the position of the unseen hand; (2) what, if anything, is in that hand; (3) what the drawn Person is doing with that hand, if anything. If the Person is drawn with a hand and arm outstretched, the examiner tries to learn what the Person is reaching for or pointing to. If the drawn Person appears to have his gaze focused upon something, the examiner asks the S to tell what that something is.

If any part of the House, Tree, or Person touches, or appears to extend beyond, the top, bottom, or either side margin of the drawing form page, the examiner asks how far the House, Tree, or Person extends beyond the page.

If the Tree has been drawn to consist only of a stump, the examiner asks the S to show how tall the Tree once was and tell what happened to it.

Schizophrenics often accept as reasonable such questions as: "Which is the good side of this Tree and which is the bad side?" and

"Which is the male side and which is the female side of the House?"

Obviously the Post—Drawing Interrogation session could be expanded almost indefinitely. However, any great amount of questioning beyond the formal 60 questions may be best reserved, in most instances, for subsequent interview sessions.

To recapitulate: the intent of the Post—Drawing Interrogation is two-fold: (1) to afford the S with ample opportunity to project verbally his feelings, attitudes, needs, and so on, into his descriptions of and comments upon a dwelling-place, a living or once-living inanimate thing, and a living or once-living human being, respectively; and (2) to afford the examiner the opportunity to clarify aspects of the drawn wholes not clear to him.

Phase Two, Step One: Chromatic Drawings *

Present the S with a set of eight or more wax crayons: red, green, blue, yellow, brown, black, orange, purple, and others. The examiner asks him to identify them by color. If the S cannot do this, it is imperative that the examiner test more formally for color blindness in the S.

Next present the S with a new drawing form with only page two visible and *House* at the top of the page from the S's view. Ask the S to draw as good a House as he can using any crayons available to him. The S is not asked to draw "another" House, for this might make him think he should not duplicate his achromatic House; the S is allowed full freedom of color choice. Be sure no pencil is available to the S. Tell the S he is not to erase in this step.

After giving the S these instructions, the examiner turns to page 4 of the Scoring Folder and records (as in Phase 1, Step 1) initial latency period. time consumed, detail sequence (noting carefully colors used for each detail and colors selected but not used), spontaneous comments, emotional manifestations, etc.

Instructions for the drawing of the chromatic Tree and chromatic Person are the same as for the achromatic Tree and achromatic Person except the S is told he may use whichever crayons he wishes.

After the S completes his chromatic House, Tree, and Person, have him draw a sun and a line to represent the ground in each drawing in which he has not already done this spontaneously (note which were induced).

Phase Two, Step Two: Post—Drawing—Chromatic—Interrogation

If the S is not too fatigued when he has completed his chromatic

---

* The author again acknowledges his indebtedness to Mr. John T. Payne for suggestions concerning the advisability of securing drawings in color which led to the development of the Chromatic Phase of the H—T—P.

drawings, and rapport is excellent, and time permits, the full P—D—I may be used.

In any event, the examiner asks the following "formal" questions, which constitute the usual chromatic P—D—I.

Person

1. *Is that a man or a woman (or boy or girl?)*
2. *How old is he?*
3. *Who is he?*
4. *What is he doing? (And where is he doing it?)*
5. *How does he feel? (Why?)*
6. *What sort of Person is he?*
7. *What is the weather like in this picture?*
8. *What does that Person need most? (Why?)*
9. *What kind of clothing does that Person have on?*

* * * * * * * * * * * * * * *

Tree

1. *What kind of Tree is that?*
2. *How old is that Tree?*
3. *Is that Tree alive? (If not, what part is dead and what caused it to die, and will that Tree ever come to life again, and when?)*
4. *Which does that Tree look more like to you: a man or a woman?*
5. *What is there about it that gives you that impression?*
6. *What is the weather like in this picture?*
7. *Show me in what direction the wind is blowing?*
8. *What does that Tree need most? (Why?)*

* * * * * * * * * * * * * * *

House

1. *How many stories does that House have?*
2. *Whose House is that?*
3. *If that were your own House and you could do whatever you liked with it:*
   (a) Which room would you take for your own? (Why?)
   (b) Whom would you like to have live with you? (Why?)
4. *What is the weather like in this picture?*
5. *What does that House need most? (Why?)*

The examiner asks additional questions needed to (1) make clear the S's intent; (2) identify and account for, as far as possible, conceptual differences between achromatic and chromatic drawings; (3) make possible the quantitative and qualitative analyses; (4) ascertain the significance to the S of unusual or bizarre details; absence of essential details; unusual proportional, spatial or positional relationships of the wholes or parts thereof; (5) identify, if possible, the person, persons, or objects not part of the drawn chromatic House, Tree, and Person.

The examiner concludes the session by (1) asking the S to indicate in his achromatic and chromatic drawings of the Person (by a penciled dot) the location of the Person's pelvic crest (to enable an accurate quantitative scoring of points 323 II, III, and IV) and (2) noting if the S is dextral or sinistral so a more accurate qualitative evaluation of profile presentation of the wholes may be made.

Group Testing

Materials needed:

For group testing the examiner needs the same materials as for *Individual Testing* with one possible exception: the "Two Copy Drawing Form" — devised by Western Psychological Services — may be substituted for the standard drawing form used in the *achromatic* Phase so a permanent record of an S's erasures will become available; otherwise these data would not be derivable from the group-obtained drawings obtained by use of the standard drawing form.

Administration:

Ss should be seated far enough apart to provide a feeling of privacy (and make it difficult, if not impossible, for one S to copy or be influenced by another's production).

Phase One, Step One: Achromatic Drawings

The examiner gives each S a drawing form and tells the *Ss* they will be expected to make, in pencil, as good a freehand drawing as they can of a House, a Tree, and a Person in that order. They may erase as much as they wish without penalty; and take as much time as they choose. Each S should notify the examiner as soon as he has completed a given drawing so the examiner can record the time.

In certain instances, however, it may be necessary to set a definite overall time limit (preferably not less than 30 minutes for each set of drawings: achromatic or chromatic). In such cases, the examiner tells the Ss of the time limitation before they begin.

Before instructing the Ss to start, the examiner demonstrates the proper page of the drawing form on which each whole is to be drawn.

The examiner records the time used by each S in drawing each whole, emotions shown by individual Ss, questions asked, or comments of Ss before or during the drawing period.

Phase One, Step Two: Post—Drawing—Interrogation: Achromatic

With literate subjects, of dull average intelligence or better, there is no reason to forego a P—D—I because group procedures were used.

When all Ss complete their achromatic drawings, the examiner distributes the four-page Group P—D—I Folder and instructs them to write their answers to all questions contained therein. He stresses it is important they answer questions in the order in which they appear in the folder, explaining that the letters *P, T,* and *H,* respectively, refer to Person, Tree, and House, in that order. He tells the Ss they can ask for clarification of any question which is not clear.

The Group P—D—I Folder has the same questions as the individual P—D—I Folder except: (1) questions T5-I and T5-II read, "If you said.........."; (2) the letters *A, P,* and *R,* or combinations thereof, in brackets do not appear after the questions; (3) the printed directions instructing the S to draw a sun and groundline are omitted; (4) questions H17 and T23 are not given; (5) the directions for securing a floor plan of the House and comments on supplementary questions are omitted.

Questions are spaced farther apart than on the individual P—D—I folder to allow each S ample space for his answers. However, if the space is not sufficient, an S should be provided with additional paper and instructed to identify by letter and number each question he answers on the sheet provided him.

Phase Two, Step One: Chromatic Drawings

When all the achromatic P—D—I questions have been answered, the examiner collects the drawings, P—D—I folders, pencils and erasers. He gives each S the standard drawing form and a set of crayons containing at least the eight colors: red, green, yellow, blue, black, brown, orange and purple. He asks the Ss to identify the red, green, blue, and yellow crayons in that order, by making a check mark with the crayon in the lower left corner of the drawing form's front page.

The examiner tells the Ss they are to draw as good a House, a Tree, and a Person as they can, using any crayons they wish. He should be very careful *not* to ask for *"another* House, Tree, and Person". He tells the Ss they are not allowed to erase and asks them (as in Step One of Phase One) to notify him as soon as a given whole has been completed.

The examiner records, as in the achromatic drawing step, time used by each S for each drawing, emotions shown, questions asked, or comments made by any S (identifying the S) before or during the drawing period.

Phase Two, Step Two: Post—Drawing—Interrogation: Chromatic

After all Ss complete their chromatic drawings, the examiner distributes the Chromatic P—D—I form and instructs the Ss (as in Step Two of Phase One) to write their answers to all questions in the order the questions appear.

In many instances, in group procedures, the graphic portion of the H—T—P is all that is sought, since the Group H—T—P often is but one of several abbreviated procedures used. In such cases, of course, Step Two (P—D—I) of each Phase is omitted. Occasionally, when time is of the essence, even the chromatic drawings will not be obtained.

It is the author's conviction that no group-obtained H—T—P protocol is as informative as one obtained by the standard individual examination method: nonetheless, Cassel, Johnson, and Burns (1), Cowden, Deabler, and Feamster (2), and Hammer (3) have presented evidence that in certain circumstances it is possible for group-administered H—T—P's to provide even richer, more openly expressed diagnostic and prognostic graphic material than is obtained in individually administered H—T—P's. One thing is certain: both methods are of value.

Chapter Bibliography

1.   CASSEL, R. H., JOHNSON, A. P. and BURNS, W. H. Examiner, Ego Defense, and the H—T—P Test. *J. Clin. Psychol.* XIV, 157—160.

2.   COWDEN, RICHARD C., DEABLER, HERDIS and FEAMSTER, J. HARRY. The Prognostic Values of the Bender-Gestalt, H—T—P, T. A. T., and Sentence Completion Test. *J. Clin. Psychol.* XI, 3, July, 1955, 271—275.

3.   HAMMER, EMANUEL F. *The Clinical Application of Projective Drawings.* Springfield, Ill. Thomas, 1958.

Chapter 4   Quantitative Scoring

Once the chromatic P—D—I has been administered and the interview ended, the first step in the analysis and evaluation of the graphic and verbal materials obtained from the S is the quantitative scoring of the achromatic and chromatic drawings. The upper portion of page 2 of the Scoring Folder has a tabulation form on which are recorded items of detail, proportion, and perspective which the S used in producing his House, Tree, and Person, in accordance with the factor symbol assigned each item in the quantitative scoring tables in this chapter.

To facilitate scoring, items listed in these tables are arranged in order of details, proportion, and perspective for House, Tree, and Person, respectively.

In any set of drawings the examiner may find items for which no scoring or only some scoring is provided, but not scoring which covers the case in point; such items are to be evaluated from a qualitative standpoint only. Occasionally, during the P—D—I an S adds to his drawing. If the item is added spontaneously, and not as a result of the interrogation, it should be treated as if produced during the regular drawing phase and be scored quantitatively if the quantitative scoring system provides for it. If, however, the item were added during tne P—D—I. as a result of the question (for example, an S draws the roots of his Tree after T19 had been asked, or draws clothing after P20), the item is appraised only from a qualitative standpoint.

In short, the examiner scores quantitatively only items the S produces spontaneously and for which provision is made in the quantitative scoring tables.

When an S draws more than one achromatic or chromatic House, Tree, or Person, the examiner observes the following rule: if an S abandons a House, Tree, or Person, as incomplete and then draws what he indicates is to him a finished whole, the examiner scores quantitatively the finished whole; if an S draws what he indicates is a finished whole, and then perseverates by drawing one or more similar wholes (or even several), the examiner scores quantitatively only the first completed whole. The others, however, are appraised qualitatively.

When an S has rejected (totally or in effect, as by degrading) one or more of the wholes, the examiner will evaluate this reaction to the drawing of the rejected and/or degraded whole qualitatively and estimate the S's I.Q. on the basis of his drawings of the wholes not rejected or degraded, making use of the method of appraising I.Q. by *percentage* of raw G, recognizing that less than the usual number of wholes have contributo to the final score.

If it is learned that a drawn whole is a stereotype or a reproduction of a learned figure ("Teacher makes us draw them that way"), the examiner may treat the figure qualitatively only (and estimate the I.Q. on the basis of the score obtained by the subject on the other two wholes), or he may ask the subject to draw another whole.

It has been found that certain details have differential value from the standpoint of the intellectual level of function only when they appear in the drawings: for example, an elliptical face for the Person with the horizontal dimension the greater. Certain details have differential value only when *not* shown: for example, window panes. Some details have no quantitative significance as far as the intellectual level of function is concerned: such as smoke issuing from the chimney. Certain details have differential value only when considered in relation to other details: a Person drawn "full-face" but with only one eye (and no attempt by the S to account for the absence of the other eye).

The proportional relationship between certain pairs of items has differential weight: the width relationship between face and trunk of a Person drawn "full-face." However, the proportional relationship between other pairs of items apparently has no quantitative significance (area of chimney compared with area of roof, unless the former is greater than the latter, which has not yet been seen). The "area" of the chimney in this instance is that portion of the chimney above the baseline of the roof. Poor proportional relationship is more easily and accurately evaluated than good proportional relationship and usually appears to have greater differential value.

Certain perspective "good" points, as motion in the Person, and certain perspective "flaw" points (attachment of arms of the Person to the head) have high quantitative differential value.

In constructing this relatively objective quantitative scoring system, it was very difficult to divorce the measurement of "architectural artistry" which is presumed to be a highly specialized and specific ability, from the appraisal of good proportional relationships.

A progressive increase has been found in the number and quality of details presented as one goes from drawings of Ss at the imbecile level to those at the superior level. There seems to be an equally progressive increase in the recognition of the element of proportion from the moron level upward. The matter of perspective becomes of differential value at the moron level in a negative way (slow diminution of number of perspective "flaw" points), but from the dull average level through the superior level there is an ever increasing use of "good" perspective points.

SCORING INSTRUCTIONS

To become familiar with the descriptive matter in the quantitative scoring tables, the examiner should inspect carefully the plates containing drawings which illustrate the quantitative scoring points specifically (not every possible scoring point is illustrated but the great majority seem to be covered, and a careful study of these plates and the ten illustrative cases in the appendix should make quantitative scoring a simpler and easier task.)

Wherever a scoring item has subheads designated by *Arabic* numerals, *only one subhead* is scored, for subheads so designated are presumed mutually exclusive; wherever the scoring item has subheads designated by *Roman* numerals, however, *any or all* of the subheads so designated may be scored when in drawings.

To illustrate what is involved in the quantitative scoring of a set of drawings let it be assumed in part that the examiner is scoring a House with a trapezoidal roof (material is *not* indicated); a chimney (material *is* indicated by a careful outlining of the bricks) with smoke pouring from it.

The examiner enters a "1" in the box immediately to the right of the factor symbol A2 in the vertical column headed Det. (details) to credit the drawing of a trapezoidal roof, and another "1" in the box immediately to the right of the factor symbol S1 to credit the showing of chimney material. There is no scoring for the omission of roof material however (only its presentation has differential value); no credit is given for presenting a chimney, since only the absence of a chimney has differential weight; and no credit is given for drawing smoke. (It was found that chimney smoke was drawn by 40% of the standardization Ss of the moron group, and by 35% of the Ss of the above average group, but by varying lesser percentages of the Ss of the other groups.)

In scoring the examiner goes through the scoring tables, item by item, scoring only items which the S presented spontaneously and for which scoring is provided, and omitted items for which scoring is provided.

After entering all scorable items for the House, the examiner totals the raw D, A, and S scores in the vertical columns and the D3, D2, D1, A1, A2, A3, S1, and S2 scores on the horizontal lines; he later does the same for the Tree and Person. This done, he enters the grand total for the horizontal rows in the vertical column headed *Grand Total Raw* and follows by compiling the *grand total weighted score* in the last vertical column to the right. This last is done by multiplying the *grand total raw* D3 score by five, the D2 by three, and the D1 by one; the sum of these equals the *weighted flaw score*. The examiner then multiplies the *grand total raw* A1 score by one, the A2 score by two, the A3 score by three, the S1 score by four, and the S2 score by five; the sum of these is the *weighted good score*.

The examiner then (1) enters in the appropriate spaces on the tabulation sheet the S's raw D, raw A, and raw S scores; (2) calculates the percentage of raw G by dividing the sum of the raw A score and the raw S score by the sum of the raw D, A, and S scores; (3) enters the weighted "good" and the weighted "flaw" scores in the appropriate spaces: (4) computes the net weighted score by subtracting the weighted "flaw" score from the weighted "good" score (at times the result will be a negative figure); (5) refers to Table 4 and derives an I.Q. figure for the *percentage of raw G score*, the *net weighted score*, the *weighted "good" score*, the *weighted "flaw" score*, respectively.

After he has done this, the examiner will use the Means Table of the tabulation sheet. He enters a check in the box most closely approximating the S's *grand total raw score* for each of the various factor levels. In this Means section a plus sign following a number indicates that the average S of that specific intellectual and factor level produced a fraction more than the whole number given, but not a sufficient amount to justify the use of the *next higher* whole number; a minus sign following the figure indicates that the average S at that particular intellectual and factor level scored slightly less than the whole number indicated in the box in question, but not sufficiently less to justify the use of the *next lower* whole number.

Referring again to the case of Mr. N., the first illustrative case: Mr. N's *grand total raw scores* were: No D3's, two D2's, five D1's (total of seven D's) seven A1's, twelve A2's, eleven A3's (total of thirty A's); ten S1's and three S2's (total of thirteen S factors). To enter these upon the Means Table one would place an X in the *average* column for the D3 line, an X on the line between *dull average* and *average* for the D2, and an X on the bar between *average* and *above average* for the D1. (The lowest intellectual level for the D3 was selected, even though all average, above average, and superior Ss, as a rule, show no D3 factors, because Mr. N's D2 and D1 scores indicated less than above average function in the "flaw" area.)

The examiner places an X in the *superior* column for the A1 score; an X in the *above average* column for A2, and an X in the *superior* column for A3. The X for the A1 score is placed in the *superior* column rather than in the *moron* column, because it is indicated by the High A2 and A3 scores, in this instance, that the lessened frequency of the presentation of A1 factors represents a superior rather than a deficient function (examination of the Means Tables reveals there is a rapid tapering off of A1's from the *dull average* level upward; A1 factors are replaced by A2, A3, and S factors).

For the S1 factors the examiner enters an X in the box in the *superior* column and likewise for the S2, placing the letter X to the right of the box in the latter case in indicate that better than superior presentation of S2 factors is present.

Finally the examiner records Mr. N's raw D, A, and S scores on the Means Tables, by placing an X on the line between *average* and *above average* for his total D score, and X's in the *superior* column to represent his total A and S scores.*

When the examiner completes his quantitative scoring of the achromatic drawings, he turns to page 3 of the Scoring Folder and does the same for the chromatic drawings.

---

* See Figure 1 which gives Mr. N's Scoring Folder Sheet as it appeared after all Quantitative Scoring had been done.

CASE 1. – K. N. –

TABULATION SHEET

Factor Symbols	HOUSE				TREE				PERSON				Grand Total Raw	Grand Total Weighted
	Det.	Prop.	Persp.	Total	Det.	Prop.	Persp.	Total	Det.	Prop.	Persp.	Total		
D3....	0	0	0	0	0	0	0	0	0	0	0	0	0	x 5 = 0
D2....	1	0	0	1	0	1	0	1	0	0	0	0	2	x 3 = 6
D1....	1	0	1	2	0	0	0	0	1	0	2	3	5	x 1 = 5
Total D...	2	0	1	3	0	1	0	1	1	0	2	3	7	Total Flaw 11
A1....	0	0	0	0	0	1	0	1	4	2	0	6	7	x 1 = 7
A2....	3	1	0	4	2	2	1	5	1	2	0	3	12	x 2 = 24
A3....	0	0	0	0	2	0	1	3	4	1	3	8	11	x 3 = 33
Total A...	3	1	0	4	4	3	2	9	9	5	3	17	30	64
S1....	6	0	0	6	2	0	0	2	1	0	1	2	10	x 4 = 40
S2....	2	0	0	2	0	0	0	0	1	0	0	1	3	x 5 = 15
Total S...	8	0	0	8	2	0	0	2	2	0	1	3	13	Total 55 Good 119

MEANS

Classification	Imb.	Mor.	Bord.	D. Av.	Av.	Ab.Av.	Sup.
Raw D3........	3+	1+	1-	1-	0	0	0
Raw D2........	9	7	5	3-	1+	1-	1-
Raw D1........	13	12	11	9	7	4	3
Raw A1........	6	9	10	11	10	9	
Raw A2........	4-	6	7+	10	11	11	10+
Raw A3........	2	2	4	4	8	9	11+
Raw S1........	1-	1-	1+	2-	4	7	10
Raw S2........	0	0	0	0	1-	2	2
Total Raw D..	25	20	16	12	9	5	4
A..	12	17	21+	25	29	29	
S..	1	1	1	2-	4	9+	12
Percentage Raw G..	34%	47%	58%	68%	79%	90%	93%

	Details		Proportion		Perspective
Good	Sup.	Good	D. Av.–Av.	Good	Av.
Flaw	Av.–Ab. Av.	Flaw	Ab. Av.	Flaw	Av.–Ab. Av.

	House		Tree		Person
Good	Sup.	Good	Sup.	Good	Av.–Ab. Av
Flaw	Av.	Flaw	Ab. Av.	Flaw	Av.–Ab. Av.

ADULT NORMS TABLES

Adult I. Q.	Per Cent Raw G	Net Weighted Score	Good Score	Flaw Score
25	1	-65	10	75
30	9	-55, -56	13	69
35	18	-45, -46	17	63
40	26	-35, -36	21	57
45	33	-25, -26	25	50
50	40	-15, -16	28	44
55	44	-9	30	39
60	48	-2	32	34
65	52	+4	35	31
70	56	12	39	27
75	61	19	43	24
80	65	27	48	21
85	70	35	53	18
90	74	43	59	16
95	78	54	66	12
100	82	64	74	10
105	85	73	81	8
110	88	82	89	7
115	90	92	97	5
120	92	102	106	4
125	94	111	114	3
130	96	121	122	2
135	98	130	131	1
140	100	140	140	0

SUBJECT'S SCORE		COMMENTS:
D	7	
Raw A	30	
S	13	
Per cent Raw G	86	
Net weighted	108	
Good	119	
Flaw	11	

Figure 1.

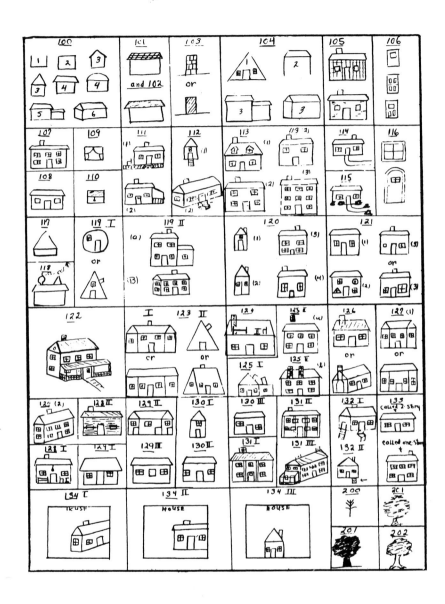

Illustrating Scoring Points

Figure 2A

Illustrating Scoring Points

Figure 2 B

Illustrating Scoring Points

Figure 2 C

QUANTITATIVE SCORING POINTS

HOUSE

Details

100:　*Roof:*
　　(1)　No roof at all.. D3
　　(2)　One 1-dimensional roof..................................... D2
　　　　Note: If the S draws a multi-storied building and calls
　　　　it an apartment house, the score should be A2 as in
　　　　100 (4). The score also should be A2 if the S has
　　　　drawn a House of the "ultra-modern" type with a flat
　　　　roof.
　　(3)　One 2-dimensional roof, inverted—V (triangular) in
　　　　shape.. A1
　　　　Note: The S need not draw a baseline to the inver-
　　　　ted—V to secure an A1 credit.
　　(4)　One 2-dimensional roof, rectangular, semi-elliptical, or
　　　　trapezoidal in shape (breadth greater than height)...... A2

　　　　A *porch* roof does not qualify as a "roof".

　　(5)　Two 2-dimensional roofs, both rectangular, e.g., the
　　　　roof of the main portion of the House and extending
　　　　wing of that House... A3
　　(6)　Two (or more) 2-dimensional roofs, one or more rectan-
　　　　gular and one an inverted—V (triangular) or two trape-
　　　　zoidal. One roof must be over an endwall, the other
　　　　over a sidewall... S1
　　　　Note: If 2 endwalls and a sidewall are shown simul-
　　　　taneously do *not* score item 100, *regardless of the
　　　　roof types.*
101:　*Roof Material* indicated in any recognizable way (as by
　　shading, blocking, diagonal lines, etc.)—not *all* the mate-
　　rial need be shown... S1
102:　*Chimney:* No chimney shown...................................... D2
　　Note: If the S indicates his House is located in a section of
　　the country in which central heat, stove heat, or fireplace
　　heat is not needed, do not score here.
103:　*Chimney Material* shown in any recognizable way, as by out-
　　lining of individual bricks, shading, etc. —not *all* the mate-
　　rial need be shown... S1
104:　*Wall:*
　　(1)　No wall shown... D3

(2)   No baseline shown for wall D2
      Note: Do not so score if the bottom of the page is
      used as a baseline.

(3)   Two walls shown: the main portion of the House and
      an extending wing or side; or a side and an end of the
      House.. A3
      Note: Do not score if a sidewall and *two endwalls*
      are shown simultaneously.

105: *Wall Material* shown in any recognizable way and either
      completely or partially... S2
      Note: When in doubt as to S's intent, ask S for clarification.

      A *louvre* shown in an endwall is not considered wall material.

106: *Door:*
      (1)   No door shown.. D3
            Note: If the S has presented a one-walled House and
            no door, the examiner should ask the S whether he has
            presented the front or the side wall of his House; if S
            says "Front," or "Back," the item is scored D3; if S
            says, "Side," do not score. For any House showing
            an endwall and a sidewall, but no door, the score
            always is D3.
      (2)   A door with a window, or panels, or both.................. S1
107: *Window:*
      (1)   No window shown... D3
      (2)   More than two windows shown (an opening in a door is
            not considered a window)..................................... A2
108: *Window Panes:* No window panes shown in any way (no
      mid-window cross-bar, no rectangular subdivision, no shad-
      ing — to indicate light on a glass surface — etc.)................ D1
      Note: Score D1 if *any* window is drawn without panes, even
      though other windows have panes.
109: *Window Curtains* shown in any recognizable way............... S1
110: *Window Shades* or *Venetian Blinds* shown in any recogniz-
      able way... S1
      Note: The examiner must not assume that the mid-window
      crossbar is the lower edge of a shade.
111: *Porch:*
      (1)   Porch shown, but without pillars or railings.............. S1
      (2)   Porch with pillars and/or railings.......................... S2
            Note: To be scored as a "Porch", the delineated
            area outside the door must be at least twice as wide
            as the door itself, if the Porch is on the front of the
            House; and it must be at least three times the width
            of a step if shown at the end of the House.

112:   *Steps:*
    (1)   Ladder-like steps (no depth to step tread shown).......   D1
    (2)   Two-dimensional step or steps (3-dimensional effect)...   S1
113:   *Stories:*
    (1)   One and a half stories...   A2
    (2)   Two-story House..   A2
    (3)   House with more than 2 stories S2
        Note: Scoring is based on what is drawn; *not* what the S says he drew.
        Note: The attic of a House is *not* construed as a half- or full-story unless the S states it is occupied by a person.
114:   *Walkway* from door of House..   S1
    Note: To avoid confusing a set of steps with a walkway, the examiner always asks the S what he intended to present.
115:   *Shrubbery* beside the House or bordering the walkway to the House...   S2
    Note: This is not scored for trees.
116:   *Facings* of door, window, or windows shown.....................   S1

Proportion

117:   *Roof to Wall:* Obvious malproportion of roof to wall over which it is drawn (roof definitely larger in area than wall)...   D2
118:   *Chimney:* one-dimensional, oval, triangular, or any unconventional shape...   D2
    Note: It was impossible to establish criteria for a well proportioned chimney on the basis of a height-to-width ratio since a satisfactory chimney might range from a simple, tubular iron stove-pipe to a full-length, elaborate stone affair.
119:   *Wall:*
    I.   Wall not rectangular in shape.................................   D3
        Note: Scored for *each wall* not rectangular, but the examiner must not score this merely because the S, through inability to draw, was unable to make precisely right-angled corners.
    II.   (a) Primary wall height greater than breadth, or primary wall approximately square......................   A1
                Note: By "primary" wall is meant the larger wall, if the presentation is front and a wing or wings; the wall most nearly facing the viewer, if the presentation is end and side.
        (b) Primary wall breadth greater than height...........   A2

Note: The *height* of a wall is the distance from a wall's base to the eaveline of the roof.

120:     *Door:*

    (1)   A door with area greater than one-third area of wall in which it appears..... .... D3

    (2)   One-dimensional door (represented by a single vertical line); a door with lower portion not rectangular...... D2

    Note: Before scoring, the examiner must make certain by post-drawing interrogation, that the S did not intend this to represent an open 2-dimensional door.

    (3)   *"Miniscule"* door: obviously too tiny for wall in which it is drawn; much smaller in area than an ordinary single window of the same story and wall................ D2

    (4)   Door too small for wall in which drawn, but not *miniscule:* a door with height less than a window in the same story of the same wall.................................. D1

    Note: Window's *height* means the vertical dimension of the window itself, *not* distance from ground to top of window.

121:     *Window:*

    I.   Malproportion (as to size) between windows of same type in same story of same wall.............................. D2

    Note: In case of doubt, the examiner questions the S as to type his odd-sized window is supposed to be: the conventional small bathroom window or the stair-landing window, for example, are not scored D2. Slight differences due to poor drawing ability are not penalized.

    II.   Window, except attic or stairway, any shape except square or rectangular......... .... D2

    Note: Glass in, about, or over doors is *not* construed a "window".

    III.   Window too small or too large for wall it appears in.... D1

    Note: Scored D1 for each story of each wall in which the too small or too large window or windows appear— not D1 for each window of the same story and wall— and item is scored leniently (only gross malproportion merits such a score).

122:     *Porch:* broader than wall to which it is attached, but not continued along a sidewall or endwall (in short, not L-shaped).. D1

Perspective

123:     *Roof:*

    I.   "Double perspective" (three roof sections shown simultaneously): two inverted—V (triangular) roofs and one rectangular or trapezoidal roof; in short, the roofs

over a sidewall and both endwalls are shown, or in effect, and simultaneously.................................... D1
Note: Score D1, too, if one roof is drawn when both an
end and a sidewall or two endwalls and a sidewall are
presented, or if one wall is drawn with a roof and two
end-gables over it.

II.   "Roof-walling": lines of an inverted—V roof brought
down to the baseline of the House, without altering
angular relationship of the lines, so the roof, in effect,
functions also as a wall..................................... D2

124: *Roof Transparency:* a roof which permits objects within the
House or rear wall of House to be seen, for example (sky-
lights are excepted)................................... D2
Note: Not scored if the S has made an attempt to draw roof
material, as by lining, shading, etc,. even though the viewer still "sees through" part of the roof.

125: *Chimney:*

I.   "Roof-angled" chimney: with vertical axis not paral-
lel to vertical axis of House (most frequently seen
with an inverted—V roof)..................................... D2

II. (a) Chimney malplaced: as suspended over roof of
House D2
     (b) Chimney malplaced: as projecting through *eaves*
of roof over front door, or above windows of first
and second stories sharing a common vertical
axis....................................... D1

126: *Chimney Transparency:* part of roof, wall, or both, or anything else, is seen through the chimney.......................... D1
Note: Do not score if the S has made any attempt to indicate presence of chimney material.

127: *Wall:*

(1)   "Double perspective": sidewall and both endwalls
are presented simultaneously............................... D1

(2) Satisfactory wall-corner angulation at junction of endwall and sidewall S1
Note: Do not score S1 when "double perspective" is
shown.

128: *Wall Transparency:*

I.   Wall transparency: objects within House, or other
walls, seen through a wall D2

II. Wall material transparency: a log, for example, continued across a window, without the S's noticing anything incongruous in such a continuation.................. D2

129: *Door:*

I.   Door "roof-topped": a door with lower roof line of
House, the "eavesline," as its upper margin D3

    II.   Door "wall-sided": a door with wall's vertical end-line as one of its lateral margins...........................   D3

    III.   Door malplaced: a door, for example, unnaturally far above the groundline and no steps leading to it (score leniently)...   D1

130:   *Window:*

    I.   Window "roof-topped": a window with lower or upper roofline of House for its upper margin.....................   D2

    II.   Window "wall-sided!": a window with a wall's vertical endline for one of its lateral margins......................   D2

    Note: Do not score if S says House is ultra-modern with windows which occupy a corner of a wall.

    III. Window (or windows) malplaced in wall or roof. For example: two windows of same type in same story of same wall, but not in same horizontal plane............   D1

    Note: Score (for each subhead) once for each story of each wall so affected.

    Note: The note to item 121-I applies here.

131:   *Porch:*

    I.   Porch one-dimensional in effect; indicated for example, by vertical pillars drawn as if flat against House, with no attempt to indicate depth — as by a porch floor.......   D1

    II.   Transparency of porch pillar.................................   D1

    Note: D1 is scored for *each* porch pillar exhibiting a transparency.

    III. Transparency of porch roof.................................   D1

132:   *Steps:*

    I.   Steps shown in different plane from that of House......   D1

    II.   Steps malplaced (attached to House at point with no means of entrance, or with no porch, or attached to House definitely below a door's sill)......................   D1

133:   *Stories:* House not of number of stories stated by the S in response to P—D—I...   D3

134:   *Placement of the House on the page:*

    I.   House "paper-chopped" (House extends beyond page's top, bottom, or lateral margins). D2

    II.   House "paper-based" (bottom margin of page serves as vertical end-line of a wall of the House D1

    III. House "paper-sided" (lateral margin of page serves as vertical end-line of a wall of the House)..............   D1

    Note: The baseline of a House is the line, or its equivalent, indicating the point at which the base of the wall of the House makes contact with the ground.

    IV.   Vertical disparity less than one inch......................   A3

    Note: By "vertical disparity" is meant the difference between (a) distance from top margin of page and uppermost point of House's roof (not the chimney) and (b) distance from bottom margin of page to point of House's baseline nearest bottom of page.

Note: Do *not* score this item if the S has turned the page so the long axis of the page, as first presented, no longer pertains.

TREE

Details

200:    *Trunk* one dimensional (consisting of only a single vertical line) D2

201:    *Bark* shown on trunk in any recognizable way, partially or completely. *Not* credited if trunk is one-dimensional S1

202:    *Roots:* Two-dimensional roots shown by actual and irregular taper into the ground S1

203:    *Baseline:*

     (1)   No baseline shown (even for trunk), and trunk not "paper-based" D1

     (2)   Baseline consisting of a continuation of the lines forming the sides of the trunk into horizontal lines extending laterally away from each other; *or* Tree "paper-based". A1

     (3)   Baseline shown for trunk only (base of trunk closed); *or* Tree "boxed" (as potted plant, or Christmas Tree on a wooden base); *or* Tree drawn as if suspended in midair with roots dangling.................................... A2

       Note: Do not credit for a one-dimensional trunk.

     (4)   Baseline for trunk and beyond. May consist of:

       (a)   A line that crosses the trunk at its base and extends toward the lateral edges of the page on either side.

       (b)   A short line closing the trunk at its base and another line indicating a groundline (scored as "by implication" if shading is about the Tree at or near its base).

       (c)   An attempt to draw grass.

       (d)   A long line in front of or behind the Tree to indicate ground (even though base of trunk of Tree is not closed)... A3

       Note: Do *not* score if this line was induced at conclusion of P–D–I.

204:    *Branches:*

     (1)   No branches shown, specifically or by implication..... D3

     (2)   1-dimensional branches....................................... D1

     (3)   2-dimensional branches drawn A2

     (4)   2-dimensional branches indicated by unshaded impli-

cation (as by oval, circular, or deltoid figure having
only a perimeter line)... A2

    (5)   2-dimensional branches indicated by shaded implica-
tion (as No. 4 but with figure at least partly shaded).. A3
Note: If two or more types of branch depiction are
employed, credit S with factor rating for method *last*
used.

205:   *Branch System:*
    (1)   No branch system shown. For a branch *system* to be
scored there must be more than branches radiating from
a trunk; there must be a branch-from-branch radiation.. D1
    (2)   Branch system wholly 1-dimensional, or wholly 2-di-
mensional.. A1
    (3)   Actual 2-dimensional branches tapering into 1-dimen-
sional twigs A3
    (4)   Branch system shown by unshaded implication (oval,
circular, or deltoid figure having a perimeter line
only)... A2
    (5)   Branch system shown by shaded implication (as in
No. 4 but with figure at least partly shaded)............. A3
Note: If two or more types of branch systems are employed, credit S with factor rating for method *last* used.

206:   *Foliage:*
    (1)   No foliage shown by individual leaves, by shading,or
by verbal designation.. D1
    (2)   Actual 2-dimensional or acicular leaves drawn (scored
if one 2-dimensional leaf-bud is drawn)................... A2
Note: Fruit does *not* qualify as foliage.
    (3)   Foliage provided by unshaded implication. (Branch
system and foliage indicated by oval, circular, or deltoid figure having a perimeter line only) A2
    (4)   Provision for foliage by verbal designation A2
Note: The S may provide by "verbal designation" for
foliage on a deciduous Tree drawn leaf-bare by saying: "That's a dead Tree," or "It's winter now,"
spontaneously prior to the P—D—I question "Is that
Tree alive?" or in response thereto.
    (5)   Foliage provided by shaded implication (as in No. 3
but with shading, which need not be completed)........ A3
Note: If two or more methods of presenting foliage are
employed, credit S with factor rating for method *last*
used.

207:   *Branch System Baseline* not shown. The blank or shaded
figure (oval, deltoid, or circular) which implies the presence
of a branch system not closed (across the trunk) at its base. D1
Note: If the branch system is 1-dimensional, 2-dimensional,

or 2-dimensional and 1-dimensional, this point is not scored.

208:     *Grass* at base of Tree in a recognizable way. If in doubt, question the S...   S1

Proportion

209:     *Trunk:*
     (1)   Width of trunk greater elsewhere than at its base.......   D2
     (2)   2-dimensional trunk with height at least twice the width and width never greater than at base of trunk....   A2
            Note: Where trunk is drawn as covered by a shaded branch system, or covered by an unshaded branch system, score A2.

210:     *Branch:*
     I.   Width of a 2-dimensional branch greater elsewhere than at point of its junction with trunk.........................   D2
     II.   Length of a 2-dimensional branch less than its width.   D2
            Note: Item II is not scored if the S remarks the branch has been cut off.
     III.   Width of a 2-dimensional branch greater than the trunk's width...   D2

211:     *Branch System:*
     I.   The width of the branch system at its widest point not greater in dimension than full height of Tree............   A2
            Note: Do *not* score if Tree is ''paper-chopped'' or ''paper-sided.''
     II.   (a) Any 2-dimensional branches with a 1-dimensional trunk..   D2
            (b) All branches 1-dimensional with a 2-dimensional trunk..   D1

212:     *Actual Height of Tree Drawn:*
     (1)   Height of drawn Tree less than 1¼ inches...............   D2
     (2)   Height of drawn Tree greater than 7½ inches............   D1
     (3)   Height of drawn Tree between 1¼ and 7½ inches......   A1
            Note: By ''actual height'' is meant distance from tip of Tree to portion of trunk's base nearest the page's base (does *not* include root structure). Does not include any S-described extension of the Tree beyond the page's top or bottom.
            Note: These scores hold only if the standard 8½'' x 7'' H—T—P form sheet is used.

Perspective

213:     *Roots:* shown below ground line, ''in effect'' (as by ground transparency), or as if Tree miraculously were suspended in

		midair without a ground line	D2
214:		*Baseline:* A Tree with no trunk baseline and no branch system baseline; a Tree which is two 1-dimensional Trees, since trunk lines do not join at any point, even at the tip of the Tree...	D2

215:     *Branch Attachment:*

      (1)   Branch attachment to trunk or other branch segmental (as if both units were drawn separately, then attached without either becoming an integral part of the other).....   A1
            Note: 1-dimensional branches are construed as segmentally attached to a trunk or to each other.

      (2)   Branch-trunk or branch-branch attachment "fluid" in in some instances, but not throughout Tree (as by implication and *without* a branch system baseline)........   A2

      (3)   Complete fluidity of branch-trunk and branch-branch attachment actually or by implication (shaded or unshaded)...   A3

216:     *Placement of Tree on Page:*

      I.   Tree "paper-chopped": any margin of the page chops off any part of Tree..   D2

      II.   Tree "paper-topped": uppermost part (or parts) of Tree extends to page's upper margin, but does not seem to extend and is not said by the S to extend beyond the margin or margins....................................   D1

      III.   Tree "paper-sided": a lateral margin of Tree extends to the page's lateral margin— or lateral margins, but does not seem to extend and is not said by the S to extend beyond the margin or margins......................   D1

      IV.   Tree "paper-based": bottom margin of the page serves as a baseline for Tree's trunk......................   D1
            Note: Proper scoring of 216-I and 216-IV depends upon S's reply to questioning in the P−D−I.

      V.   *Vertical Disparity*
          (a) 2½ inches or more........................ ....   D1
          (b) 1½ inches to less than 2½ inches A1
          (c) Less than 1½ inches.....................................   A3
            Note: By "vertical disparity" is meant the difference between the distance from the top margin of the page to the uppermost point of the Tree and the distance from the bottom margin of the page to the point of the trunk's base *(not the roots)* nearest the bottom of the page.
            Note: Do not score this item if the S turned the page so long axis of page, as first presented, no longer pertains.

217:     *Type of Tree:* Tree clearly of another type than that specified by the S in P−D−I.....................................   D1

Type means only *evergreen* or *non-evergreen* and is not construed to mean specific subspecies as, for example, maple.

PERSON

Details

300:    *Eyes:*

    I. (a) Eyes not shown D3

       (b) Incorrect number (as 2 in full profile or 1 with full face)... D2

    II. (a) Eyes shown by dots, hollow circles, ovals, squares, or horizontal lines (only one line for each eye).... A1

       (b) Eyes with 2-dimensional socket, and pupils indicated by dots or circles (or, as by implication, with eyes hidden by a hand).......................... A3

         Note: Do not score if head is drawn so only back is seen.

301:    *Nose:*

    (1)   Nose not shown... D3

    (2)   Nose shown by a single, straight vertical line or a single dot (with head full-face)............................ D2

    (3)   Nose shown as a triangle, oval, square, or a circle.... D1

    (4)   Nose shown in full-face by two dots, circles, or ellipses, or 2 unjoined vertical lines; by a < (in profile). A1

    (5)   Nose shown as conventionally 2-dimensional (as by two vertical, parallel lines joined at the bottom, or two vertical, unjoined, parallel lines with two dots between the lines at their lower end, or by a single vertical line curving at its lower end).............. A2

    (6)   Definite "flaring" of nostrils in a conventional 2-dimensional nose S1

        Note: Do not score if head is drawn so only back is seen.

302:    *Mouth:*

    (1)   Mouth is not shown.... .... D3

    (2)   1-dimensional mouth (one thin horizontal line only: reshading is construed as implying 2-dimensional intent and is not scored D1).................................. D1

303:    *Chin:*

    (1)   Indicated in full-face by distinct and careful lineation. The chin must be clearly defined for credit here........ S1

        Note: This item is *not* scored leniently.

    (2)   Chin indicated clearly with head in profile A1

    (3)   Mandibular line shown with the head in profile: "jaw line" is continued horizontally or obliquely toward

back of head and is more than a mere continuation of
chin-into-neck line.. S2

304:   *Ears:*
    (1)   Ears not shown D1
        Note: Do not score here if Person is a female and
        hair on head is so drawn that ears - even if presented -
        could not be seen because of the hair.
    (2)   Ear convolutions shown clearly (a dot or circle will
        not suffice).. A3

305:   *Hair:*
    (1)   No hair shown on head or face............................. D2
        Note: Do not score if position of hat may be pre-
        sumed to hide hair.
    (2)   Hair shown in more than one place on the head, as by
        eyebrows (or eyelashes) and hair on top of the head,
        and mustache, or by any other combination involving
        the head... A2
        Note: If the person is drawn full-face *both* eyebrows
        must be shown for A2 credit.

306:   *Neck:*
    (1)   No neck shown.. D2
        Note: Do not score if neck is wrapped in a scarf.
    (2)   1-dimensional neck... D1
    (3)   2-dimensional neck... A1

307:   *Trunk:*
    (1)   No trunk shown... D3
    (2)   1-dimensional trunk (as in a "stick-man").............. D2
    (3)   2-dimensional (circular, oval, triangular, or boxlike
        in shape)... D1
    (4)   2-dimensional trunk of conventional shape.............. A1

308:   *Shoulders:*
    (1)   No shoulders shown (or trunk is 1-dimensional, circu-
        lar, oval, triangular, or box-like in shape).............. D1
        Note: If no arms, not even stumps of arms, there are
        no shoulders.
    (2)   Shoulders drawn (in full-face presentation credit *only*
        if *both* are drawn)... A1
        Note: To be credited only when there is an obvious
        rounding from the horizontal downward into the perpen-
        dicular (for the lateral margin of the trunk) in full or
        partial full-face presentation; in profile presentation
        uppermost margin of arm must approximate base of
        neck line.

309:   *Arms:*
    (1)   No arms shown.. D3
    (2)   Incorrect number of 1-dimensional or 2-dimensional

arms shown, and presence of only one arm not verbally and logically accounted for.................................. D3

Note: Only one arm need be shown if Person is in profile.

(3) 1-dimensional arms D2

310: *Hands:*

(1) Mitten-like, bar-like, or circular hands without fingers.. D2

(2) Mitten, bar-like, or circular hands with 1-dimensional fingers D1

(3) 2-dimensional wrist clearly shown by width of forearm at wrist end being narrower than at elbow and then widening towards the fingers, or a joint indicated by a change in direction of the long axis of a 2-dimensional forearm at the appropriate point A3

Note: Score A3 if the S draws his Person so Person has hands in pockets, or hands behind back, for example. The examiner should ask (when in doubt) if hand is gloved.

311: *Fingers:*

(1) No fingers shown.. D3

(2) 1-dimensional fingers, but improper number (as six)... D2

(3) 1-dimensional fingers of proper number shown actually or by implication (as with hand partly in a pocket)..... D1

(4) 2-dimensional fingers shown, but in improper number.. D2

Note: To be scored 2-dimensional, length of finger must exceed its breadth.

(5) 2-dimensional fingers shown in proper number. This is credited if hand is drawn at such an angle that *all* fingers cannot be seen, but the finger (or fingers) visible is 2-dimensional...................................... A2

Note: If the Person is drawn so both hands are visible, both hands must have proper number of 2-dimensional fingers to score A2.

Note: Score A2 if the Person is drawn with hands in pockets or a muff, or with hands behind the back, etc.

(6) Thumb shown as distinct from other fingers.............. A3

Note: Credit if a straight line drawn across the proximal ends of the other four fingers will pass distally to to the proximal end of the supposed thumb. Do not score if such a line intersects thumb's proximal end or passes proximally to it.

312: *Elbows:* Elbow joint indicated clearly by flexion of a 2-dimensional arm (and whole arm must be more than a single ellipse) at proper point or by careful outlining of joint, if arm is not flexed.. A3

313:    *Legs:*
        (1)   No legs shown D3
        (2)   Incorrect number of legs whether 1-dimensional or
              2-dimensional and absence of a leg not logically ac-
              counted for verbally D2
              Note: One leg suffices if the Person is drawn in full
              profile.
        (3)   1-dimensional legs D2
314:    *Knee Joint:*   presented by flexion of leg at proper point or
        by a recognizable outlining of joint S1
        Note: Do *not* credit for 1-dimensional leg.
315:    *Feet:*
        (1)   No feet shown D3
              Note: Do *not* score if only the toes are shown, even
              though they project from the leg.
        (2)   1-dimensional feet, or 2-dimensional feet with incor-
              rect number of toes D2
        (3)   Golf-club-head, oval, or square feet without heel D1
        (4)   Heel clearly shown if foot drawn in profile, or correct
              number of 2-dimensional toes shown (or shoe clearly
              outlined) if foot drawn pointing anteriorly A1
              Note: Score A1 if feet are hidden by a long evening
              gown or, for example, by a table at which the Person
              sits.
316:    *Clothing:*
        (1)   No clothing shown, and no sexual organs drawn to in-
              dicate that presentation in the nude was intended D2
        (2)   Clothing suggested (as by shading, by a bottom trou-
              ser - or a bottom dress-line, by a belt, hat, or row of
              buttons), but neither trousers nor dress is satisfacto-
              rily outlined throughout D1
        (3)   Minimum conventional clothing shown (trousers for a
              male; dress for a female) and/or more complete cloth-
              ing suggested A1
        (4)   Person nude with sexual organs drawn, or well clad;
              there must be a coat or a shirt *and* trousers, *and*
              shoes for the male; a dress and shoes for the female;
              (the shoe must be fully outlined, unless hidden as by
              a dress of floor-sweeping length) A3
              Note: The unclad Person drawn in profile may be pre-
              sumed, in certain instances (as with the back partly
              turned toward the viewer), to have adequate sexual
              characteristics by implication— but before allowing
              credit the examiner should be satisfied as to the S's
              intent; in full-face presentation all *sexual organs* must
              be drawn or concealed by other parts of the body.

317:      *Additional Details* as a cane, basket, roller skates S1
        Note: The essential point is that the object be relevant to
and "tie in" with what the Person *may be* (sword for soldier),
or may be doing (horse for Person riding).

Proportion

318:      *Facial Inter-part Proportion:*
       (1)   Less than 3 of the following points are positive: that
is, eyes and mouth of greater width than height, and
ears and nose of greater height than width D1
            Note: If the Person is drawn with head in profile, and
the eye shown is more than a dot, the width of the eyes
and mouth may be assumed to be greater than their
height. And if the hair on top of the head is in sufficient profusion to cover the ears, the unseen ears may
be assumed to have greater height than width.
       (2)   Three plus: If any 3 of the above proportional require-
ments are met A1
       (3)   Four plus: If all the above proportional requirements
are met S1

319:      *Head Proportion:*
       (1)   Face (full-face presentation) an oval with horizontal
measurement greater than its vertical measurement,
or face in profile with vertical dimension markedly
exceeding the horizontal dimension, or vice versa D1
       (2)   Face (full-face presentation) a circle or almost square.. A1
       (3)   Face (in profile) with vertical and horizontal measure-
ments approximately equal.................................... A2
            Note: "Vertical" = tip of chin to top of forehead:
"horizontal" = center of forehead to occipital bulge.
       (4)   Face (full-face presentation) a vertical oval............. A3

320:      *Arms:*
       (1)   Forearms (one or both) wider than upper arm............ D2
            Note: To be scored leniently — not for minute dif-
ferences.
       (2)   Arm Taper: forearm narrower than upper arm. If both
arms are shown, *both* must taper to secure credit A2

321:      *Leg:*
       (1)   Lower leg's width greater than upper leg's width D2
       (2)   Satisfactory leg taper from thigh to ankle. Scored only
if a sufficient portion of the *unclad* leg indicates
good taper. If both legs are presented, both must
taper to secure credit A2

322:     *Dimensional Scatter Between the Extremities:*
    (1)   2-dimensional arms with 1-dimensional legs.............. D2
    (2)   1-dimensional arms with 2-dimensional legs............. D2
323:     *Ratios:*
    I.   *Face-trunk ratio*:as to width (with entire Person in full-face).
        (a)   Trunk's width less than width of face................ D2
        (b)   Trunk's width approximately that of the face....... D1
        Note: Width of face and trunk is the largest horizontal measurement of each.

    II.   *Head-trunk ratio:* (as to height) Head measurement is taken from tip of forehead to lowest point of chin with mouth closed (if mouth is open, the point should be approximated); trunk measurement is taken from lowest point of chin to top of pelvic crest (in Persons drawn clothed, this will be at approximately lower margin of belt; in Persons drawn nude, it will be slightly above hip joint.
        (a)   H:T: :1:3 or more, *or* T:H: :1:1 plus............ D1
        (b)   H:T: :1:2 or more but less than 3, *or*
               H:T: :1:1 or more but less than 1½................. A1
        (c)   H:T: :1:1½ or more but less than 2................. A2
        Note: Ratios under (a) mean the trunk measurement is 3 times that of the head, *or* the head measurement is greater than that of the trunk . The ratio under (c) means the measurement of the trunk is at least one and one-half times that of the head, but not quite two times that of the head.
    III.   *Arm-trunk ratio:* (long axis dimension) If arms are unequal in length, take the dimension of the longer arm *(arm dimension* is distance from tip of shoulder to point of finger farthest therefrom):
        (a)   T:A: :1:2 or more, *or* A:T: :1:1 plus............ D2
        (b)   T:A: :1:1½ or more, but less than 2................ D1
        (c)   T:A: :1:1 or more, but less than 1½................ A2
    IV.   *Trunk-leg ratio:* (long axis dimension) If legs are unequal in length, take dimension of longer leg *(leg dimension* is distance from tip of pelvic crest to point of foot farthest therefrom):
        (a)   T:L: :1:4 or more, *or* L:T: 1:1: plus D2
        (b)   T:L: :1:2 or more, but less than 4................. D1
        (c)   T:L: :1:1.. A2
        (d)   T:L: :1:1 plus, but less than 2..................... A3
        Note: In a poorly drawn Person it may be impossible for the examiner to determine the pelvic crest's location without asking the S where the hip joint of his Person is: the pelvic crest would

be a trifle above that point. *If the pelvic crest's position cannot be determined even by questioning, do not score the ratios involving the trunk's long axis dimension.*

Perspective

324:   *Arm-to-Trunk Attachment:*
  (1)   Arm-trunk attachment *segmental,* as if the arms were drawn separately from the trunk, then glued on: there is, in short, no appearance of continuation of the shoulder line into the arm. 1-dimensional arms *always* are considered segmentally attached...................... D1
  (2)   Both arms springing from a common or nearly common source.. D1
  (3)   "Ribbon attachment" of arm or arms to trunk: in such instances the arm looks as if squeezed out of the trunk, like a ribbon of toothpaste from a tube: there is almost always a marked widening of the arm as it leaves the trunk... A1
  (4)   Complete "fluidity" of arm-trunk attachment: there is a continuation of the upper shoulder line into the outer arm line; in short, the arm becomes an extension of the shoulder. (If both arms are shown, both must have fluid attachment to secure credit here)............. A3

325:   *Malplacement of Arms:*
  (1)   Arm or arms attached to head or neck...................... D2
  (2)   Arm or arms attached to trunk below the shoulder level... D1
        Note: If both types of presentation are employed score D2.

326:   *Position of Arms:*
  (1)   *With body presented in full-face:*
        (a)   Both arms extended laterally and approximately at right angles to trunk or upward......................... D1
        (b)   One or both arms extended laterally at less than right angles to trunk, but not straight down at the sides... A1
        (c)   One or both arms straight down at the sides of body... A2
        (d)   With one or both arms (2-dimensional) flexed....... S1
              Note: If two types of depiction are employed, credit the type with the higher factor rating.
  (2)   *With body presented in profile:*
        (a)   Arm or arms extended forward or backward and/or

        upward... D1
        Note: If one arm is extended pointing toward
        something, score A3.
    (b) Arm or arms extended forward or backward, at
        less than right angles to trunk but not straight
        down A1
    (c) Arm or arms hanging straight down at sides A2
    (d) Arm or arms (2-dimensional) with elbow flexed S1
        Note: If two types of depiction are employed,
        credit the type bearing the higher factor rating.

327:   *Finger Attachment:*
    (1) More than one finger shown protruding from the side
        of the arm D2
    (2) Fingers shown protruding from end of forearm D1
        Note: Do not score 327 if any attempt to produce a
        hand was made.

328:   *Mal-attachment of the Legs:*
    One or both legs attached to head or neck of the Person or
    joined to trunk in some abnormal fashion......................... D3

329:   *Placement of the Person on the Page:*
    I. "Paper-chopped" (a margin of the page "chops" off a
        portion of the Person)... D2
    II. *Vertical Disparity:*
        (a) 2 inches or greater... D1
        (b) 1 inch to less than 2 inches A1
        (c) Less than 1 inch.. A3
        Note: By "vertical disparity" is meant the dif-
        ference between distance from top margin of page
        and uppermost point of the Person's skull (*not
        the hat*) and distance from bottom margin of page
        to point of the Person's foot nearest the bottom
        of the page.
        Note: Do not score this item if the S has turned
        the page so the long axis of the page, as first
        presented, no longer pertains.

330:   *Method of Presentation of Person:*
    (1) Head drawn in profile; body in full-face.................. A2
    (2) Full or partial profile for face and body.................. A3

331:   *Animation of Person:* Figure is doing something besides
    standing (sitting, walking, running, riding, throwing, writ-
    ing, for example)... S1

332:   *Type of Person:*
    I. Person not recognizable as of sex specified by the S
        in his P—D—I (induced) or if the S cannot or will not
        specify the sex D2
    II. Person recognizable as of an age markedly different

from that specified by the S in his P—D—I (induced)...   D2
Note: This point must be appraised leniently or the
examiner will find hinself estimating artistry rather
than concept.

333:    *Transparency:* of a body part or of clothing: score once for
each "transparency" of body or clothing, except a pair of
shoes lacking complete "top lines," which is counted as
only one transparency..   D1

Transparency is the inability of an exterior or superim-
posed substance or object to conceal or cover, actually or
in effect, objects conventionally perceived as beneath or
behind the cover and, therefore, concealed by the cover.

The H—T—P is not, and never was intended to be, merely an *intelligence test* in the usually accepted definition of that term.

H—T—P derived I. Q.s are only signposts, albeit valuable ones.
The I. Q.s of such well-recognized tests of intelligence as the Wechsler-
Bellevue and the Stanford-Binet, on the contrary, are presumed to stand
on their established merits.

But the differences between the H—T—P and an intelligence test
per se make a comparison of I. Q.s derived from both sources an extremely
useful procedure. For example, if the Wechsler I. Q.s are mildly depressed,
but the H—T—P I. Q.s are sharply depressed and there is wide scatter
among them, a good measure of the effect of a personality disturbance upon
the S's intellectual efficiency could be presumed to exist.

In comparing H—T—P derived I.Q. scores with those derived from
formal tests of intelligence, these points must be kept in mind:

(1)   The H—T—P is almost entirely unstructured, whereas
the formal intelligence test is almost completely struc-
tured--relatively speaking.

(2)   The H—T—P evaluates intellectual function as *one
aspect* of the total personality constellation of the S,
in a setting designed to be emotion-arousing. The formal intelligence test, on the other hand, measures
intelligence nearly in isolation and in a setting designed to be little emotion-arousing.

(3)   H—T—P I. Q.s are often highly vulnerable to depression by non-intellective factors. The I. Q.s of more
formal tests of intelligence are relatively more stable.

(4)   There is no age-correction factor applied to H—T—P—
derived I. Q.s

(5)   Ss with formal art training probably will produce higher
H—T—P I. Q.s than those without such training, as
Bieliauskas and Bristow[1] have shown.

It probably would be more accurate to refer to H—T—P I. Q.s as
E. Q.s (Efficiency Quotients).

Empirical evidence accumulated over the past twenty-five years
suggests the following (in each instance the H—T—P I.Q. referred to is the
Per Cent of Raw G I.Q.):

(1)   For most endogenous mental defectives the H—T—P I.Q. is
higher (not infrequently 10 points higher) than the Stanford-
Binet or the Wechsler-Bellevue Verbal or Full I.Qs. This
appears due to the fact that many endogenous mental defectives find verbalization difficult because of their limited
vocabularies, and find tests such as solving arithmetic problems and detecting similarities most troublesome.

(2)   For exogenous defectives the disparity usually favors verbal tests—and the depression of the H—T—P I.Q. appears
to depend upon the degree and type of the organic component and its involvement of the motor areas.

(3)   For many pseudo-mental deficients, the H—T—P I.Q. is so
much higher than the Stanford-Binet or the Wechsler-Bellevue
Verbal or Full I. Q.s as to be striking; apparently such individuals find it possible to reveal potentials on the H—T—P,
as on the Rorschach, more easily than upon the more formal
and structured tests.

(4)   In cases where verbalization is markedly interfered with (as
in certain schizophrenias), the H—T—P I.Q. tends to be
much higher than the Stanford-Binet or the Wechsler-Bellevue
Verbal or Full I. Q.s presumably because drawing for such
Ss is a far more acceptable and usable medium of expression than is speech.

(5)   In cases where organic deterioration has occured or is occurring from an average intelligence level, the H—T—P I.Q.
tends to be lower than the Stanford-Binet I.Q. or Wechsler-
Bellevue Verbal I.Q: in such cases, the Stanford-Binet and
the Wechsler Verbal I.Q.s appear to represent residuals, the
H—T—P I.Q. to indicate deterioration. In some cases where
concept formation is sharply affected, the H—T—P I.Q. ap-

1. Bieliauskas, V. J. and Bristow, Robin B. The Effect of Formal Art Training upon the
Quantitative Scores on the H—T—P. J. Clin. Psychol., 1959, 15, 57-59.

pears to show deterioration in a prognostic rather than a diagnostic sense.

(6) The H—T—P I.Q. of the markedly depressed, or psychoneurotics who exhibit much anxiety or depression, or both, usually is lowered markedly and is believed to represent in striking fashion the interference with intellectual efficiency which is brought on by anxiety and/or depression.

(7) The H—T—P I.Q. of obsessive-compulsive neurotics may be enhanced by the "quantity necessity" of such Ss which may lead to tremendous detail production resulting in a spuriously high H—T—P I.Q. score.

(8) The H—T—P I.Q. of negativistic or psychopathic Ss may be spuriously low because of either their;

   (a) Refusal to draw one or more wholes (usually the Person), or;

   (b) Caricaturing or otherwise degrading one or more wholes (as by drawing a "stick-man" for the Person).

Intelligence Levels Depicted by H—T—P Drawings

Each of the following H—T—P sets of "wholes" — House, Tree, Person — was drawn by a different person. No set of "wholes" in its entirety is "typical" for a given intelligence level. Nor is it likely that any one person will produce three H—T—P "wholes" of the same calibre.

The following series of drawings is presented for two reasons:

1. To illustrate types of drawings at different intelligence levels.
2. To illustrate factors of detail, proportion, and perspective which tend to differentiate intelligence levels.

Adult Imbecile

Adult Moron

Adult Borderline

Intelligence Levels

Figure 3 A

Adult Dull Average

Adult Average

Adult Above Average

Adult Superior

Figure 3 B

Table 4

Adult Norms

Classification Level	Adult IQ	Per Cent Raw G	Net Weighted Score	Good Score	Flaw Score	Adult IQ
Imbecile	25	1	−65	10	75	25
	30	9	−55, −56	13	69	30
	35	18	−45, −46	17	63	35
	40	26	−35, −36	21	57	40
	45	33	−25, −26	25	50	45
Moron	50	40	−15, −16	28	44	50
	55	44	−9	30	39	55
	60	48	−2	32	34	60
	65	52	4	35	31	65
Borderline	70	56	12	39	27	70
	75	61	19	43	24	75
Dull Average ..	80	65	27	48	21	80
	85	70	35	53	18	85
	90	74	43	59	16	90
Average	95	78	54	66	12	95
	100	82	64	74	10	100
	105	85	73	81	8	105
	110	88	82	89	7	110
Above Average..	115	90	92	97	5	115
	120	92	102	106	4	120
Superior	125	94	111	114	3	125
	130	96	121	122	2	130
	135	98	130	131	1	135
	140	100	140	140	0	140

Table 5

Means For Quantitative Standardization Groups By
Intelligence Level, Raw Scores, And Percent Of Raw G I.Q.

Classification	Imb.	Mor.	Bord.	D. Av.	Av.	Ab. Av.	Sup.
Raw D3	3+	1+	1-	1-	0	0	0
Raw D2	9	7	5	3-	1+	1-	1-
Raw D1	13	12	11	9	7	4-	3
Raw A1	6	9	10	11	10	9	8
Raw A2.	4-	6	7+	10	11	11+	10+
Raw A3	2	2	4	4	8	9	11+
Raw S1..........	1-	1-	1+	2-	4	7	10
Raw S2..........	0	0	0	0	1-	2	2
Total Raw							
D	25	20	16	12	9	5	4
A	12	17	21+	25	29	29	29+
S	1	1	1	2-	4	9+	12
Percent of							
Raw G IQ	40	58	72	83	97	117	130

Table 6

Mean Raw "Good" and "Flaw" Scores on Details, Proportion,
Perspective of Quantitative Standardization Groups by Intelligence Levels

	Imb.	Mor.	Bord.	D. Av.	Av.	Ab. Av.	Sup.
Details:........							
Good.........	6	7	10	13	17	23	25
Flaw..........	12	9	7	5	4	2	0
Proportion:							
Good..........	4	6	7	8	10	10	10
Flaw..........	5	4	3	2	1	1	1
Perspective:							
Good..........	2	4	5	5	6	6	7
Flaw..........	8	7	6	5	4	2	2

Table 7

Mean Raw "Good" and "Flaw" Scores on House, Tree, Person of
Quantitative Standardization Groups by Intelligence Levels

	Imb.	Mor.	Bord.	D. Av.	Av.	Ab. Av.	Sup.
House:							
Good.........	3	4	4	5	7	10	11
Flaw	6	5	3	3	3	2	1
Tree:							
Good.........	4	4	7	7	8	8	9
Flaw.........	4	4	3	3	1	1	1
Person:							
Good.........	6	10	12	16	19	21	22
Flaw.........	15	11	10	7	5	2	1

Table 8

Coefficients of Correlation Between H–T–P
Percent of Raw G I.Q. and I. Q. s of Other Tests

Group	Test	No. Cases	Pearson r	P.E.r
A	Otis, Higher...................... 30	30	.41	±.1024
B	Stanford-Binet, Forms L&M 26	26	.45	±.1054
C	Wechsler-Bellevue, Verbal I.Q........ 100	100	.699	±.034
C	Wechsler-Bellevue, Performance I.Q... 100	100	.724	±.032
C	Wechsler-Bellevue, Full I.Q. 100	100	.746	±.029
Total		356		

Table 9

Comparison of Measures of Central Tendency and Variability *

Group	Test	No. Cases	Mean I.Q.	Range	S.D.
A	Otis, Higher I.Q................... 30	30	121	98-144	11.07
	H–T–P *percent of raw G I.Q.*.......		114	83-140	12.48
B	Stanford-Binet, Forms L&M I.Q...... 26	26	47	25--65	9.71
	H–T–P *percent of raw G I.Q.*.......		53	33--81	13.39
C	Wechsler-Bellevue, Verbal I.Q....... 100	100	74	44-132	20.60
	H–T–P *percent of raw G I.Q.*.......		73	35-133	23.10
C	Wechsler-Bellevue, Performance I.Q.. 100	100	69	34-120	21.95
	H–T–P *percent of raw G I.Q.*.......		71	35-115	21.32
C	Wechsler-Bellevue, Full I.Q......... 100	100	70	35-125	23.29
	H–T–P *percent of raw G I.Q.*.......		73	35-133	23.36
Total		356			

---

* Group A was composed of medical students of the School of Medicine of the University of Virginia, all young adults. Group B was composed of mentally deficient, epileptic, and psychotic in- and out-patients of the Lynchburg State Colony, all young adults. Group C was composed of white adults examined individually at the Lynchburg State Colony or one of its Mental Hygiene Clinics; all Ss were maladjusted, epileptic, mentally deficient, psychoneurotic, or psychotic; Ss were studied in chronological order of their examinations: Ss of each of the three C groups were not entirely comparable, however, as the first hundred patients had not all been tested by the full Wechsler. Ages in Group C ranged from 15 to 65 years.

Comparison of the H—T—P *per cent of raw G* I.Q. with I. Q.s obtained by the same Ss on other more structured and stable tests than the H—T—P and designed specifically to measure intelligence, offers evidence that the H—T—P appraises general intelligence. (See Tables 8 and 9). It is patent, however, that the H—T—P's approach to this appraisal is quite different from that used by intelligence tests in general.

The Correlation coefficients between the H—T—P *per cent of raw G* I.Q. and the I. Q.s on the three Wechsler-Bellevue Scales presumably were depressed somewhat for adults of advanced age since the Wechsler I. Q.s automatically were "corrected" for a decline in efficiency due to advanced age; no such "correction" was used in estimating the H—T—P I. Q.s

Later studies by the author seem to indicate that correlations of this magnitude may be expected only when: (1) Ss are relatively free of personality flaws; (2) Ss are so deteriorated and/or maladjusted that all test scores are depressed thereby. The H—T—P I.Q. should never be appraised in isolation, so to speak, and without careful qualitative evaluation of the non-intellective factors which analysis of H—T—P drawings may indicate to have influenced the I.Q.

The H—T—P is not a highly refined measure of intelligence, as shown by the fact that the Norms Table I. Q.s represent the range Q1 to Q3 for the respective intelligence levels (in brief. there is much overlap), but this need not be surprising in view of the fact that it would be almost impossible to devise a less structured test of intelligence.

H—T—P I. Q.s quickly reflect the effect which non-intellective factors of Ss' personalities have upon their intellectual functions. Such I. Q.s will not have and must not be expected to have the stability of I. Q.s obtained from formal intelligence tests. A careful examination and appraisal of the H—T—P—derived I. Q.s when compared with those of the Wechsler and similar tests will provide useful diagnostic and prognostic data.

Chapter 5   Quality of the Quantity *

The second procedure in the analysis of an S's graphic material involves the *qualitative* appraisal of the various *quantitative* scores. This step, called "The Quality of the Quantity", serves to bring into closer and more efficient relationship the quantitative and the qualitative scoring systems, and provides the examiner with valuable information concerning the internal consistency of an S's graphic performance.

The appraisal of the quality of the quantity of a set of H—T—P drawings is divided into five major steps.

Step 1:   This involves an evaluation of the degree of the disparity between the I.Q. scores by pairs. The Percent Raw G and the Net Weighted I.Q.s constitute the first pair; the Good and the Flaw I.Q.s, the second.

While no true dichotomy is posited in either instance, the scores appear to have somewhat different qualitative implications. The Raw G I.Q., derived from raw points only, without consideration of more than their gross differentiation as Good and Flaw, respectively, seems largely to represent the present qualitative level of an S's creativity and productivity.

The Net Weighted I.Q., derived by subtracting the weighted Flaw score from the weighted Good score and thus according each factor point a more refined differentiation, seems to emphasize the S's potential level of function (which may or may not be realizable).

In the majority of cases the Net Weighted I.Q. is from 1 to 10 points above the Raw G. Whenever these two scores are within five points of one another, they may be regarded as representing stable function. This stability of function, however, may represent (a) an over-all depression of

* This material was first published in condensed form in an article entitled "The Quality of the Quantity of the H—T—P" in the Journal of Clinical Psychology, Vol. VII, No. 4, October, 1951.

function due to a personality disturbance of long-standing, or (b) "normal" stability.

If the Net Weighted I.Q. is 15 or more points above the Raw G, the S may not be functioning at the qualitative level of which he is capable. If the Raw G I.Q. is several points above the Net Weighted I.Q., the S has what may be called "quantity necessity" (at times it seems to represent maximal efficiency). If the disparity is 15 points or more in favor of the Raw G, pathoformicity is suspected, and with the quality of behavior that much below quantity, a regression is implied, whose probable permanence depends on other factors.

In appraising the *percent of Raw G* I.Q. score of Ss of above average or superior ability, the examiner must remember the percentage method of arriving at that score may penalize the S. In such instances, the *net weighted* I.Q. score seems more closely to approximate the S's level of intellectual function as appraised by the H—T—P. For instance, there are Case A and Case B: A scored 4 Ds, 25 As, 10 Ss; B scored 5 Ds, 30 As and 17 Ss. Although B scored 5 more As and 7 more Ss than A, he received the same *percent of Raw G* I.Q. score (115) as A because of the one additional D factor. The quantitative difference between A and B, however, was reflected by their *net weighted* I.Q. scores of 115 and 134, respectively.

The examiner should bear in mind that the *percent of Raw G* I.Q. score usually will be less resistive to depression by emotional and/or organic factors than the *net weighted* score I.Q. because the percentage method of deriving the former reflects more quickly the presence of additional D factors than the subtraction method used to derive the latter score. The *percentage Raw G* I.Q. takes into consideration only "good" points and "flaw" points, as such, without consideration of their relative qualitative values.

For the second pair of I.Q.s, the Good and the Flaw, no real dichotomy is believed to exist, but there is some qualitative difference. The Good I.Q. score, estimated solely on the weighted Good points, seems to stress the S's productivity, since it is a measure of his expression of details, their size, and their spatial relationships in the drawings of House, Tree, and Person. By generalization, then, it seems to express the degree to which the S is able to act and interact in his environment.

The Flaw I.Q., based on the measureable errors an S commits in producing his H—T—P, stresses his power of criticality; it largely emphasizes his ability to appraise reality aloofly, objectively, analytically.

The Good I.Q. score usually is higher than the Flaw I.Q. If it is 15 points or more higher, one suspects the S's general behavior would be vacillant and at times inefficient because of the great striving on the one hand and the lower level of analytic judgment on the other. If the Flaw I.Q. is 15 points or more higher than the Good, one suspects the S's failure to function socially at a level commensurate with his critical judgment might be due to hypercritical attitudes.

At times it is found the Flaw I.Q. has been so depressed by 2 or 3 D3s it cannot be regarded representative of the S's critical level: but the presence of such gross errors in judgment has pathological implications. H—T—P I.Q.s, like all H—T—P items, are regarded only as sign posts to be interpreted in light of all qualitative and quantitative factors elicited.

Where the four I.Q. scores vary widely, the presence of a personality maladjustment to which the S is reacting in an impulsive, more or less disorganized fashion, is suggested.

Step 2:   First this involves an appraisal of mean score patterns: appraisal of factors making up the four I.Q.s. First, the examiner determines the relative part played in the production of the Flaw I.Q. by the raw D scores which represent the S's misuse or omission of details, and/or his faulty assignment of proportional and spatial relationships to them in the drawings of House, Tree, and Person. By generalization D scores are regarded as qualitative representations of an S's level of critical judgment in life situations. The D1 factors represent minor flaws, the D2s and D3s imply, respectively, strongly pathoformic and pathological (if not pathognomonic) errors in critical judgment. A complete absence of D-factors is regarded with suspicion, for it implies a hypercriticality possibly more crippling than helpful.

Next the examiner appraises the raw A-score and S-score patterns to determine their respective roles in the production of the Good I.Q. score. The S's A-scores reveal his grasp of the details essential to the productions of House, Tree, and Person and their proportional and spatial relationships, and by generalization A-scores seem to indicate an S's ability to deal with the more concrete and elemental aspects of reality. An S whose Good I.Q. score is made up largely of A1s and A2s is one whose major interests are relatively simple, immediate, and material. An S's S-scores, which represent his use of enriching details, and more refined and elaborate proportional and spatial relationships in the drawings of House, Tree, and Person, from a qualitative standpoint seem to indicate the ability of the S to deal with the more abstract and abstruse aspects of everyday life. The S whose Good I.Q. score is in large measure made up of S1s and S2s* is likely to be an individual whose interests are more intellectual than material; and the greater the number of Perspective factors in the S-score, the greater the likelihood the S is more flexible and resourceful.

If there is more than adjacent level classification scatter between the D-scores, the A-scores, and the S-scores, respectively, with the latter the highest as to level, the examiner will suspect severe personality distur-

---

* As a rule there will be more material shown by shading in the chromatic series than in the achromatic (apparently the whiteness of the enclosed space is enhanced by the greater contrast between crayon and background). S-scores for material, therefore. have a lower qualitative "value" in the chromatic H—T—P than in the achromatic H—T—P.

bance. It is postulated, in such instances, that the A-scores represent basic ability and the widely disparate D-score indicates current depression of function.

An examiner may find an S with D-scores in a higher classification level than either A-score or S-score, in which instance he might presume presence of a personality factor which had enhanced the S's need for meticulosity and criticality and at the same time inhibited the production of "good" factors which, in turn, would have produced a relatively high A-score and S-score.

In the second part of Step 2 the so-called consistency of performance is appraised by evaluating the *classification level spread* of the individual means scores. A "normal spread" involves from 3 to 4 adjacent classification levels. Seventy-six percent of Ss in the quantitative standardization group had raw scores with no greater scatter than three adjacent classification levels. A spread of less than 3 adjacent levels carries qualitative implications of pathoformic constriction of function. The greater the spread beyond 4 adjacent classification levels, particularly if more than one factor level is involved, the greater is the qualitative implication that the S's behavior is characterized by impulsivity and widely divergent levels of efficiency of function.

In appraising *grand total raw* scores scatter, however, the examiner should bear in mind: (1) *any* S may score one D3 or one S2 without such a score being significant; (2) when an individual has a high A3, S1, and S2 factor score, a low A1 and A2 score does not necessarily indicate great scatter, for in such instances the ordinarily shown A1 and A2 items of Details, Proportion, and Perspective have been replaced by factors of higher quality value; (3) one or more S-factors may appear in drawings of low grade mental defectives and a few D-factors almost always appear in drawings of persons of superior intelligence (in fact, a total absence of D-factors may be regarded as highly suspicious, since it implies a meticulosity and excess of critical faculty which may be severely handicapping).

Step 3:   This involves inspection and evaluation of scores for Details, Proportion and Perspective: first, the Good score against the Flaw score in each category is appraised, next, the quality of the categories in relationship to each other is weighed.

The Details Good score is the raw score measure of the S's concept of the elements necessary to the production of a satisfactory House, Tree, and Person. By extension this score qualitatively is an index of the S's ability to recognize the elements of everyday life and employ them conventionally. The Details Flaw score, which is the raw score measure of the S's ability to avoid mistakes in using Details in the H—T—P, qualitatively is a measure of an S's ability to appraise critically the elements of reality in general.

The Proportion Good score is the raw score measure of the size relationships which the S assigns to the Details in constructing a whole, and the size of the drawn whole* in relationship to the drawing form page. It seems, qualitatively speaking, to be a measure of an S's ability to make efficient use of his judgment in the solution of the more basic, concrete, and immediate problems of everyday living.

The Proportion Flaw score, the measure of the S's ability to avoid mistakes in assigning proportional relationships to the Details and his wholes, becomes qualitatively an index of his ability to subject to aloof, critical judgment the more basic problems presented by his environment. "Logic-tight compartments" may depress this score.

The Perspective Good score is a raw measure of the S's concept of: (1) spatial relationships of elements making up each whole; and (2) relationship of each whole in symbolic time and space to other objects in the environment. Qualitatively it seems to be an index of the S's ability to function in the more abstract and broader relationships of everyday life. In short, it is considered, in part, a measure of an S's functioning insight. The Perspective Flaw score, a raw score measure of an S's ability to avoid mistakes in assigning spatial relationships to the Details, and the total figure, by extension, becomes a measure of the S's critical insight into his environment and those sharing it with him.

If the Perspective Flaw score is the only one of the six Good and Flaw scores of high calibre, the examiner should check to see if the apparent high quality is not due to the absence of any attempt to show Perspective and therefore to be regarded as spurious.

In none of these comparisons, of course, is any strict dichotomy implied, but the Good scores seem to emphasize the level of doing, acting, and interacting; the Flaw scores, the level of aloof thinking and analysis. A disparity of one classification level between the Good and the Flaw scores in a given category seems to have no significance. The greater the disparity beyond this, however, the greater is the degree of presumed pathoformicity.

In interpreting Details, Proportion, and Perspective patterns, the examiner must remember that, from a developmental standpoint, initially a child is conscious of details only, and a limited number at that. Later, as he adds to his Details vocabulary, he increasingly becomes aware first of the Proportional and then the spatial relationships of those Details.

In the H–T–Ps of Ss of limited intelligence, Perspective may well be the first to undergo qualitative loss under the impact of anxiety, and so on; in those Ss in whom Perspective has been well and long developed (as in many of above average intelligence), however, Proportion may well be the first to suffer from pressure.

Not all presentable Details, or all of their respective size and/or spatial relationships, can be scored by the H–T–P quantitative scoring

---

* All else being equal, chromatic wholes usually are larger than achromatic wholes (in part, presumably, because crayon lines are coarser than pencil lines).

system. Score patterns for Details, Proportion and Perspective must, therefore, be interpreted qualitatively in light of what *cannot* be scored as well as what can be scored.

Step 4:   In this step the S's raw "good" and "flaw" scores for House, Tree, and Person, separately, are compared to determine the respective parts played by the disparate wholes in the production of the total score. To obtain these scores the examiner turns to the tabulation sheet and takes the sum of the raw A-scores and S-scores (for Details, Proportion, and Perspective) and the sum of the raw D-score (for Details, Proportion, and Perspective) for House, Tree, and Person, respectively. Table 7 shows average scores made for the disparate wholes by Ss of the quantitative standardization group.

The House, as a dwelling, seems to arouse a mixture of conscious and unconscious associations concerning home and interpersonal relationships of the most intimate type. For the child it seems to stress adjustment to siblings and parents, especially the mother; for the adult, adjustment to the domestic situation in general, and more specifically spouse and children (if any).

The S's Good score for the House is a raw score measure of ability to recognize and present commonly accepted elements in the picture of a House and organize them into a whole using satisfactory size and spatial relationships. Qualitatively it is an index of the S's ability to function efficiently under the stresses and strains of intimate human relationships. The House Flaw score, raw score of an S's ability to avoid mistakes in organizing Details into a House, is generalized into a qualitative measure of ability to analyze critically problems created by the home situation.

The Tree, which seems to arouse less conscious and more subconscious and unconscious associations than the other two wholes, is a graphic expression of the S's felt experience balance and his view of his personality resources.

The Good score for the Tree is the raw measure of the S's ability to recognize and employ elements commonly making up a Tree and organize them into an adequate whole. From a qualitative standpoint, it appears to be a measure of the S's resources for deriving satisfaction in and from his environment.

The Flaw score for the Tree is the raw measure of the S's avoidance of mistakes in developing his concept of a Tree. Qualitatively it is an index of the S's ability to evaluate critically his relationships to his environment.

The drawing of the Person appears to arouse more conscious associations than the other two wholes. Also, it affords the S an opportunity to express more directly his "body-image".

The Good score for the Person is the raw measure of the S's ability to recognize and use Details commonly representing a human figure and organize them into an acceptable whole. By extension this score appears to be an index of the level and degree of the S's function in interpersonal relationships in general and often specifically.

The Person Flaw score, raw measure of the S's skill in avoiding mistakes in producing his Person, from a qualitative point of view seems to be a measure of the S's ability to subject himself and his relationships to people to adequate objective critical evaluation.

Again, no dichotomy is postulated between the Good and the Flaw scores, but the Good score seems to emphasize the level of action in the particular area of sensitivity; the Flaw score, the level of the S's ability to appraise that area objectively and critically. A disparity of one classification level between the Good and the Flaw scores in a given area seems to have little, if any, meaning. A disparity greater than that, however, has increased pathoformic implications in direct relationship to the increased disparity.

In appraising the S's scores for House, Tree, and Person, separately, it must be remembered: (1) the majority of Ss obtain a higher score on the Tree than upon the House or the Person (in part, because almost anything can be a satisfactory likeness of a Tree, which is why few "flaw" factors are identified for the Tree). This means, therefore that when scores for the Tree are *lower* than for the House and Person, pathoformicity is to be regarded as that much greater; (2) the House may be the most difficult whole for an S, because people usually do not "doodle" houses and drawing the House, therefore, is a new and difficult task; or it may be the easiest of the three wholes, if it represents the House the S would like most to have, and therefore, is one to which he has given much thought; (3) the Person may be the easiest whole to draw, because the drawn Person represents a stereotype the S has produced many times, or it may be the most difficult whole because: (a) it represents a person in his environment whom the S hates or fears, or both; or (b) some organic disturbance prevents the S from receiving the kinesthetic cues he otherwise might receive which could lead to a better drawing. If questioning reveals the S has drawn a particular Person many times, the examiner accords less weight to its quantitative scores than if the Person were drawn spontaneously.

If an S secures his highest "whole" scores for the House, and his scores for the Tree are relatively inferior, while those for the Person are still lower, the examiner might suspect this progressive score depression to be due to: (a) a depression of mood concomitant with early fatigue; and/or (b) a progressively increasing negativism.

If the S secures his lowest "whole" scores for the House, and scores for the Tree are higher, while those for the Person are still higher, the examiner might suspect the initial lowering of efficiency to be due to: (a) initial test-situation fright; and/or (b) a present difficulty in adapting to new situations.

When clinical evidence suggests that scores for the Tree should be depressed, the fact that they remain high appears to indicate the S still blames almost everything and everyone but himself for his dilemma. When scores for the Tree are: (1) the lowest of the whole scores; and (2) well below the S's known usual level of function, the prognosis is least likely to be good.

In almost no instance will all three wholes be of the same quantitative calibre. A disparity greater than one classification level from whole to whole, however, leads one to suspect the S's scores for the whole most adversely affected presumably were influenced by something represented by that whole, actually or symbolically. To illustrate: (1) relatively low scores for the House might indicate the S felt constricted by any four walls within which he had to stay, or it might indicate conflict with someone in that House; (2) comparatively low scores for the Tree might imply the S felt his environment to be unsatisfactory, or himself in conflict with the individual represented by the Tree for the S:: (3) low scores for the Person might signify the S shunned interpersonal relations in general or relations with the individual (or individuals) represented by the drawn Person.

Step 5: Part one of this final step is a comparison of the quality of the quantity of the achromatic and chromatic materials; this comparison is believed to provide prognostic as well as diagnostic data.

Theory suggests (and the validity of this belief has empirical support) that (1) the achromatic H—T—P reveals characteristics (behavioral, attitudinal, emotional, etc.) an S presently uses in meeting and dealing with problems of life; (2) that characteristics revealed in the chromatic drawings are likely to be more basic to an S's personality since (a) chromatic drawings are produced after the S has drawn these same objects before and been questioned directly and indirectly concerning them at considerable length (an experience calculated to activate the non-intellective factors in the personality which might enhance or impede efficiency of function); and (b) the adult S in Western culture has become somewhat conscious of the aesthetic value of form and is compelled to use crayons, inferior drawing tools with childhood associations, and is not permitted to erase.

If the S is mildly maladjusted, his chromatic H—T—P ordinarily differs little from his achromatic H—T—P, quantitatively and qualitatively (neither will be more than mildly pathoformic); but if he is seriously maladjusted, many pathoformic characteristics shown in the achromatic H—T—P will appear, often exaggerated, in the chromatic H—T—P and still other pathoformic characteristics may be seen.

The author believes the colors of the chromatic series (red, black, green, yellow, blue, orange, brown, and purple) represent external emotional stimuli to the S. If when an S is mildly fatigued physically and emotionally aroused he uses color easily and conventionally in producing his House, Tree and Person, there is reason to assume strong integrating forces are present in his personality.

If, however, he eschews the use of colors, his ability freely to make warm, sharing, personal relationships is subject to doubt. If an S uses colors expansively and unconventionally, one suspects a pathoformic inability to exercise control over emotional expression. And if in either of these two instances the use of Details and/or the assignment of Proportional and/or Perspective values to the Details in the given wholes were of lower quality than in the achromatic drawings, the prognosis would be poorer.

The second part of Step 5 depends upon the existence of previous H—T—P protocols with which to compare present drawings. Perhaps the most rewarding use of the H—T—P technique is its use longitudinally to accumulate samples of an S's behavior at periodic intervals so progress or regress (with or without therapy) can be identified and evaluated.

Summary

Appraisal of the quality of the quantity enriches the H—T—P protocol by providing: (1) a qualitative extension of the quantitative values and (2) an objectification of qualitative material thus making for more accurate comparisons of (a) achromatic and chromatic H—T—P sets and (b) H—T—P sets in longitudinal relationship - with but little additional consumption of time.

Chapter 6   Qualitative Analysis and Interpretation

The final approach to the appraisal of an S's achromatic and chromatic drawings of House, Tree, and Person, and his spontaneous and induced comments concerning them is qualitative analysis and interpretation. Of the three systems of analysis presented in this Manual, this is the most productive of valuable diagnostic and prognostic material.

It involves the evaluation of (1) the *graphic productions* from the major standpoints of Details, Proportion (size relationships), and Perspective (spatial relationships) and the minor (but only *relatively* minor) standpoints of Time Consumed, Line Quality, Criticality, Attitude, Drive, and Color; (2) the *verbal phase* from the minor point of view of Drawing Phase Comments and the major approach, Post-Drawing Interrogation; (3) the *total concepts* - graphic and verbal.

The clinician using this system, however, should bear in mind that:

(1)   No single sign itself is an infallible indication of any strength or weakness in the S.

(2)   No H—T—P sign has but one meaning.

(3)   The significance of a sign may differ markedly from one constellation to another.

(4)   The amount of diagnostic and prognostic data derivable from each of the points of analysis may vary greatly from S to S.

In over twenty-five years of H—T—P clinical use, the author has found no valid reason to doubt the correctness of the postulate that no H—T—P sign has a fixed and absolute meaning. Equally, there has been no reason to doubt that all signs by reason of form, function, size, type, color, proportional or spatial relationship, or other characteristic or combination of characteristics, have an *inherent symbolic meaning (or meanings)*. As an example: because of its shape (and at times other characteristics) the chimney often is seen as a phallus -- and treated accordingly -- by a sexually maladjusted S.

1. DETAILS

In general, the type and the number of details used, the method of presenting them, the order of producing them, and the emphasis placed upon them may be regarded as an index of the S's recognition of, concern with, and reaction to the elements of everyday living.

A. TYPE AND QUANTITY

1. *Relevant Details:* these, by definition, constitute integral parts of the drawn whole. They are of two kinds:

(a) *Essential:* the primary or basic details--the absolute minimum.

The House must have at least one door (unless only the side of the House is presented and such a presentation is itself pathoformic); it must have one window, one wall, and a roof (unless it is identified as a tropical dwelling or something of that sort) and it must have a chimney or means of egress for smoke. If electric heating becomes used more commonly, ultimately the chimney may no longer be considered an essential detail.

The Tree must have a trunk and at least one branch.

The Person must have a head, a trunk, two legs and two arms, unless the position is such that only one of each can be seen and such a drawing is itself pathoformic), or the absence is accounted for in some way, as by an amputation(which is itself also pathoformic). For facial characteristics, there must be two eyes, a nose, a mouth, and two ears, unless the position is such that the ears could not be seen, or their absence is accounted for verbally, as by mutilation, for instance.

• The absence of even a single essential detail is regarded as serious; the implications for pathology are greater the more essentials there are missing and more wholes there are involved. Less than average, or a bare minimal use of essential details, particularly for the House and the Tree, suggests withdrawal and/or conflict in the area represented or symbolized by the detail, or the whole from which it is missing. Excessive use of essential details (as by perseveration) implies overconcern with what may be represented or symbolized by the detail in question.

(b) *Non-essential:* the secondary basic details which complete and enrich the drawing.

Examples are: for the House, window curtains; material indicated (by careful drawing out or shading) for the wall, chimney, or the roof. For the Tree, there are foliage (drawn out in careful detail or implied by shading,) a branch system (either detailed or shaded), bark, etc. For the Person, there are a neck, hands and feet, hair, clothing, etc.

In general, limited use of non-essential details implies good reality testing; a sensitive, probably well-balanced interaction with the environment. Excessive use of detailing suggests pathoformic overconcern with the environment or the area symbolized or represented by the details used or associated with.

2.   *Irrelevant Details:* there are details which are not an integral part of the House, the Tree, or the Person. In many instances they enrich the drawings but are produced by the S of his or her own volition, and not at the examiner's request. They may be classified as: (a) Nearby and (b) Distant.

Examples of *Nearby* irrelevant details for the House are shrubs, walkway, grass; for the Tree they are grass, birds perched on branches; for the Person they are a ball, a dog on a leash, a bicycle, etc. *Distant* irrelevant details would be the sun, moon, clouds, and/or birds in the sky, mountains, background, etc., for the three wholes.

Limited use of irrelevant details implies a mild basic insecurity-- a need to structure the situation more securely; to "tie into" the environment, particularly if the irrelevant details are of the *Nearby* variety. Excessive use suggests a pathoformic to pathological "free-floating" anxiety (or conflict) in the area symbolized by the detail or details or a strong withdrawal need (particularly when the irrelevant details tend to obscure the whole).

3.   *Bizarre Details:* these suggest a major personality disorder, since almost invariably they are produced by Ss whose reality-testing is pathologically deficient. Examples of bizarre details would be: (a) obviously human legs supporting a House; (b) eyes, nose, and mouth drawn upon the sun (except in drawings made by young children). Bizarre details rarely are seen: often what at first glance appears to be bizarre detailing is later found to be bizarre proportional or spatial relationship or method of presentation.

General Comments: "Quantity Necessity" (the depiction of an excessive number of details) appears always to be pathoformic--if not pathological--since it indicates a compulsive need to structure the entire situation (the type of details employed may aid in establishing a specificity of sensitivity).

Obsessive-compulsives tend to draw a large number of relevant details. The drawings of Ss in a manic state are characterized by a vast amount of irrelevant detailing (some may even be comments written on the drawing form.

If an S employs a bare minimum of details, the examiner would wish to confirm or rule out the presence of: (1) mental deficiency; (2) a diminution of intellectual efficiency which might or might not be irreversible; (3) a strong withdrawal tendency; and (4) a deep depression of mood.

B.   PRESENTATION METHOD

The examiner should appraise carefully the S's method of presenting his details.

Details may be shown in a number of ways ranging from the direct concrete to the implied abstract.

1.   *One-dimensional:* almost never does one find a one-dimensional detail used for the House, but a Tree composed of a one-dimensional trunk with one-dimensional branches is not unusual, and at times the Person is drawn with a circle or oval for a head, but with the trunk, the arms, and legs all one-dimensional. In general one-dimensional details are used by relatively low-grade mental defective Ss or organics who were of higher intelligence but have greatly deteriorated.

2.   *Two-dimensional;* most dull average to average adult Ss draw Houses, Trees, and Persons with all details two-dimensional. At times less imaginative and/or less flexible adult Ss of above average or superior intelligence do likewise.

3.   *Full shading:* by shading an entire wall of the House an S can imply the presence of wall material; by shading the entire branch area of the Tree, he can indicate that the Tree has branches and foliage without producing each branch and leaf; by shading the entire trunk of the Person, the S can show that the body is clothed.

4.   *Partial Shading:* a few diagonal lines across a window can imply glass; a few random lines across the trunk of a Tree can indicate bark; a series of lines across the legs of the drawn Person suggests a dress.

5.   *Positionally:* if the Person is drawn in profile, one must assume that the Person has two eyes and two ears, though only one of each may be visible.

Some clinicians hold that Ss who use shading always are anxious. While this may be true in some projective techniques, it is not so in the H–T–P.

"Healthy" shading is produced quickly, lightly, and with few random strokes, and the S does not return to and reinforce it from time to time.

"Unhealthy" (pathoformic) shading is characterized by one or more of: unwarranted use of time, excessive force, over-meticulosity, inferior control, and reinforcement.

"Healthy" shading implies: (1) a fairly high level of intellectual function (since it involves abstraction); (2) a relatively high degree of sensitivity (but not vulnerability) in the S's relationships with his environment. *"Unhealthy" shading suggests, at best, an unfortunate hypersensitivity and, at worst, a crippling anxiety.

C.   DETAIL SEQUENCE

The order in which the S produces the items of detail for his House. Tree, and Person may, in a sense, be regarded as an index of his recognition of and conformity to convention.

The examiner should record the S's detail sequence, for once the whole is completed, deviations from the average in the order of detail presentation will be lost if an adequate record has not been made at the time of performance.

Most Ss begin the House in one of two sequences; (a) the roof, a wall (or walls), a door and a window (or windows), or a window (or windows) and a door, and so on; or (b) the baseline, a wall or walls, the roof, and so on.

• Insecure Ss have been found to draw symmetrically at times (two chimneys, two windows, two doors, etc.)

Seriously maladjusted Ss at times draw segmentally (detail by detail without consideration for the relationship of the details to each other or the finished whole.

A pathoformic sequence for the House would be one in which the door or windows of the ground floor was the last or almost the last detail drawn and might imply: (a) a distaste for inter-personal contacts; (b) a tendency to withdraw from reality.

A clear pathological detail sequence--believed to be almost pathognomonic of organicity--is the "2-Plane" method of presentation. The S starts as though he were going to make a conventional 3-dimensional reproduction of a House, but ends by producing, in effect, a blueprint of the floor plan.

The sequences for the Tree usually are: (a) the trunk, the branches and the branch system and/or the foliage (drawn actually or by implication), or (b) the tip of the Tree, the branches (by shaded or unshaded implication), the trunk, the trunk's base.

A pathoformic sequence of detail presentation for the Tree, which may be called "contaminated", is one in which the S begins making good use of implication, but ends by drawing 1-dimensional or 2-dimensional branches in vague fashion and without erasing his original production.

A pathological sequence is: two-dimensional branches, one below the other (to the left) beginning at the top of the Tree, then similar branches to the right, but without the branches joining one another or the trunk, then two trunk lines not joined at top or bottom and not touching the proximal ends of the branches; then a single peripheral line joining the outer tips of the branches, but not touching the trunk lines at any point.

In most instances the Person is produced about as follows: the head, the features (eyes, nose, etc.); the neck, the trunk, the arms (with fingers or hands), the legs and feet (or legs and arms transposed in order), and so on.

A pathological sequence in the production of a Person; the S begins the drawing with a foot, and draws the head and facial characteristics last.

Delayed presentation of facial characteristics may connote: (1) a tendency to deny receptors of external stimuli; (2) a desire to postpone identification of the Person as long as possible.

As a rule, details once drawn are left as completed and not returned to. Details drawn in multiplicity, (as all the windows of a given story) usually are completed before another specific detail is introduced (except, of course, that panes may be drawn in each window after that window's frame has been produced).

Any marked deviation from the average sequence, involving (1) an unusual order of presentation: (2) a compulsive return to something previously drawn, with erasure and/or redrawing; or (3) a reinforcement of the drawing (drawing over and over the outline of a detail) is clearly pathoformic.

If the completed whole drawing gives no indication that a deviant sequence has been used, the S may be credited with ability to recover, but nevertheless the examiner must not discount the pathoformicity of the organizational difficulty shown.

The examiner should determine if deviations from the ''normal'' in detail sequence are due solely to basic intellectual incapacity (as in drawings of organic mental deficients) or to vacillation and indecision due to an emotional disturbance or an organic change and represent a beginning difficulty in organization.

D.   EMPHASIS

The S may indicate in a number of ways that a specific detail, or combination of details, has special significance for him--that it is not for him solely a part, or combination or parts, of the drawing of a House, Tree, or Person.

He may express his emphasis *positively:*

(1)   By overtly exhibiting emotion before, during or after drawing the detail or combination of details, or while commenting upon it or them during the drawing or in the Post-Drawing Interrogation.

The examiner must not assume, however, because the S exhibits emotion while drawing, that the emotion is evoked by the detail being drawn: it may be an anticipatory reaction to something the S will draw, or a delayed reaction to something previously drawn.

(2)   By presenting a detail or combination of details in a deviant sequential order.

(3)   By exhibiting unusual concern over the presentation of a detail or combination of details by:

(a) erasing excessively -- particularly when the erasure is not followed by improvement in form, or

(b) by returning to the detail or detail combination one or more times during the drawing of the given whole or subsequent whole, or

(c) by use of excessive time in drawing the detail or combination of details.

(4) By presenting the detail or combination of details in a deviant or bizarre manner: for example, an S who was or has been recently of dull average intelligence or better, draws arms protruding from his Person's head.

(5) By perseverating in the presentation of a detail (as by drawing each brick of a three-story House).

(6) By making a frank comment (spontaneously or as the result of being questioned by the examiner) concerning a detail or detail combination.

(7) By using traumatic detailing: that is, by producing a Tree trunk bearing a jagged scar. The examiner must bear in mind that an S will not symbolize in this way or in a similar manner a traumatic past event unless *he* feels that the event was psychologically traumatic. The examiner should not assume, because an S's history contains an incident which the examiner feels is traumatic, that the S also will have found it traumatic. The author recalls an S who had had no less than three episodes which most psychologists would consider deeply scarring experiences; this S drew a Tree with a trunk containing a deep scar, yet when he was asked to account for the scar, he said nothing about the three episodes in question. Instead, he related what most would regard as a trivial occurrence in his childhood. There was no question, however, that for him this childhood event had been a harrowing experience.

The S may express emphasis *negatively:*

(1) By omitting one or more "essential" details.

(2) By presenting incompletely a detail or combination of details.

(3) By commenting evasively, or flatly refusing to comment upon a detail or detail combination in the P—D—I.

E. CONSISTENCY

If the S presents all essential details for his Houses, ordinarily he may be expected to do likewise for the Trees and Persons. If the S embellishes his drawings of the House with a number of non-essential details, he usually will embellish his Trees and Persons in similar fashion. In short, a reasonable amount of consistency in the use of details is to be expected from whole to whole.

Variations from this "normal" behavior *per se* are significant. The significance depends upon the detailing that is deviant and the degree of the significance depends upon the magnitude of the variance.

* * * * * *

In the 1948 edition of the H—T—P Manual, an attempt was made to present examples of interpretation under each of the qualitative scoring points. Students complained, and with justice, that these examples were not sufficient to provide a comprehensive picture of the scope and intricacy of the method of interpretation.

In this edition, the author presents most of the principal *inherent symbolic meanings*.

Students should bear two points in mind, however; (1) the statements which follow concerning interpretations are positive only in order to conserve space; interpretations must be presumed to be preceded by such qualifying remarks as: "There is good reason to believe that. . . ."; and (2) the interpretations given must be treated with extreme caution, never accepted as appropriate for a given case without careful consideration of other signficant data in the case.

HOUSE

A. Relevant Details

Sound empirical evidence exists for the assumption that the roof represents the areas of thinking and phantasy when the House is considered a psychological self-portrait of an S.

Roof material frequently is indicated by methods ranging from meticulous outlining of each shingle to a few scattered strokes of the pencil implying the presence of a material.

The interpretation of all "material" is based on the method of production, the character of the detailing, the time used in presentation, and the presumed meaning of the area covered. Easily and noncompulsively drawn material appears to indicate a mild awareness of surface differentiation and a good capacity for well-balanced interaction with the environment; meticulous detailing implies obsessive-compulsive tendencies; deep shading connotes anxiety or tension.

Emphasis on the eaves of the roof by reinforcement or extension beyond the walls implies an over-defensive, usually suspicious, attitude.

The roof and wall, or walls, of the House seem to depict crudely the S's ego; symbolically the strength or weakness of the roof and walls corresponds to that of the ego. The peripheral boundaries of the personality are represented by the peripheral boundaries of the wall and the roof. Over-emphasis of these peripheral or "containing" lines is believed to indicate a conscious effort to maintain control. If the peripheral lines are faint and inadequate, a feeling of impending breakdown, of weak ego control is implied. If the baseline of the House is the first detail drawn and/or if it is emphasized by reinforcement, feelings of insecurity may be presumed to exist.

Material is drawn less frequently for the walls than for almost any other part of the House, large or small.

● Rain spouts and gutters connote a heightened attitude of defensiveness (and usually suspicion), with a concomitant effort to channel off unpleasant stimuli.

The door or doors of the House afford a mode of ingress or egress (the front door usually represents both and equates with accessibility; but the back and the side door usually seem to emphasize egress: escape).

Emphasis upon the door's facing or upon locks and/or hinges seems indicative of a defensive sensitivity. Emphasis upon the knob suggests an overconsciousness of the door's function and/or phallic preoccupation, or both.

The window or windows of the House provide less direct and less immediate modes of interaction with the environment than the door. If the S draws no window panes and no window interstices indicating the presence of glass and makes no attempt to indicate glass by drawing a few lines across the pane to denote shadow it is assumed that the S has definite oppositional tendencies since, in effect, he is saying, "I'll make it impossible for you to see in."

A multiplicity of window interstices which makes a window appear to be barred, may be an expression of a feeling that the room behind that window is a prison to him. ●

Emphasis upon window locks implies an over-defensive attitude.

If windows are decorated with shutters, shades, or curtains which are not closed or drawn shut, it usually is implied that there is a consciously controlled interaction accompanied by some anxiety. If all three are shown, however, the S probably is too defensive.

If some windows are shown with shades or curtains, while others are not, and some have panes and others do not, specific post-drawing interrogation is indicated to determine the cause of this disparity. To ascertain the conflict so symbolized, the examiner seeks to find which room is behind the window which differs, who occupies tnat room (if it has an occupant) and the kind of room it is (whether it has an occupant or not). The attitude of the S to this room's occupant (as Father) or the room's function (as bathroom) may clearly and fully account for the deviant presentation.

If many windows are drawn (and without shades, curtains or shutters), it is assumed the S tends to behave bluntly and directly (many windows indicate a willingness to make contact; the absence of shades, curtains, etc., implies that the S feels no need to mask his feelings). A multiplicity of windows with shades, etc., on the other hand, implies over-concern about the S's interaction with his environment.

General emphasis upon windows and doors by reinforcement and without much detailing connotes concern over interaction, but suspicion is aroused that the concern may be partially based upon an orificial fixation.

Sexually maladjusted Ss tend to see doors and windows as oral, vaginal, and/or rectal substitutes.

The chimney that is drawn quickly, easily, and well implie s that the S has satisfactory sensual maturity and balance.

The omission of the chimney does not represent as serious a maladjustment as does an overemphasis of the chimney by (1) size enhancement; (2) reinforcement; (3) difficulty in presentation (as by erasure without subsequent improvement); (4) malplacement; (5) bizarre presentation, or any combination thereof.

Material is drawn more frequently for the chimney than for any other detail of the House except window panes indicated by window interstices.

Smoke from the chimney has no quantitative value, but sometimes it has high qualitative value: when it is produced in great profusion the implication is that there is considerable inner tension, presumably occasioned by unsatisfactory relationships with those with whom the S lives.

While there is good clinical evidence that the chimney is not necessarily a sexual symbol, in a restricted sense, there is equally good evidence that sexually maladjusted Ss tend to view it as a phallus and behave accordingly.

B. Irrelevant Details

In general, irrelevant details indicate that an S needs to structure the environment more completely, which, in turn, connotes feelings of insecurity and inadequacy. The more profuse the irrelevant detailing is, the more intense is the presumed feeling. Usually the better the irrelevant details are organized and the more intimate their relationship is to the House, the greater is the likelihood that the anxiety, such as it is, is well channelized and well controlled.

The more the irrelevant details dwarf the whole, by number, size, or placement, the greater is the presumed pathoformicity.

A brief consideration of the apparent meaning of certain specific irrelevant details follows:

(1) *Nearby:*

> *Mid-wall Line:* Occasionally an S emphasizes the fact that his House has two stories by drawing a horizontal line or two separating the second story from the first. This suggests an undesirable compartmentalization of the personality with em-

phasis on the soma.

Groundline: The spontaneously produced groundline seems to represent a need by the S to "tie" his House into something more tangible than space.

Walkway: A walkway easily drawn and well proportioned lends reality and depth to a drawing and seems to imply that the S exercises control and tact in his contacts with others. A long walkway suggests lessened accessibility.

Trees: If drawn near or about the House, they frequently represent persons with strong positive or negative valence for the S. It is imperative that the examiner in the P—D—I secure the identification of such person or persons, if possible.

Shrubs: Shrubs drawn near the House imply a felt need to erect ego-defensive barriers, to make contact with others in a somewhat formalized fashion. At times, shrubs constitute an attempt to impress the examiner with the S's affluence. Like Trees, they may represent persons. This usually is not the case, but its possibility always is explored in the P—D—I.

Flowers: Tulips or daisy-like flowers occasionally are drawn about the House -- usually by schizoid or very young "normal" subjects. Dr. Richard Ledgerwood, in a study of the spontaneous drawings of schizophrenics at the Eastern State Hospital, Williamsburg, Virginia, found such flowers commonly produced.

Shadows: Shadows are interpreted as representing a conflict situation which produces anxiety at the conscious level when they are drawn spontaneously and before a sun has been produced; such a shadow is evidence of a subconscious recognition of the presence of something not in the drawing (sun) otherwise there could be no shadow; and the shadow, being on the ground, indicates its existence in reality, the conscious area.

Degrading Details: An out-house may be placed beside a House that is otherwise a mansion; or a large garbage can may be placed on a front porch. Such irrelevant details usually symbolize feelings of aggressive hostility, at times partially internalized.

(2)   *Distant:*

Sun: The sun is always sought if it has not already been drawn spontaneously (usually it must be induced for the achromatic House). It appears to represent the figure of greatest authority or emotional valence, positive or negative, in the S's environment.

Clouds: Clouds appear to indicate generalized anxiety as in the Rorschach; they are perhaps more significant when drawn spontaneously in the H—T—P than when they are seen in the Rorschach.

Mountain: Mountains in the background suggest a defensive attitude and a need for dependence, often maternal dependence.

Rain or Snow: Neither is seen often. Each implies a strong need for the graphic expression of the S's feeling of being subjected to powerful and oppressive environmental pressures. Snow has greater implications for pathology than rain.

To repeat: the more remote the relationship of the irrelevant details to the House, the more generalized is the anxiety presumed to be; the more the irrelevant details tend to dwarf the whole by profusion, size, or place, the greater is the pathoformicity.

TREE

A. Relevant Details

The branches and the branch system of the Tree are believed to represent the S's resources for seeking satisfaction in his environment. Overemphasis of the branches on the left side of the Tree by number, size, or both, suggests a personality imbalance occasioned by a tendency to seek too strongly for immediate, frank, emotional satisfaction. Overemphasis of the branches on the right side, suggests imbalance produced by a too strong tendency to avoid or delay emotional satisfaction. and, instead, to seek satisfaction through intellectual effort (if the S is of low level intelligence, still further conflict is self-evident). Absolute symmetry of the branch structure implies feelings of ambivalence; an inability to grant dominance to any course of action.

Partially drawn 2-dimensional branches *and* shading, and branches presented by shading which is easily and quickly drawn, appear to represent the most mature adjustment. 1-dimensional branches definitely indicate that the S's satisfaction-seeking resources are inferior, particularly if there is no branch system. By *branch system* is meant a branch-to-branch organization, not a Tree with branches which join the trunk but are not connected to one another.

Branches indicated by unshaded implication carry the connotation of oppositional tendencies.

"White shading", rarely seen, suggests schizoid thinking. In such 'Tree the white space is given an implied solidity by having parts of 2-dimensional branches showing through the white space, in effect, at intervals.

2-dimensional branches drawn like clubs or fingers and with

little organization imply strong hostility. Phallic-like 2-dimensional branches suggest castration fear. 1-dimensional or 2-dimensional branches which tend to turn in toward the Tree's center, instead of conventionally extending outward as they go upward, imply strong intratensive ruminative tendencies and have been seen only in Trees of obsessive-compulsives. Branches drawn as 2-dimensional, thick and short,,and as if cut off near the trunk, may imply suicidal tendencies. Branches drawn as if the S intended them to be 2-dimensional but which are not "closed" at the distal end, usually are drawn by Ss with little control over the expression of their drives.

Broken or dead branches are believed to represent traumatic experiences felt as such by the S.

Reinforcement of the branches connotes a feeling of inadequacy in satisfaction seeking.

The Tree trunk appears to be an index of the S's feeling of the basic strength of his ego. Reinforcement of the peripheral lines of the trunk implies a conscious need to maintain integrity. Faint peripheral lines suggest a feeling of impending breakdown.

Bark, if easily drawn, implies a well-balanced interaction. If it is drawn consistently or very heavily, anxiety is presumed to be present. If it is meticulously and painstakingly produced, the S may be compulsively overconcerned with his relationships with his environment.

Vines on a trunk or vine-like bark have been found to represent an S's feeling that (1) he is losing or has lost control of certain compelling drives; and/or (2) others are aware that he has forbidden ideas and/or needs.

Shading is used more frequently on the Tree than on the House or Person.

Scars on the trunk are believed to represent experiences in the past which the S feels were severely traumatic. One cannot assume that events recorded in the anamnesis actually were experienced as such by the S. They will be represented symbolically only if the S found them scarring to a degree which demands graphic portrayal.

A psychoneurotic woman interpreted a knothole which she had drawn with great care as representing the scar left by a concealed (from the examiner) suicidal attempt made some years before.

Leaves are cosmetic and functional. Cosmetically they decorate and cover the skeleton of the Tree; functionally they serve to make the most immediate and direct contact with the environment.

If 2-dimensional leaves are meticulously and painstakingly drawn, obsessive-compulsive characteristics are presumed to be present.

Fruit commonly is drawn by children and occasionally by pregnant adults.

Ss with advanced organicity often draw a Tree with a 1-dimensional trunk and tortuous 1-dimensional branches which do not form a system.

The "key-hole" Tree, with no line closing the base of its circular, unshaded branch structure and no line closing the base of its trunk, implies strong oppositional tendencies. It is as if the S says: "I'll draw as little as I can to make a recognizable Tree".

Nigg's Tree is like a "key-hole" Tree except that its unshaded branch structure has a saw-toothed edge and to some degree resembles the jaws of a nutcracker. This Tree usually is produced by Ss with rigid, compartmentalized personalities.

The Tree (and particularly its trunk) is readily seen as a phallic substitute by sexually maladjusted Ss. One disturbed male drew his trunk as an obvious penile shaft penetrating the feathery branch structure, an equally obvious hirsute vaginal orifice.

Roots which taper easily and gently into the ground imply good reality contact; talon-like roots that seem to clutch the ground rather than enter it, argue for the presence of strong paranoid, aggressive attitudes. Roots that are obviously beneath the ground but that are visible, strongly suggest a pathological reality-testing flaw.

B. Irrelevant Details

(1) *Nearby:*

Groundline: A groundline is drawn spontaneously more frequently for the Tree than for the House or Person.

An arc-like groundline, with its center the point of greatest elevation, implies maternal dependence, with feelings of isolation and helplessness, if the Tree is relatively small and/or inadequately organized; *but* if the Tree is rugged and large, the primary implication is that the S has strong needs for dominance and exhibitionism.

When the groundline is produced in the form of a box which has no relationship to the Tree, the reality testing of the S obviously is inadequate. Adult Ss who draw a gaily ornamented Christmas Tree suggest the presence of well-developed narcissism, regressive tendencies, plus a strong need for nurturance.

Shadow: The author has seen only two Trees drawn casting a shadow. The interpretation in each instance was that the shadow represented an anxiety-binding factor at the conscious level. The reasoning was that the shadow represented an unsatisfying relationship in the psychological past which was felt in the psychological present. Its existence at the conscious level was postulated because the shadow was on the ground, presumed to represent reality. Preoccupation was suggested, since the shadow presumed the existence on an unseen element, the sun, which, in turn, has qualitative significance as power. In each case, this interpretation was supported by strong objective evidence elicited from other sources.

Birds and Animals: Not infrequently an S embellishes his drawing of a Tree with one or more birds or animals. Occasionally, on interrogation, the S identifies the bird or animal as a person with high positive or negative valence for him, usually negative. Even when identification cannot be obtained, cautious interpretations, based on the characteristics of the bird or animal, or its action in the drawing, can be made. The implications of a buzzard hovering over the Tree, or a horse with tail raised and about to defecate on the Tree, are obvious. More subtle is the drawing of a Tree with a squirrel's head protruding from a hole in the trunk, which was interpreted as symbolizing a feeling that a segment of the personality unhappily was free from control and had destructive potentialities. In this case it was obsessive guilt feeling.

Persons: A person drawn near the Tree (and this is rarely done) seems always to have significance. One severely disturbed S with an unhappy relationship with his father drew a huge Tree lying on the ground, with a man, identified as the S's father standing beside it with axe in hand. Occasionally a human face is drawn in the branch structure, recognized later by the S. Such faces usually have strong negative valence for the Ss.

Trees: It is believed to be pathoformic if an S produces one or more additional Trees spontaneously. It is not unusual for a maladjusted child to draw two Trees and identify them, respectively, as his or her father and mother.

(2)   *Distant:*

Sun: The sun seems to have the same meaning in the drawing of the Tree as in the drawing of the House, but an S can express feeling more strikingly by its use in the drawing of the Tree.

As a rule, other *Distant* irrelevant details appear to have the same meaning in the drawing of the Tree as in the drawing of the House. (See discussion thereunder.)

PERSON

A. Relevant Details

The head is believed to represent the area of intelligence (control). and phantasy

Emphasis on the peripheral lines of the head suggests strong efforts to maintain control in the face of disturbing phantasy (or obsessive or delusional ideation).

Emphasis upon the face implies a conscious effort to maintain an acceptable social front.

A delay in the presentation of facial characteristics connotes a desire to delay as long as possible the final identification of the Person.

The eyes, receptors of visual stimuli, are perhaps the most revealing detail of the facial constellation. They are usually the first facial details drawn by the young child. If the eyes are drawn as hollow sockets, with no attempt made to indicate the eyeball or pupil, the implication is a marked reluctance to accept stimulus from the eye. Eyes drawn closed imply a stronger desire to avoid unpleasant visual stimuli. Complete ommision of the eyes is pathological and the presence of visual hallucinations should be suspected.

Overemphasis of the nose (a prominent phallic substitute) suggests phallic preoccupation and possible castration fear.

The mouth, presumably the receptor of the earliest pleasurable sensations (in point of life age), also may be an instrument of aggression: the likelihood of the latter is enhanced if teeth are presented prominently.

Overemphasis of the ears usually is seen in Persons drawn by paranoid Ss. Such Ss may be expressing almost overwhelming desires to hear distinctly what they feel others are saying about them. Underemphasis may indicate a desire to shut out criticism. Omission of the ears suggests the presence of possible auditory hallucinations but the ears frequently are omitted by well-adjusted Ss of low intelligence. The relative pathoformicity of such an omission, therefore, depends in part on the S's intellectual level.

A schizophrenic small girl drew a Person whose face had eyes only. The eyes implied a suspicious watchfulness; the absence of the nose, ears, and mouth, symbolized her limited contact with reality; the absence of the mouth also pointed up her reluctance to communicate.

The chin is believed to be a masculinity symbol. Overemphasis on it implies a need for dominance, often social more than sexual, and underemphasis implies a feeling of impotence, again often more social than sexual.

Hair is presumed to be an expression of virility and virility striving; on the chest of the nude male it seems to be so expressive. Adolescent girls tend to overemphasize and formalize hair. Heavily-shaded hair implies anxiety over thinking or phantasy. Long and unshaded hair, as by implication, suggests highly ambivalent phantasy concerning sexual matters. Beards and mustaches are masculine symbols, phallic substitutes.

The neck as the organ joining the head (the control area) and the body (the so-called impulse area), is an index of coordination between head and body.

Failure to draw the neck in its usual sequential order (as by drawing the head, then the trunk, and joining them only later) implies conflict between control of and expression of emotion.

Omission of a chinline in full-face presentation, or a neck baseline in profile, implies an unhappily free flow of basic body drives with a probable lack of adequate control. The same implication holds, even more strongly, when the neck is omitted entirely; in such instances the S feels, so to speak, at the mercy of his body drives which threaten too frequently to overwhelm him.

The trunk is the seat of basic physical needs and drives; absence of the trunk implies a denial of body drives.

Shoulders are regarded as expressing an S's feeling of basic strength or power.

Overemphasis of the breasts of the drawn female Person, if the S is a male, suggests oral eroticism and maternal dependence; if the S is a female, exhibitionism and narcissism, and perhaps maternal dependence, are implied.

Arms are viewed as tools for attempting to control or make changes in the environment.

If both arms are omitted (and the S is not a low-grade mental deficient), a very strong feeling of inadequacy is implied, Suicidal tendencies might be present. Powerful castration fears would be suspected.

Schizophrenic Ss tend, at times, to draw arms which look like wings with short broad feathers instead of fingers at the distal end.

Hands are more refined tools for offensive or defensive action within the environment. Aesthetically satisfactory hands seldom are seen in drawings by Ss of below average intelligence. The absence of hands in drawings of Ss of a high level of intelligence implies feelings of inadequacy.

Heavily shaded hands are said to be pathognomonic of masturbatory guilt, but since such guilt is common and shaded hands are not, shaded hands should not routinely be so interpreted.

Spike-like fingers with a rudimentary hand, or drawn as protruding from the end of the forearm, connote hostility. Petal-like fingers are a more infantile presentation. Fingers drawn as 1-dimensional and enclosed by a looping line suggest conscious efforts to suppress aggressive impulses.

Drawing the fingers or the hands last, or almost last, connotes a marked reluctance to make immediate and intimate contact with the environment, at times predicated upon a desire to avoid revealing feelings of inadequacy.

Dr. Karen Machover (5) has suggested that the waist-line may be considered the coordinator of the power drives (upper trunk) and the sex drives (lower trunk). Overemphasis on the waist-line, usually expressed by difficulty in drawing a belt, or by a heavily-shaded belt, implies strong conflict between expression and control of sex drives.

The production of the lower trunk, the site of sex drives, occasions many maladjusted Ss great difficulty.

Frank presentation of the genitalia on the Person is not considered abnormal if the S is a young child.

There is reason to think however, that drawing carefully outlined genitalia on the nude Person is more pathoformic than drawing a nude Person in full-face without identifying sexual characteristics. Neither is regarded as a healthy production for an older child or adult.

Emphasis upon the buttocks of a drawn male Person by a male S makes the examiner suspect the presence of strong homosexual impulses.

Inability to close the pelvis at the base is strongly pathoformic; inability to draw the pelvis at all is pathological.

One sexually maladjusted male adult drew a nude male, omitted the genitalia and spent much time decorating his Person with a large, deeply shaded necktie, a phallic substitute.

The legs as a body's implements for locomotion may be regarded as representing the S's view of his autonomy within his environment.

Absence of the legs suggests strong feelings of constriction and probably equally strong castration feelings.

Emphasis on the knees, particularly by outlining the knee cap or joint, has been seen only in the drawings of Ss with homosexual tendencies.

Feet are refined tools for modifying and controlling locomotion and also, at times, used as assaultive weapons. Many psychologists believe the feet to be phallic substitutes.

Omission of the feet implies strong feelings of constriction.

Overdetailing of the feet, as by minute detailing of the shoe laces, toe design on the shoe, etc., suggest obsessive characteristics with a strong narcissistic-exhibitionistic component.

In general, even in the drawings of superior Ss, from an aesthetic point of view, the feet are the poorest drawn of all body details.

The vast majority of Persons are drawn as at least partly clad: therefore, clothing must be considered relevant detailing albeit of the non-essential type.

Certain items of clothing appear to have specific implications:
(1) *Belt:* Overemphasis of the belt implies sexual preoccupation and overconcern.
(2) *Tie:* Overemphais 'of a tie connotes phallic preoccupation and makes one suspect feelings of impotence.
(3) *Buttons:* A multiplicity of buttons in the drawing of a Person by Ss of average or higher intelligence suggests regression: in a child's drawing, strong dependence on the mother is implied.

Ss may indicate their views of their roles in psychosocial intercourse by the clothing they use on their Persons. A Person squatting on the ground, clad only in a loin cloth, indicates a view of one too busy contemplating to be concerned with worldly affairs which are presumably too conflict-producing for him. A Person clad in an uncommonly fancy-dress, military uniform implies that the S has well-developed feelings of superiority over his fellow men *or* powerful needs for dominance coupled with equally strong feelings of inferiority.

B. *Irrelevant Details*

Certain objects appear to be on the borderline between the relevant non-essential and the irrelevant. They bear close relationship to the S, and serve to indicate what he is doing: for example, (1) a pipe, cigar, or a cigarette, at best indicate mild oral eroticism, but if emphasized, are likely to be phallic substitutes; (2) canes, swords, axes as weapons imply the presence of aggressive tendencies (they may also be phallic substitutes).

Distant irrelevant details are not as frequently produced in drawings of the Person as of the House and Tree, but when they are, they usually appear to have about the same meanings.

Progress in Therapy

As withdrawn and/or markedly depressed patients improve in therapy, they tend to produce more details than when entering therapy. As overproductive schizophrenics, manics, or psychoneurotics improve, they tend to produce fewer irrelevant details and previously drawn bizarrities disappear.

2. *PROPORTION*

The reality and the relativity of the proportional values expressed by an S in his drawings of House, Tree, and Person reveal, in many instances, the values the S assigns to the objects, situations, persons, etc., which the drawings, or a part or parts thereof, represent for him actually or symbolically.

By extension then, the proportional values which the S employs in his drawings may be regarded as a crude index of his ability to assign objective values to the elements of reality; of his ability to make judgments easily and flexibly; of his ability to solve the more immediate and concrete problems of everyday living.

A. *Drawn Whole to Drawing Form*

This phase involves the evaluation of the size relationship of the completed whole (House, Tree, or Person) to the drawing form page.

Examples of deviation, with possible interpretations, follow.

The average whole occupies from one-third to two-thirds of the standard size drawing form page area.

From the standpoint of deviation from the average, the examiner is interested primarily in two types of space-utilization: (1) the whole which occupies an extremely small amount of the available space; (2) the whole which occupies almost all the alloted space, or may even have a portion of the whole chopped off by a border of the page.

In the first instance there is "whole-constriction" (the whole is unusually small, but it may be consistent and well-proportioned within itself); in the second instance, there is "space-constriction" (constriction of the whole by the borders of the page).

"Whole-constriction"--the tiny whole--usually is interpreted as indicating: a feeling of inadequacy; a tendency to withdraw from the environment (many schizophrenics appear to symbolize their limited interaction with their environment by drawing tiny wholes); or a desire to reject the whole or what it symbolizes for the S (rejection often is in a symbolic sense, as *House* for *home*).

"Space-constriction,"--the overly large whole, on the other hand-- may be interpreted as: (1) indicating a feeling of great frustration produced by a restricting environment, concomitant with feelings of hostility and a desire to react aggressively usually against the environment, though occasionally against the self; (2) representing feelings of great tension and irritability; (3) indicating a feeling of helpless immobility (if for example, the feet and/or a portion of the legs of the drawn Person are chopped off by the bottom margin of the form page); or (4) representing an ego-centric view of the S's importance in relation to the environment--particularly if the S is a young child.

Just as the roof plus the wall or walls is, in effect, the skeleton of the House, so the trunk plus the branch or branches or the branch system may be considered to be the skeleton of the Tree. A tiny Tree suggests strong feelings of inadequacy to cope with the environment. A huge Tree, as with a huge House, particularly one not contained within the page's borders, implies overcompensatory satisfaction-seeking in action or phantasy, or both, and connotes, at best, a hypersensitivity. The same may be said of the Person.

B. Intra-Whole

Interest here is in the identification and interpretation of any unusual size relationship detail to another detail, detail-to-detail complex, or detail to the whole House, Tree, or Person.

Examples follow of the more commonly seen deviations together with a discussion of their probable implications.

HOUSE

If the roof is overly large in relation to the rest of the House, the assumption is that the S devotes much of his time to phantasy, presumably seeking satisfaction therein.

It is noteworthy that imbeciles frequently produce Houses whose roof area is a single line only; imbeciles significantly lack the ability to phantasy to any degree.

If the horizontal dimension of the wall is overemphasized at the expense of the vertical, the S may be functioning inefficiently because the past and/or the future interferes with his attention. This S may be presumed to be vulnerable to environmental pressure since so much of him, figuratively speaking, is available for assault at the reality level. If the vertical dimension is overemphasized, satisfaction presumably is sought in phantasy, and the S, as much as possible, shuns contact with reality.

Mental deficients of the moron level tend to draw Houses with "double perspective", showing a mainwall flanked by both endwalls. Morons, perhaps sensing, at least in part, the fact that two endwalls and a sidewall cannot be seen simultaneously, tend to minimize the endwalls' width, to emphasize the mainwall. Schizophrenics, however, when employing "double perspective," tend to overemphasize the endwalls greatly as to size, or by emphasizing their details, to produce a relatively small mainwall. The schizophrenic seems to regard the endwalls as protecting the center, or mainwall, and thus indicates his heightened tendency to protect the self.

The extremely tiny door, called *miniscule* (it looks almost like a small rat hole), portrays the S's feelings of inadequacy and reluctance to make contact. A door larger than miniscule, but still very small, implies less reluctance. A very large door suggests over-dependence upon others, and overconcern about it.

Windows may vary in size without pathoformicity. As a rule, the bathroom window is the smallest in the House, except for the attic window. When the bathroom window is the largest, however, the assumption is that the bathroom's function is disturbing to the S and conflicts concerning sexual and/or eliminative functions would be suspected.

When size disparity appears among windows of the ground floor, "normally" it is the living-room window which is the largest. A living-room window small by comparison with other windows in the ground floor would make one suspect that the S had a distaste for social intercourse. Windows of the ground floor, since they are nearer to reality, imply more direct contact, are qualitatively of more importance, and are more often omitted or distorted in size or placement than are the upper floor windows by maladjusted Ss.

If the chimney is overly large, it may be presumed that the S is over-

concerned about his virility, and probably also has well-developed exhibitionistic tendencies. One temporarily impotent male symbolized his
plight by carefully drawing a massive chimney, then rendered it inadequate
by decorating it with a large diamond-shaped opening which penetrated it.

If the chimney is disproportionately tiny, the S may feel that his home
situation lacks satisfying warmth, or he may have doubts concerning his
masculinity; castration fears also may be present.

A walkway, very narrow at its junction with the House, and very
broad at the end farthest from the House, connotes an attempt to cloak
with an apparent but superficial friendliness one's desire to remain aloof.

TREE

A Tree with a very slender or tiny trunk and a large branch
structure implies a precarious personality balance because of excessive
satisfaction-seeking. A small branch structure with a much larger trunk
suggests a precarious personality balance because of frustration engendered by inability to satisfy strong basic needs.

The trunk that has a broad base but which becomes very slender a
short distance above the base, implies an early environment which at its
best lacked warm and healthful stimulation. The trunk which is narrower
at its base than at a point or points higher up, is a strongly pathoformic
sign which suggests striving beyond the S's strength, with the concomitant implication of a possible collapse of ego-control.

If two-dimensional leaves are too large for the branches from which
they grow, the S may be presumed as wishing to mask his feelings of inadequacy with a cloak of superficial good adjustment.

One psychopathic male who was afraid of his sadistic stepfather,
completed his Tree by drawing three large, upward pointing, spike-like
branches, unlike any he had previously drawn. This was interpreted as expressing symbolically a subconscious castration fear.

Another S, who had always been dominated by his powerful, aggressive mother, drew a huge sun whose rays were focused on his Tree's upper
left branch structure; the branches in that area were much smaller than elsewhere in the Tree: this expressed vividly the emotional trauma he had
suffered from his Mother.

PERSON

Well adjusted Ss of superior intelligence not infrequently draw
Persons with disproportionately large heads. Such oversized heads also
are drawn by maladjusted Ss who place undue emphasis upon intelligence
per se, or emphasize phantasy as a source of satisfaction.

The disproportionately small head often is seen in the drawings of obsessive-compulsive Ss. It may represent the obsessive's expression of a desire to deny the site of painful thoughts and guilt feelings.

Disproportionately small eyes connote a desire to see as little as possible.

An overly large mouth implies oral eroticism and/or oral aggressive tendencies.

A long, thin neck suggests schizoid characteristics.

A disproportionately large trunk implies the presence of many unsatisfied drives which the S may feel acutely. A disproportionately small trunk suggests a denial of body drives or a feeling of inferiority, or both. A tall, narrow trunk carries schizoid connotations.

Shoulder size is an index of the feeling of basic strength or power, physical as well as psychological. Shoulders which are disproportionately large connote feelings of strength or overconcern about the need for strength or power. Tiny shoulders imply feelings of inferiority.

A marked proportional difference between the right and left sides of the Person suggests sexual role confusion, specifically, and personality imbalance, in general.

Inequality in size of the shoulders and/or the arms suggests personality imbalance.

Overly long arms imply over-ambitious striving. Very short arms connote an absence of striving. Broad arms suggest a basic feeling of strength for striving. Thin arms portray feelings of weakness.

Disproportionately large hands imply impulsivity and ineptitude in the more refined aspects of social intercourse.

Tiny hands suggest a reluctance to make refined and intimate contacts in psycho-social intercourse.

Overly large breasts in the drawing of a female Person imply maternal dependence by the S; oral-eroticism would be suspected, too.

Large or over-emphasized buttocks suggest homosexual tendencies, particularly in drawings of male Persons by male Ss.

Disproportionately long legs connote a strong striving for autonomy. Very short legs imply feelings of constriction.

Disparity as to size (width, length, or both) between the legs implies ambivalence concerning the striving for autonomy or independence.

Unusually long feet imply a need for security and also suggest a need to demonstrate virility. Disproportionately tiny feet imply constriction, dependence.

C. CONSISTENCY

It is not to be expected that all proportional relationships will be consistent, but a marked deviation from the average is suspicious and the examiner should attempt to account for it.

In general, (1) a detail, detail complex, or whole of *greater* than average size implies overconcern and preoccupation with what the item symbolizes for the S; (2) a detail, detail complex, or whole of *less* than average size suggests a rejection of or a desire to reject what the item may symbolize for the S; (3) the greater the number of wholes in which deviant proportional relationship is shown, the more generalized is the disturbance presumed to be.

Progress in Therapy

As therapy succeeds for Ss who exhibited withdrawal and/or depressive tendencies:
 (1)   The wholes become larger.
 (2)   Intra-whole proportions tend to improve.
As hypersensitive, hostile and often aggressive Ss improve under therapy:
 (1)   The wholes become smaller.
 (2)   Intra-whole proportions improve.

III.   *PERSPECTIVE*

An S's use of perspective (spatial relationships) in his drawings of House, Tree, and Person, is an index of his ability to grasp and react successfully to the broader, more complex, more abstract, and more demanding aspects of life. By extension, perspective also may be regarded as a measure of an S's insight.

A.   *WHOLE TO DRAWING FORM PAGE RELATIONSHIP*

1.   *Horizontal Axis*

From a *quantitative* standpoint the horizontal placement of the whole in relation to the drawing form page's average midpoint has no specific significance. Only the whole's placement on the page's vertical axis differentiates between the various intellectual levels (and that varies for the disparate wholes).

From the standpoint of personality differentiation, however, the placement of the whole upon the page often is highly significant.

The farther the midpoint of the whole is to the left of the average midpoint of the drawing form page (see Fig. 4A), the greater is the likelihood that the S tends to behave impulsively and to seek immediate, frank, and emotional satisfaction of his needs and drives. From a temporal standpoint such an S is overconcerned with the past. He will be primarily and greatly concerned about himself. Conversely, the farther the midpoint of of the whole is to the *right* of the page's average midpoint, the more likely is the S to exhibit stable, rigidly controlled behavior, to be willing to delay the satisfaction of immediate needs and drives, to prefer intellectual to emotional satistactions.. Such as S will be overconcerned about the future from a temporal standpoint, and tend to be too concerned about those sharing the environment with him and their opinions of him.

Just as the placement of *the whole* to the left or the right of the average midpoint has the above implications, so though to a lesser degree does emphasis on items within the whole to the left or right of the midpoint of the whole itself, particularly in the Tree.

2.   *Vertical Axis*

The farther below the average midpoint of the drawing form page (see Fig. 4B) that the midpoint of the whole is located, the greater is the likelihood (1) that the S feels insecure and inadequate, and the greater the likelihood that this feeling is creating a depression of mood; (2) that the S tends to be concrete and seek satisfaction in reality rather than in phantasy. (If the whole is said by the S to extend below the page's bottom margin, the implication is that the S feels overwhelmingly constricted).

The farther above the average midpoint of the drawing form page that the midpoint of the whole is located, the greater is the likelihood (1) that the S feels that he is over-striving toward relatively unattainable goals; (2) that the S tends to seek satisfaction in intellectualization or phantasy rather than in reality.

In interpreting the placement of the Tree on the page's vertical axis, the examiner must bear in mind that "normally" the Tree is drawn higher on that axis than the House or the Person.

From the standpoint of the vertical axis *of the whole itself,* the baseline seems to represent reality, and the farther the whole goes upward from that baseline the closer it approaches the phantasy area (the feet of a standing Person, for example, are in direct contact with reality; and the head is the presumed source of phantasy).

Interpretation of vertical placement must be modified in accordance with horizontal placement, and *vice versa.*

Ss with aggressive and/or negativistic tendencies may show rejection of suggestion by refusing to accept the page in the position presented. For example, such an S seems to feel that it is a sign of weakness to accept instructions literally; he seems compelled to turn the page, even though by turning it he alters the ideal vertical-horizontal dimensional relationship and makes his task more difficult. Such page turning is assumed to be pathoformic.

Legend: _ _ _ _ _ _ = average vertical and horizontal midlines of page

_____ = actual (geometric) vertical and horizontal midlines

◯ = average midpoint of form page

☐ = geometric (actual) midpont of form page

Note: Implications concerning vertical or horizontal placement, quadrants, page-left and page-right are the same for each form page--House, Tree, and Person.

PERSON

HORIZONTAL PLACEMENT OF THE WHOLE

S Tends To:
1. *Behave impulsively.*
2. *Seek immediate, frank emotional satisfaction.*

3. *Be overconcerned with the self.*
4. *Be overconcerned with the past.*

S Tends To:
1. *Behave in stable, controlled fashion.*
2. *Be willing to delay satisfaction; to prefer the more intellectual and abstract to the frankly emotional.*
3. *Be overconcerned with the environment.*
4. *Be overconcerned with the future.*

Figure 4 A

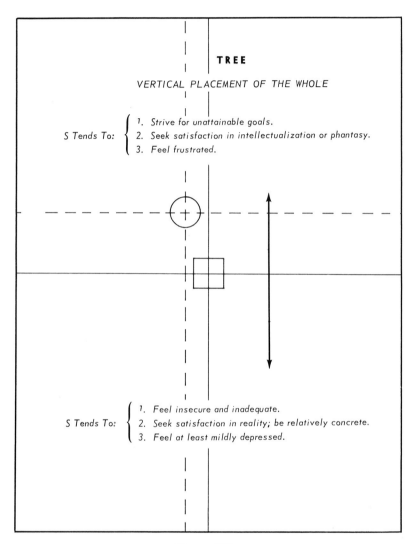

Figure 4 B

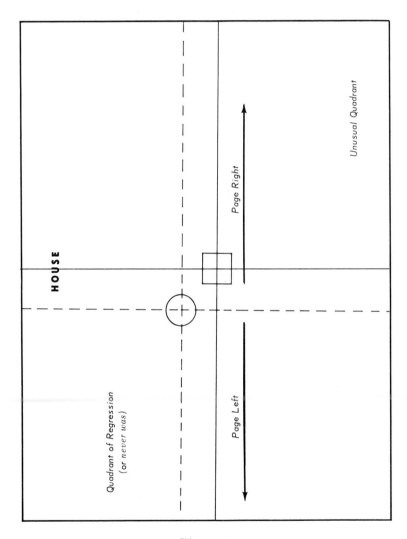

Figure 4 C

3.   *Form Page Quadrants*

From the standpoint of quadrants (see Fig. 4C) two things stand out: the upper left quadrant of the form page (particularly its extreme upper left corner) is "the quadrant of regression" Deteriorated psychotic or organic Ss most frequently place their wholes in this quadrant. This quadrant, too, is frequently the one of choice of individuals who never have attained a high level of conceptual maturity; in such cases it may be called the "quadrant of *never was.*" In the drawings of older children, placement in the upper left quadrant implies a lag in concept maturation; (2) the lower right quadrant, the "unusual quadrant," almost never has a whole placed entirely within it.

The whole whose midpoint is in the geometric center of the page (a whole that is perfectly .framed with an absence of vertical or lateral disparity) is usually produced by the S who is rigid in behavior, usually anxious and insecure.

4.   *Form Page Margins*

Deviant use of the margin or margins of the drawing form page is always significant. There are at least four such possibilities: (1) "paper-chopping" which constitutes the amputation of a part of the whole by one or more page margins; (2) "paper-topping," in which part of the whole touches the upper margin of the page, but does not appear to extend beyond it; (3) "paper-siding" in which one part or more of the whole is extended to the page's lateral margin, but apparently does not extend beyond it; (4) "paper-basing", in which the bottom margin of the form page is the baseline of the whole.

Clinical experience indicates that the following tentative interpretations may be made:

1.   "Paper-chopping" of one or more rooms of the House frequently signifies the unwillingness of the S to draw the room or rooms in question because of unpleasant associations with that part of the House and/or its customary occupant; "paper-chopping" of the Tree's top denotes a desire to seek in phantasy satisfaction denied the S in reality; "paper-chopping" of the Person, as by amputation of the feet, or the feet and a portion of the lower leg, appears to express the S's feeling of helpless immobility in his environment; "paper-chopping" of the top of the House or of the Person's head is rarely seen (it implies the presence of a pathological need to seek satisfaction in phantasy). From a temporal standpoint, "paper-chopping" of the left margin (or more) of the whole appears to connote a fixation upon the past with a fear of the future; "paper-chopping" of the right margin (or more) of the whole appears to indicate a desire to escape into the future, to get away from the past. "Paper-chopping" always is pathologi-

cal in implication.

2.   "Paper-topping" appears to indicate a fixation upon thinking and phantasy as sources of satisfaction.

3.   "Paper-siding" of a House, the use of the lateral margin of the page as a sidewall line for the House, seems to indicate a generalized insecurity; frequently it also indicates insecurity which has (a) a specific temporal meaning (page-left, for past; page-right, for future) and/or (b) a specific meaning associated with the use of the room or its customary occupant. "Paper-siding" for the Tree implies space constriction with resultant heightened sensitivity and a strong suggestion of aggressive-reactive tendencies which may or may not be well suppressed. "Paper-siding" of the Person appears to indicate a basic generalized insecurity with, at times, a more specific temporal fixation.

A whole that is "paper-chopped" on one side and "paper-sided" on the other dramatically expresses the S's feeling of overwhelming frustration with concomitant feelings of hyper-sensitivity and loss of control.

4.   "Paper-basing" of the whole appears to connote: (a) a more or less generalized insecurity; (b) a tendency to behave in concrete, unimaginative fashion; a depression of mood tone. It is the least pathological of the four deviant marginal uses.

B.   WHOLE TO VIEWER RELATIONSHIP

1.   Apparent Plane Relationship of Whole to Viewer.

The House, Tree, and Person usually are drawn as if they were on the same plane as that of the viewer: that is, the viewer (examiner). as he looks at the whole, feels it is almost on a level with him. There are two types of plane-deviation which deserve discussion:

(a) *Bird's-Eye View:* In this deviant plane relationship, the viewer (examiner) has the impression that he is looking down upon the House, Tree, or Person; as if the whole were in a valley and he (examiner) on a hillside above it.

Such a presentation of the House appears to represent (1) the S's feeling of superiority in relation to those sharing the home with him; (2) an iconoclastic rejection by the S of the common tendency to glorify the concept "home"; and occasionally, (3) frank rejection of the home and those in it.

In a study of drawings produced by a group of medical students, almost all the Houses were drawn as if they were below the viewer. The medical student group included many individuals who regarded themselves, perhaps because of their scientific training, as superior persons above the usual emotional and (to them) restrictive home ties.

The Tree drawn below the viewer appears to symbolize the S's feeling of depression or defeat.

Persons rarely are drawn as below the viewer: such a presentation is pathological.

(b) *Worm's-Eye View:* This deviant plane relationship is in direct contrast to the bird's-eye view. The viewer (examiner) feels situated below the House, Tree, or Person and looking up at the whole.

Such a presentation of the House usually represents: (1) a feeling by the S of rejection from his home, or striving towards a home or home situation which he feels unlikely to obtain; or (2) a desire to withdraw, to make limited contact with other persons.

One young mother, recently widowed, produced a carefully fenced in House which gave the viewer the definite but weird impression that at one and the same time it was both *above* and *below* him. This was interpreted as indicating the simultaneous expression by the S of her depressed mood tone and feelings of longing for the reestablishment of a home situation which had been most pleasant for her (by worm's-eye depiction), and her reactive attempt to devalue the unattainable, at least at the moment (bird's-eye view).

A Tree drawn as if it were partly up a hill seems to symbolize: (1) a feeling of striving; (2) a need for shelter and security, partly provided by the side of the hill. A Tree drawn by itself on top of a hill does not always indicate a feeling of superiority. On the contrary, it may represent a feeling of isolation, concomitant with a struggle for autonomy, since it is exposed and subject to attack by the elements.

The Person rarely is drawn as above the viewer. When it is, the implication seems to be that the S desires to hold himself relatively aloof from psycho-social intercourse, or (if the whole represents one or more persons seen as hostile) the S feels oppressed and dominated by that person or persons.

2. *Apparent Physical Distance of Whole From Viewer*

Distance may be suggested by: (1) the extreme smallness of the whole; (2) the number of details placed between the viewer and the whole; or (3) the placement of the whole atop a high hill or deep in a valley.

The House is more likely to be· drawn as distant from the viewer than is the Tree or Person, particularly if the impression of distance is produced by detailing placed between the whole and the viewer.

For example, a chronic alcoholic male drew a tiny cabin but was not content with drawing a cabin only. He drew trees near the cabin, then a large river (with an Indian paddling down it in a canoe), then a roadway between the House and the viewer. This was interpreted as an expression of a strong desire to withdraw as far as possible from conventional society; to live where he might dress and act as he pleased without fear of of criticism.

A whole whose distance is indicated by its small size only implies a strong need to keep the self aloof and inaccessible.

3.   *Position of the Whole vis-a-vis the Viewer.*

To put it simply, here the examiner is concerned with determining the degree to which the whole is presented in full-face.

(a)   *Full-face*

1. *Facade:* this presentation offers no suggestion of depth. The House has one wall only with a door; the Tree has one - or two-dimensional branches which extend laterally only and do not cover the trunk; the Person usually has arms fully extended at right angles to the trunk. The implication is that such an S essentially is rigid and uncompromising in behavior, and has a profound need to cloak his feelings of inadequacy and insecurity with this suggested willingness to face everything directly and firmly.

Occasionally a psychopathic or aggressively resistive S may draw a "stick" Person and attempt to justify his refusal to draw as good a Person as he could on the ground that a "stick" Person is acceptable in cartoons.

2. *Depth Indicated:* at worst this type of presentation implies a tendency to behave in too blunt and uncompromising a fashion.

3. *Reversed:* a Person drawn with its back to the viewer is rarely seen and is pathognomonic; such an S flatly rejects psycho-social intercourse, and in most instances reality as well.

(b)   *Profile*

The points to be determined here are the degree of departure from full-face presentation and the degree of conformity to reality.

1. *Partial:* the House may be drawn with an endwall and a mainwall and the Person as turned somewhat away from the viewer. This type of presentation suggests that the S probably is of high intelligence and has a tendency to behave in a sensitive rather flexible fashion. It is impossible to draw the Tree in profile, but at times an S will indicate in the P—D—I that he sees the Tree presenting its side to him.

2. *Complete:* the House is drawn with only one side visible and with no door in the single side presented. The Person is drawn so that only one side with one arm and one leg is seen, and there is no suggestion that another side exists.

This presentation connotes strong withdrawal and oppositional tendencies: it is seen most frequently employed by Ss with frank paranoid states. A complete profile for the House may be more serious than for the

Person, though neither is healthy.

Reversed: occasionally an S draws a House and/or a Person in profile the reverse of that which might be expected from one of similar handedness. Sinistrals, for example, customarily draw Houses with the right endwall and the mainwall showing, with the Person facing the drawing form page's right margin; dextrals do the reverse. When the S draws a profile view of a House or a Person the reverse of what one might expect of him, he is behaving in deviant fashion, yet at the same time doing something which must be difficult for him. This may be interpreted as representing the expression of hostile impulses which, however the S strives to suppress and/or sublimate.

(c)   *Deviations from Reality*

1. *Loss of Perspective:* for example: the S produces a good endwall and roof at one end then finds it impossible to produce adequate representation of depth at the opposite end of the House, and draws the vertical endline for both the roof and the wall perpendicular to the baseline. The result, in a sense, is incongruous: one end shows depth, proper angulation, etc., while the other end looks abruptly chopped off. So far, this sign has appeared only in drawings made by schizoid subjects, and seems to indicate a beginning organizational difficulty and perhaps a temporal blocking.

2. *Double-Perspective:* the House is drawn so that the mainwall and *both* endwalls are visible at the same time. In the "simple" type, emphasis by size is placed upon the mainwall, and the baseline for all three walls is a single straight line, with little or no attempt at angulation where the endwalls and the mainwall meet. This is commonly produced by adult mental defectives of the moron and borderline levels. From a developmental standpoint, it is produced by "normal" children who have progressed beyond the concept of the one-walled House with a triangular roof, but who have not yet fully grasped the superior concept of presenting endwall and mainwall with adequate angulation at the junction of the walls.

Another type of double perspective, however, is produced mainly by schizoid individuals: the endwalls are emphasized in size, the size of the mainwall is diminished. At times the endwalls are given material, while the mainwall is left blank; the baseline, surprisingly, may be well angulated. This patently is a pathological production

3. *Triple-Perspective:* in this rarely seen type of deviant presentation, the S attempts to show all four sides of his House simultaneously. In so doing, he appears to express symbolically his feelings of crippling exposure to environmental pressures and his overconcern about what others think of him. In brief, he tries to structure completely all superficial aspects of the self (viewing his House as a psychological self-portrait).

4. *Two-Plane Effect:* Ss undergoing organic deterioration may find it difficult to maintain the concept of a three-dimensional House and instead produce a "two-planed" affair. Initially, the House is started as if the conventional three-dimensional picture of a House were to be drawn; ultimately, however, the S draws what is tantamount to a blueprint of the House.

5. *Blueprint:* occasionally an S will from the beginning produce a blueprint or floor plan of his house. The "blueprint" House always appears to reflect the presence of a severe conflict in the home situation. By this floor plan presentation the S may structure the entire situation and, in effect, lay bare to the examiner the relationships involved. The tendency of such Ss to illustrate their feelings toward the problems presented by the various rooms (living room, meeting people; bedroom, sex; bathroom, elimination, hygiene, etc.), or their customary occupants by unconsciously altering the rooms' size, and occasionally their true location, is startling..

6. *Bizarre Presentation:* a clearly pathological presentation was drawn by a psychotic epileptic with mild organic deterioration who produced the mainwall and endwall of a cabin, but drew them as separate entities *several inches apart*, because, as he said, the two walls could not be seen simultaneously because of the thick undergrowth near the cabin. But he drew no undergrowth!

The so-called "schizophrenic" Tree expresses accurately and symbolically the basic splitting of the schizophrenic's personality. See the achromatic and chromatic Trees of *Case B* (Chapter Seven).

A Person drawn with the head, arms, and upper trunk suspended over two unattached legs illustrated one S's frantic attempts to deny his sexuality.

C.   INTRA-WHOLE

Here the examiner primarily is concerned with evaluating and interpreting the spatial relationships of detail to detail, detail-to-detail complex, and detail to whole.

HOUSE

The roof of a House may extend to the ground and become, in effect, a wall as well as a roof. This type of House (roof-walled) is produced by schizophrenics who thus seem to be stressing symbolically the fact that their worlds are largely worlds of phantasy.

A huge chimney drawn like a silo beside the House but not attached to it expressed one S's phallic preoccupation and his inability to accept his sexual drives.

The roof-angled chimney, projecting at right angles to the sloping line of a triangular roof, almost never is seen except in the drawings of normal "young children" or of older mentally deficient or markedly regressed Ss.

If the House is drawn so that the placement of the windows does not conform from wall to wall in respect to a given floor, as in *Case A,* (Chapter 7), definite organizational difficulty is suggested which could be one of the first manifestations of an incipient schizophrenia.

Occasionally the House's windows are drawn as open. If the House is said to be occupied, this connotes a high degree of relaxed accessiblity; but if the House is said to be unoccupied, a striking lack of ego defense is presumed to exist. In each case the interpretation made is subject to modification by the S's description of the weather in the drawing.

If the door is placed high above the House's baseline and not approached by steps, the S (at best) is somewhat inaccessible. The higher the door is above the baseline and the more remote the relationship of the steps (if any) is to that door, the more pronounced is the S's need to dictate the terms upon which he will make contact with his environment.

If a door is drawn as open and usually it is not so drawn, it is thought to express a strong need to receive warmth from without, or a need to demonstrate accessibility, *if the House is said to be occupied,* If the House is said to be vacant, however, it connotes a strong feeling of a lack of ego defense. Again, the S's description of the weather pertaining could modify the interpretation.

The House that has a pair of large steps leading to a blank wall only indicates that the S is highly ambivalent about making contact with those in his immediate surroundings.

The House that has no baseline, or is suspended over a groundline, suggests that the S's contact with reality is at least pathoformic.

A young, unmarried, pregnant girl experienced great difficulty in drawing a porch. Finally she drew it jutting out at an odd angle from the House toward the right of the page. This was interpreted as expressing symbolically her reluctance to accept a smaller extension of herself (baby) in the future (page's right).

An irrelevant Tree drawn close to the House often represents the S himself and can portray the S's strong feelings of rejection by his parents and his great need for their affection. Placement of a Tree close by the House and in the immediate proximity of shrubs (later identified as siblings) can express an S's need for acceptance by his brothers and/or sisters.

TREE

The greater the flexibility of the Tree's branch structure, and the better its organization, the greater is the presumed ability of the S to obtain satisfaction from and in his environment, all else being equal.

A Tree drawn with its branch structure leaning to the left suggests an imbalance of the personality produced by a desire to secure frank, immediate, emotional satisfaction. A Tree that has a branch system leaning toward the right implies an imbalance of the personality because of a fear of frank emotional expression with a concomitant overemphasis upon intellectual satisfaction.

The groundline, spontaneous or induced, although it is a detail, always should be considered under perspective especially in relation to the Tree, since it serves to structure the placement of the whole, and at times enhances sharply the impression of distance and/or height or depth. An arc-like groundline seems to connote strong feelings of dependence, usually on the mother figure, unless the whole is relatively large and well detailed, in which case needs for exhibitionism and/or dominance may be suspected. A groundline that slopes upward toward the right connotes a feeling that the future promises to be difficult and much striving will be needed (*but* the S is willing to strive); a groundline that slopes downward to the right, however, seems to imply a pessimistic view of the future, and a lessening of the will to struggle.

A strong need for affection may be expressed by branches reaching appealingly toward the sun.

A sun drawn below the Tree patently is a bizarre production.

If the Tree is drawn suspended above a groundline and its only contact with that groundline is by thin, tenuous roots, the S's contact with reality presumably is equally tenuous.

One psychopathic male adult drew his Tree so that it looked like a person sitting on a stump. On one side of the pseudo-human figure the buttocks were emphasized; on the other side there was a projection which greatly resembled an erect phallus. In the P—D—I the S stated frankly that the Tree reminded him of a male, and he called attention to the anatomical characteristics mentioned above.

PERSON

A Person drawn as facing in opposite directions simultaneously seldom is seen. However, a graduate student who was doing poorly in school and having much conflict, drew his Person with the head facing the left; the neck with a prominent Adam's-apple facing the right; the shoulders facing the left; the lower portion of the trunk facing the right; the knees facing the left; and the feet facing the right: A more expressive illustration of crippling ambivalence would be difficult to find.

A Person drawn with the back of the head toward the viewer seems clearly pathognomonic of paranoid-schizoid withdrawal. Aversion of the head--not profile presentation, but as if the head were still further turned away from the viewer--implies serious evasion and withdrawal, but it is not as pathological as the back of the head presentation.

The position of the ears, as extended horizontally or vertically, may enhance the impression of suspicious listening.

Phallic preoccupation is presumed to be present if the nose is turned up in a full-face presentation.

One S expressed a tendency to exclude visual stimuli and seek satisfaction in phantasy by drawing his Person's eyes turned inward: In the P—D—I he commented that he was watching himself think.

Well-drawn, neatly rounded shoulders imply a smooth, flexible, well-balanced expression of power. Sharply squared shoulders connote over-defensive, hostile attitudes.

The position of the arms can be revealing: relaxed, flexible arms indicate good adjustment. Tense arms, held tightly to the body, suggest rigidity.

Arms folded across the chest connote suspicious, hostile attitudes. Arms drawn as behind the Person's back imply a reluctance to meet one's fellow men halfway.

Arms crossed so that the hands are folded over the pelvis constitute the "pelvic defense position", a presentation which is frequently employed by sexually maladjusted females, and involutional melancholics.

Severe pathology is indicated when the arms are so drawn that they are not an integral part of the trunk but, instead, seem to extend across the back of the trunk, then forward on either side, and somehow appear to be forcing the Person forward: These are called "compulsive" arms and they imply that the S at times finds himself acting in an uncontrolled fashion.

The connotation of the clenched fist is obvious. See *Case A* (Chapter 7).

Hands drawn in the pockets connote controlled evasion; but this interpretation may be modified by the S's statement of the contents of the hand or pocket.

One obsessive-compulsive neurotic woman, who was rebelling bitterly against femininity in general, and her lack of physical charm in particular, drew a beautiful young girl with the dress so draped that the figure appeared to have a large, erect penis. In the P—D—I, the S strongly supported the examiner's previously formed impression that she suffered with penis-envy.

If the legs are drawn tightly together in a frozen attitude, rigidity and tension are patent, and there may be sexual maladjustment, too.

A broad-based stance may represent defiance or a strong need for security, or both, depending upon other factors.

If the legs are chopped off by the page's bottom edge, the S's feeling of a lack of autonomy probably is almost overwhelming. When the legs are drawn as paper-chopped, the examiner should have the S indicate how far below the page's bottom he sees the legs extending.

The position of the feet can be most expressive. For instance, a Person drawn on tiptoe might connote a tenuous grasp upon reality or a strong need for flight. In the drawings of Ss of average or higher intelligence, feet drawn as pointing in diametrically opposite directions, with the Person in full-face, indicate ambivalent feelings.

D.   TRANSPARENCY

The S who draws his House, Tree, or Person so that some object ordinarily considered to be covered by something is still visible commits a serious reality-testing flaw. Since transparencies imply a failure of the critical function, they are assumed to provide in the drawings of those not mentally deficient an indication of the extent to which personality organization is disrupted by the presence of functional or organic factors, or both. The pathological significance of the transparencies presented may be gauged in part by: (1) their number (2) their gravity. Examples follow.

HOUSE

Transparency of the wall of the House is a grave violation of reality seen only in drawings of mental defectives or rather seriously disturbed Ss.

A highly intelligent, hostile, young boy drew a House with the furniture in an upper story bedroom visible through the wall (not through a window). Among other things in the room there was a large bed occupied by a female figure: in the P—D—I he stated that the figure was his critically ill mother. Actually, at this time, the mother was in good health.

If a chimney at the back of the House is visible through both the front and the back walls, the S drawing this may be presumed to have an overwhelming phallic preoccupation and feel that this preoccupation is obvious to others.

If the chimney is transparent or has no depth, phallic denial, representing feelings of impotence and/or fear of castration, may be present

TREE

Roots shown as if the ground were transparent is pathological; the more so if the S was or is of high intelligence

PERSON

The most common and least significant transparency for the Person is an arm seen through a covering sleeve. However, the presence of pathology is very strongly suggested when the heart and lungs are drawn as visible.

E. MOVEMENT

In most drawings there is no graphic suggestion of movement·in the environment, as the wind blowing, or the whole in motion, as a Person running.

However, on occasion, motion is expressed in the drawings of House, Tree, and Person: the frequency of such expression is in the order Person, Tree, and House.

The interpretation of movement involves a consideration of (1) the intensity or violence of the motion; (2) the pleasantness or unpleasantness presumably involved in the movement; and (3) the degree to which the movement is voluntary.

Illustrations and their presumed implication follow.

HOUSE

The House usually is drawn as upright and intact. Any depiction of movement, as the roof flying off, the walls toppling over, etc., is pathological and expressive of a concomitant collapse of the ego under the assaults of extra-personal or intra-personal pressures, or both, depending upon the S's accounting for the collapse of the House.

One schizoid patient drew a rudimentary House with the chimney and roof on the ground, blown down by a tornado, she stated. Several weeks later she went into a catatonic state.

Feelings of environmental pressures can be expressed symbolically by smoke which instead of rising straight up from the chimney veers to one side, indicating that the wind is blowing. The magnitude of the *pressure* (wind) can be expressed by the degree of deviation of the smoke from a direct, or almost direct, upward course; the magnitude of the S's *feelings* frequently is revealed by the quantity of the smoke.

If the smoke indicates that the wind is blowing from page-right to page-left, it is presumed that the S views the future pessimistically. If the smoke is blowing from page-left to page-right, the intensity of the wind would need to be greater than that from right to left if pathoformicity were to be suspected, since left to right is the conventional direction of force. Smoke very seldom is drawn blowing from both left *and* right. Such a presentation is bizarre and has been produced only by psychotic Ss.

When an S depicts his House in motion (and such movement is catastrophic) as tilting or collapsing, the examiner regards such a depiction as pathological.

TREE

The Tree is drawn in motion more often than the House. Usually it is obvious that a strong wind is blowing since the Tree is drawn as bending to one side before it: here the suggestion is that the S is subjected to extreme environmental pressures, but he still resists and struggles to maintain his balance.

A life-term prisoner indicated his shattered ego status by drawing a large, barren Tree broken off halfway up from the ground, with the Tree's tip touching the ground.

The Tree drawn with its leaves dropping may express the S's impression of being stripped psychologically, losing his ability to hide his thoughts and emotions; and strong guilt feelings may be present, also. The S also may believe that he is losing his ability to make more refined and delicate adjustments to his environment.

Dependent children tend to draw apple Trees, to show their feelings of rejection by drawing the apples as falling or as fallen.

Several women have stated that falling leaves symbolized their menstrual function.

Falling branches express an S's certainty that he is losing his ability to cope with environmental pressures.

PERSON

Movement for the Person need be neither pathoformic nor pathological. On the contrary, movement can indicate the S's feeling of satisfactory adjustment: a Person walking easily and relaxed bespeaks good adjustment, for example.

Controlled running, as in a footrace, implies a strong need to achieve. "Blind" running, however, makes one suspect that the S might well be prey to panic states at times.

One epileptic S drew a Person falling in a seizure. A maladjusted young boy stated his Person was skating on very thin, rough ice, with many holes in it.

A paranoid schizophrenic drew two Persons; one upright, the other prone; said that the prone figure had just been shot by the standing figure.

A man who had found himself several times about to assault with a pocket knife a fellow workman who had annoyed him, voluntarily committed himself for observation. At his first interview with a psychologist, he drew a Person playing basketball, but with the Person's back almost completely toward the viewer. There was a strong suggestion that the Person was playing by himself. Two weeks later, the S drew a rigid, powerfully-shouldered, boxer with his back turned toward the viewer. Shortly after this the S was diagnosed as suffering with paranoia and he was institutionalized.

F.   CONSISTENCY

Consistency at all times is not expected from the standpoint of perspective, since there are many opportunities for the expression of in- dividual differences. As a matter of fact, absolute consistency is ap- parently indicative of pathology. Nonetheless, one should expect a reason- able amount of consistency. Unfortunately the term "reasonable amount" cannot be given a really satisfactory and objective definition.

IV.   TIME CONSUMPTION

An evaluation of the time used by the S and the use made by him of that time during the drawing phases of the H—T—P and the subsequent P—D—I can provide valuable information concerning the significance to the S of the six wholes and their respective parts.

A.   CONSUMED TIME VERSUS QUALITY OF DRAWING

If a whole is of superior quality, the examiner need not be sur- prised to find the S taking a rather long time in its production. Much de- pends on how concrete the detailing is: the more the S uses implication, the less time he will take. The acid test is the answer to the question: "Do the number of details and the method of their presentation justify the time consumed?"

If the total time used for House, Tree, and Person series, achro- matic or chromatic, is less than two minutes or more than 30 minutes, the examiner may suspect that an abnormal factor is interfering with the S's efficiency.

Schizophrenics are at both extremes of the time scale: those who draw quickly seem to do so to rid themselves rapidly of an unpleasant task. Those who use an excessive amount of time may do so because of their obvious reluctance to produce anything, or because of the intense emotional significance of the symbolism involved, or both. Manics may take a great deal of time because of the wealth of irrelevant detailing which they draw. Obsessive-compulsives, too, consume much time because of their tendency to produce meticulously all possible relevant details.

B.   INITIAL LATENCY

Anastasi and Foley (1), in their study of the spontaneous drawings of the "abnormal", found that the "abnormal" tended to have a longer initial latency than the "normal". Since, however, their Ss were permitted to decide what their first drawing would be, it cannot be assumed that the same relationship exists between the "normal" and the "abnormal" on the H−T−P. However, evidence acquired on the H−T−P thus far suggests that only the "abnormal" require any appreciable time in which to get "set" for the task before beginning to draw. If an S does not begin to draw his House, Tree, or Person within 30 seconds after receiving instructions, the examiner should regard the delay as pathoformic. Such a delay strongly suggests conflict, and the examiner should try to identify in the P−D−I the factors that produced this conflict.

C.   INTRA−WHOLE PAUSE

An intra−whole pause is a cessation of drawing for more than a few seconds at a time, once the task has been undertaken. An intra−whole pause of more than 5 seconds may be regarded as *prima facie* evidence of conflict, in the absence of evidence to the contrary.

The part of the whole being drawn, just drawn, or subsequently drawn, usually offers some clue as to the cause of the conflict. For example, sexually maladjusted Ss frequently pause for a time, when the waistline of the Person is reached, before drawing the pelvis, an area of conflict to them.

D.   COMMENT PAUSE

If the S pauses while commenting spontaneously during the drawing phase or while responding to questioning during the P−D−I, it is suspicious and probably indicates a blocking. But the examiner should conduct follow-up questioning to determine that it did not indicate that (1) the S was too concrete to do the abstracting required or (2) the S was so imaginative he was having difficulty deciding which of several replies to use.

E.   CONSISTENCY

The examiner may expect to find the S exhibiting a reasonable consistency. But in estimating consistency of time consumption, the examiner must remember that ordinarily the House and the Person require more time for adequate production than the Tree, since much of the Tree can be produced easily by implication, and since the details for the Tree, unless the S is over-meticulous and insists on drawing out carefully each two-dimensional leaf, are fewer than for the House or the Person. A major consumption of time under any of the foregoing headings, however, may be presumed to indicate that the S has strong positive or negative feeling toward the drawn whole or some part of it, or the concept symbolically represented by the whole or some part of the whole. Extremely scant consumption of time appears to indicate rejection of the task and/or rejection. of the object, idea, or situation symbolized by the whole for the S.

V. LINE QUALITY

A. MOTOR CONTROL

The average person has little difficulty drawing relatively straight lines. His "corners" are rather sharply defined, and his "curved lines" free-flowing and controlled. Impairment in motor control, as shown by deviations from the foregoing descriptions, suggests a functional personality maladjustment or a central nervous system disorder; and the degree of deviation may be a partial measure of the magnitude of the functional or organic disturbance. Individuals who have spent much of their lives performing heavy manual labor cannot be expected to manipulate a small and relatively delicate tool such as a pencil or crayon with the facility shown by a clerk. The examiner must be careful not to assume that ineptitude due to occupation is symptomatic of an organic nervous disease such as early arteriosclerosis.

B. FORCE

Heavy black lines drawn by an S who does not suffer from a central nervous system disorder are appraised in accordance with the generality and the specificity of their employment. For example: (1) if heavy lines are drawn throughout a whole, a generalized tension may be presumed to be present, and if heavy lines appear in all six wholes organicity would be highly suspect. (2) if such lines are used in the presentation of a specific detail within a whole, the examiner may presume (a) a fixation upon the object so drawn, (the hand of the Person being viewed as a source of guilt, for example) and/or (b) hostility, suppressed or overt, against the detail drawn or what it symbolizes; (3) if the heavy lines are the peripheral lines of the House, Tree, or Person, and the other lines within the wholes are not as heavy, one might suspect that the S is striving hard to maintain ego integrity, a fact of which perhaps he is unpleasantly aware; (4) if the heavy lines are the baselines and the topmost lines as well, of the House or Tree, the suggestion seems to be that the patient is struggling to maintain contact with reality and to suppress a tendency to secure satisfaction in phantasy; (5) a very heavy groundline usually is interpreted as representing feelings of anxiety occasioned by relationships at the reality level; (6) heavy lines used to outline the roof only suggest (viewing the House as a self-portrait) emphasis upon phantasy as a source of satisfaction with concomitant feelings of anxiety.

Extremely faint lines, if they are used throughout all wholes, are indicative of a generalized feeling of inadequacy accompanied by indecision and fear of defeat. If the lines become fainter from House through Person, one might suspect the presence of generalized anxiety and/or depression. If the faint lines are used in depicting certain details only within a whole, they are believed to represent a reluctance by the S to express the details in question because of what they represent to him actually or symbolically.

C.   TYPE

(The use of shading was discussed under I *DETAILS*, subhead B. Presentation Method, q.v.).

Decisive, well-controlled, free-flowing lines tend to imply good adjustment. Broken, indecisive lines, or lines which are continuous only because they have been frequently reinforced usually are pathoformic. Individuals with artistic training frequently begin by drawing vague lines which they later erase but use as "guide lines". This is not a pathoformic usage. But a line that is broken or hatched initially and which becomes continuous later only because of repetitive reinforcement is pathoformic.

The rigid, straight line frequently is an overt expression of internal rigidity. Usually the curving line is a healthy sign, although it may indicate distaste for convention and/or restriction.

D.   CONSISTENCY

The House, as a rule, requires straight lines only. The Person generally demands many curved lines. The Tree usually requires a combination of the two. Variation from the conventional type of line for a given whole apparently is pathoformic; so is marked type and force vacillation with a whole.

VI.   CRITICALITY

By *criticality* is meant: (a) the critical attitude of the S toward the task, and (b) the effort of the S to better something that he himself has criticised as incorrect or inadequate.

The ability to view one's work objectively, to criticise it, and to learn from that criticism is one of the first intellectual functions to suffer from the presence of strong emotionality and/or organic processes. Therefore, it is clinically profitable to analyze the flaws identified by the S in his drawings of Houses, Trees, and Persons, to determine his remedial steps and how successful they were.

A. VERBAL

Verbal criticism can be of several types: (1) spontaneous comment used to denounce the H–T–P as unfair; (2) the S may attempt to excuse what he regards as his ineptitude by remarking that, when he went to school, students were not taught to draw, or his hands have grown stiff with age, or by making some equivalent comment; (3) the S may say, "See! This is all out of proportion", or, "I am nervous; look how crooked these lines are." Only types (2) and (3) are real criticisms, and only (3) reveals critical ability. Some comments of these types are common. However, when they are excessive, they are pathoformic, particularly when there is no concomitant or subsequent attempt at correcting the verbally identified flaw or flaws.

B. ACTIVE

Active expression of criticality may involve: (1) abandonment of an incompleted whole with resumption of the drawing elsewhere on the drawing form page, without erasure of the abandoned whole. This is pathoformic, since it constitutes a negativistic reaction. (2) erasure without attempt at redrawing. This usually is restricted to one detail which apparently has aroused a strong conflict; the S can produce the detail once, but not twice; (3) erasure with redrawing. If the redrawing results in improvement, it is a favorable sign. It may, however, be pathoformic, if the attempts at correction represent hypermeticulosity, a futile attempt to attain perfection, or if there is erasure followed by deterioration of form quality, which implies: (a) an extremely strong emotional reaction to the object drawn or its symbolization; (b) the presence of an organic deteriorative factor; or both.

Persistent erasure and redrawing of any part of the whole strongly suggests conflict with the detail as an actuality or as a symbol.

C. CONSISTENCY

Clinical experience appears to justify the assumption that the well-integrated individual's self-critical attitude remains reasonably consistent throughout the production of the six drawings. Obviously the drawings will vary in meaning from S to S. The detailing needed for their satisfactory production, etc., also will vary, but there is no reason why the standard of excellence set by an individual should not maintain constancy, all else being equal. Absence of any effort at correction by Ss of average or higher intelligence is almost always a pathognomonic sign, unless the productions are of high quality, of course.

VII.   ATTITUDE TOWARD THE TASK

The attitude of an S toward the H—T—P as a totality indicates his willingness to accept or reject a new and perhaps difficult task; his attitude toward each whole will be influenced by the associations aroused by the whole or a part or parts thereof.

A.   WHOLE TASK

The continua described here begin with "reasonably willing acceptance", and branch off in two directions: (1) through eager acceptance to hyperegotism; and (2) through indifference, defeatism, and abandonism, to frank rejection. Rarely will an organic's feelings of impotence when faced with a task demanding creativity compel him to reject the H—T—P completely. Rarely will a hostile S flatly refuse to undertake the H—T—P: However, such Ss may reject all other attempts at a formal psychological examination.

Extreme variation from reasonable willingness is regarded as suspicious. However, mild changes in attitude are to be expected: For example. many Ss of average intelligence and well-integrated personalitities rebel initially, but gradually become more receptive as they realize that the task is not too difficult.

B.   SPECIFIC WHOLES

Marked variation from reasonably willing acceptance of any of the six tasks (Houses, Trees, and Persons) is pathoformic, and may be pathological.

The Person is the whole by far the most frequently rejected. There appear to be several reasons for this: (1) many maladjusted Ss have their greatest difficulties in interpersonal relationships; (2) drawing the human figure seems to arouse more associations at the conscious, or near-conscious level, than the House or the Tree; (3) acute body-awareness does not contribute to the comfort of maladjusted Ss.

In the absence of conflict, frustration, etc., there seems to be no reason to believe that an S's attitude toward the individual wholes will vary widely: It did not happen with the reasonably well-adjusted Ss of the quantitative standardization group.

VIII.   DRIVE

A.   AMOUNT

The examiner will wish to assess, albeit crudely, the drive of the S and be alert for evidence of psychomotor increase, decrease, or fluctuation, and the point or points of occurrence.

B. SPECIFIC WHOLES

The H—T—P tends to arouse great emotionality and affords the examiner an opportunity to keep the S under close inspection (the S often is not aware of this). The H—T—P provides the examiner with valuable clues concerning the S's stimulability and ability to inhibit impulses.

C. CONSISTENCY

The average individual shows mild fatigue by the time he completes his achromatic Person. Marked fatigability, however, is pathoformic and indicates the presence of a depression of mood which may or may not be accompanied by other factors producing a diminution of efficiency.

Ss who are initially disturbed but who calm down quickly and work efficiently, presumably suffer from test-situation fright: this is not pathoformic.

Marked psychomotor increase is presumed to be pathoformic. It suggests excessive stimulability with concomitant limited inhibitory power. A persistent psychomotor decrease suggests a deep depression of mood or crippling abulia.

Scatter is highly suspicious. Presumably it may be explained by the individual's reaction to the whole being drawn or discussed, or some part or parts thereof.

IX. COLOR

In the standard chromatic H—T—P, the S is provided with eight wax crayons (red, blue, yellow, green, brown, orange, black, and purple)* with which to draw the House, Tree and Person.

Although the principal purposes of administering the chromatic H—T—P are (1) to make the examination a miniature longitudinal study (see Postulate XIII) and (2) to provide data on which to base a more accurate appraisal of the depth and probable permanence of the dynamic material elicited, appraisal of the S's use of color *per se* may provide additional diagnostic and prognostic data.

Students often are tempted to make sweeping interpretations of the meanings of different colors. This is both dangerous and futile. The literature is replete with "meanings" of colors, but in each case close examination reveals that the "meaning" is not that of the color only, but that of the color, *plus* the object colored, plus the surroundings.

For example: Grassy, wind-swept savannahs are described as a

* If a greater range of colors can be provided the examiner is urged to use it.

luscious, pleasing green. Dank, stagnant pools have surfaces described as coated with an ugly, green slime. In each case the color is *green*, but the "meaning" is certainly not the same. In short, color should be treated as having no more significance than a qualifying adjective unless (1) its use does not conform to convention and/or reality; (2) a color tends to dominate the form of the detail with which it is used; (3) color is used in scatter fashion: That is, any color besides black is used for one or more but not all the details in a whole, or for one or two wholes, but not all three.

A.   CHOICE

The slower and more indecisive the S is in selecting his crayon for a detail, detail-complex, or whole, the greater is the likelihood that the item to be produced has more than average significance for him.

B.   APPLICATION

1.   *Method:* If an S uses a black or brown crayon only and employs it as a pencil, he may be assumed to be emotion-shy at best.

In general, shading is used more often in the chromatic than in the achromatic drawings. The interpretation of shading depends, as in the achromatic series, on the way the shading is drawn, plus the degree to which it conforms (in choice of the color used) to convention and reality.

2.   *Amount:* As a rule Ss use more colors for the Person than the House, and more for the House than for the Tree. Anxious, color-shy Ss use the black (or occasionally the brown) crayon only, and produce, in effect, a second achromatic series but with the enclosed white space enhanced. Highly emotional Ss use many colors. In general, children use colors, particularly the "bright" colors, more freely than adults. This is in line with the belief that emotional responses precede intellectual responses on the maturation scale. Regressed Ss use color more freely and less critically than non-regressed Ss, with an accompanying loss of interest in form *per se*.

If more than three-fourths of the area of the drawing form page is colored, the S may be presumed to lack adequate control of emotional expression. This interpretation is subject to modification by other factors (as are all other interpretaions from H–T–P data).

3.   *Control:* In the absence of motor damage, shading which "spills" over the peripheral lines of a whole implies a tendency toward making impulsive responses to additional stimuli.

C.   CONFORMITY

1.   *To Convention:*

The following table may help in appraising the S's conformity to convention in his use of color. The data are based largely on tne author's experience and are *not* finally definitive.

In each case, the color may be used to produce simple peripheral lines, or peripheral lines plus shading (as outlining a roof's shingle, then shading it with tne same color), or for shading only. It is "conventional" for an S to use the black crayon only; in other words, this is a "popular" usage.

HOUSE

Chimney: red, black, brown *

Smoke: black, brown

Roof: black, green, red, brown

Wall: black, brown, green, red, yellow, blue

Doors and Window Frames: black, brown, green, red, blue

Drapes and Curtains: any color except purple

Shutters: black, green, brown, blue, red

TREE

Trunk: brown, black

Branches: brown, black

Foliage: green, yellow, red, brown, black

Fruit: red, yellow, green

Blossoms: red, yellow, orange, blue, purple

PERSON

Head and Face Periphery: black, brown

Hair: black, brown, yellow, red

Eyes: blue, brown, black

Lips: red, black

Body Periphery: black, brown

Arms and Legs Periphery: black, brown (or the color used for the clothing which covers the arms and legs).

Hands and Feet Periphery: black, brown, (or, for the feet, the color of the shoe drawn).

Clothing: Suits: black, brown, blue

Dresses: any color (purple is rarely used, however).

Shoes: black, brown, green, red, and blue

---

* The colors in each instance are listed in descending order of frequency of use. The step intervals vary widely and are not to be given any weight.

Certain irrelevant details are so "fixed" as to color that any violation of convention in their presentation is highly significant. For example, the sun is yellow, and the sky is blue; grass is green or brown; shadows are indicated by black or blue shading.

Two soon-to-be published studies were graciously reported to the author by the respective research psychologists.

(1)   V. J. Bieliauskas of Xavier University and R. J. Ausdenmoore of the Cincinnati Board of Education investigated the color preferences of 134 male high school seniors using a *16-color* crayon set. They found that the most preferred colors for the House were black, brown, red, green and blue; for the Tree, brown, black, green and yellow-green; for the Person, black, brown and red. Black was the most frequently used color for all wholes.

(2)   Verlin Spencer investigated the use of color in the H–T–P by 148 prisoners at the California Medical Facility at Vacaville, California, (he used the Achromatic H–T–P, the 8-color Chromatic H–T–P, and the Water Color H–T–P which he designed). Spencer found that for the chromatic House the most frequently used crayons were brown, green, black and red; for the Tree, green and brown; and for the Person, black, brown, blue, orange and red.

The student is urged to familiarize himself with Isaac Jolles' "Some Advances in Interpretation of the Chromatic Phase of the H–T–P" (published in the *Journal of Clinical Psychology*, January, 1957). This paper describes the results of Jolles' study of the use of color by 200 children. Like Bieliauskas and Ausdenmoore, he used a 16–color set of crayons.

2. *To Reality:*

It is as impossible to conform literally and completely to reality with the 8–color crayon set as it is in the achromatic series. For example, life-like flesh-color is most difficult to produce. The majority of Ss use the black crayon to outline the unclad parts of the Person.

An S who becomes so color-bound that his House consists of a wall of two rows of blue rectangles above two rows of purple rectangles obviously is seriously maladjusted. So is one who draws a Tree that has a 2-dimensional trunk with 1-dimensional branches extending laterally from it from base to tip, all in blue. One psychotic epileptic drew his Person with a blue head and body, yellow arms, and brown legs.

The House may be produced in any color, with the possible exception of purple, without violating reality from a chromatic point of view.

The Person's clothing may be of any color and still conform to reality. Breaks with reality in the use of color are always to be regarded as serious.

D. SYMBOLISM

There is no evidence that any of the eight colors in the chromatic H–T–P has a fixed, specific meaning. Each color, however, appears to have at least one underlying inherent symbolic connotation, the precise determination of which depends upon how and where the color is used.

The following is presented with the strict admonition that little weight should be accorded it and that it be used with great caution.

1. *Red* appears to have sensual implications ranging in character and force from pleasantly warm to uncomfortably hot. Red seems to be the most difficult color for the emotionally disturbed to use.

2. *Green* seems to be a color which produces feelings of security, or freedom from threat. It has been called the color of balance. Since green is so profuse in nature, its use with the House and Tree is equally profuse and usually has no pathoformic implications.

3. *Blue* appears to express two needs: (a) maintenance of control; (b) avoidance of threat and stress. Like green, it is a relatively bland and soothing color.

4. *Black,* when used for shading, has a decidedly dysphoric connotation. When the sky contains heavy black clouds or the background is heavily shaded to indicate night, the dysphoria becomes almost overwhelming.

5. *Brown* is the second most frequently used color by Ss who try to avoid color. Heavy shading with brown (when not conventional, as it is for trunk of Tree) implies defensiveness and a reluctant response to additional emotional stimuli.

6. *Yellow* is believed to carry implications of a hostile attitude. It is most frequently used for drawing the sun. Its conventional use for the House is largely restricted to depicting light within the House (since this suggests that it is night time, pathoformicity is suspected). Occasionally the yellow crayon is used as a pencil to draw the Person (as many Ss use the black crayon). Usually the S who uses yellow in this atypical way, will explain his usage on the ground that yellow is the closest to white of any of the 8 colors.

7. *Orange* (seldom used) apparently has the connotation of an unhappy sensuality and hostility. It seems to imply that the S has highly ambivalent attitudes, particularly when it is used for the sun.

8. *Purple,* the least used of the colors, oddly enough has the most consistent implication: the need for power. Its use for the House or the Tree is never conventional, but it can be used realistically for the

Tree to depict blossoms.

The more deviantly a color is used, the greater is the justification for the suspicion that the meaning of the color has played some part in its use.

E.   CONSISTENCY

Marked inconsistency from whole to whole, in the use of color, demands that the examiner make efforts to learn the "why" therefor.

X.   COMMENTS

Appraisal of the S's comments is in two parts: (1) Drawing Phase and (2) Post-Drawing Phase. The latter usually is far more intricate and productive of diagnostic and prognostic material than the former.

(1)   DRAWING PHASE

The comments made by the S while he is drawing, may be either written or verbal, and almost invariably they are spontaneous.

Written comments usually consist of the names of persons, streets, trees, etc., or numbers, although they also may be geometric figures and doodlings. In almost each instance written materials are at least pathoformic. They seem to represent: (1) a compulsive need to structure the situation as completely as possible (indicative of insecurity); or (2) a compulsive need to compensate for an obsessive idea or feeling activated by something in the drawing.

At times, apparently as the result of the"pencil release factor", Ss verbalize materials hitherto suppressed or repressed. It is imperative, therefore, to analyze "drawing phase" verbal comments from several points of view:

(1) *Volume:* Tne absence of spontaneous comments, in effect, may offer supportive evidence to a suspicion that the S tends to withdraw; however, many well-adjusted persons make no spontaneous comments. The pathoformicity of the absence of spontaneous comments, in part, may be assayed by a consideration of the S's attitude toward the whole being drawn or discussed. Far more significant than the absence of comments are (1) the presence of an excessive number of comments; and (2) the verbalization of wholly irrelevant or bizarre material.

It is not uncommon for relatively well-integrated Ss of dull-average. average, or above average intelligence to use a number of "alibi" remarks, such as: "They didn't teach drawing when I went to school, or, "I never could learn to draw."

Occasionally while producing the House, Tree, or Person, Ss express feelings of anxiety, inadequacy, and hostility in such volume that the examiner cannot record them verbatim: He should do everything possible, however, to record the major theme expressed.

Samples of spontaneous comments are: ·

A 65-year old psychoneurotic woman with guilt feelings, obsessions and deep-seated suspicions of her husband's infidelity, etc., was so resistive to psychotherapy and shock therapy that a pre-frontal lobotomy was to be performed on her. On the day before surgery, while she was drawing her House she said, "That's something I never did in my life is to draw. Shall I draw it this way? (Horizontally) You wouldn't live in this. You wouldn't accept my architecture. You wouldn't accept this."

Examiner: "Why do you say that?"

S: "I don't know whether the foundation's solid, to begin with and the windows--"

Examiner (as the patient becomes tense and visibly worried by her inability to draw well): "Just do the best you can; don't worry too much about it."

S: "You're very encouraging. Let's see, my windows are not all the same. You wouldn't accept me as a carpenter to begin with. Are you looking at me? That's what puzzles me, that roof! How am I going to get my porch up there, and those steps?"

(Here the S used an eraser as a ruler and when she was told not to do this, she tried to erase everything she had drawn.)

S: "Now where's my door? I've got my windows in the wrong place. I'll put my door here; how would that do, doctor? Let's see, would I be cheating if I looked to see which side the doorknob's on? Have some steps going up to it: would that be all right? There's the foundation. Think it would be better architecture to have the small windows in the side? I believe it would. Is that a baby crying? Does it cry that way all the time? Not very neat construction that isn't. Is this a test of your nervousness? Your neatness? It could be interesting if you didn't get so nervous."

Examiner: "Why do you get nervous, Mrs. C.?"

S: "It's my nature--What time is it, have you any idea? You wouldn't live in this; foundation's not solid, not secure."

Examiner: "Why do you say that the foundation's not solid?"

S: "It was build so quickly--insecure--Oh, I envy anyone who can sit down and do what you are doing; be so sure of it. What is it? I am the master of my fate; the captain of my soul? Do you suppose it could be done for me?"

Examiner: "Why do you think it couldn't?"

S: "I think maybe it's my age--I think the physicians know what they are doing, but at my age do you suppose you can get everything back; those things that have been lost and to know at all times what you are doing?''

Her constant reference to the foundation of her House symbolized her feeling that the foundation of her home situation had been shattered by her husband's frank unfaithfulness or by her own suspicions. She was never sure just what the objective fact was.

Her outstanding symptoms, however, were marked distractability, overwhelming and painful uncertainty, and feeling of inadequacy.

Her comments were made at intervals during the 27 minutes, 35 seconds it took her to draw her House.

A young man of above average intelligence who exhibited generalized anxiety, many phobias, and obsessive-compulsive reactions, commented while drawing his Tree, (1) ''Copy? You want me to look at the paper and draw it?'', (2) ''I'd draw an evergreen, but you said you wanted a Tree.''

Examiner: ''Why do you feel that an evergreen is not a Tree?''

S: (3) ''It'd be a devil of a lot easier for me (S erased all he had drawn of the deciduous tree he had begun)..I've tried drawing this before. I had a squirrel sitting out on a post at school.'' (4) ''Now if I was drawing a Tree and putting it in the yard of my house, that's all the Tree I'd draw.''

His first comment appears to represent his strong need to have all tasks defined at great length, for he already had drawn a House, and by now should have known that the drawn wholes were to be his creations. The second comment puzzled the examiner at first, because it seemed almost bizarre. In the P–D–I however, it was found that the evergreen he drew had been drawn by him many times before; it reminded him of his mother, with whom he identified this Tree so strongly that he could not regard his Tree-stereotype as a Tree only.

His third comment reflected his pathoformic reluctance to undertake an unfamiliar task. The squirrel on the post outside the school might, he thought, be himself, for he didn't ''fit'' in with the other children much better than a squirrel would.

His last comment formally identified the location of the real Tree of which his drawing was a reproduction. In the P–D–I he could not state definitely whether the drawn Tree was in the yard of his parental home or of his present home; this Tree seemed to symbolize well his ''home-vacillation.''

A paranoid schizoid male who was temporarily sexually impotent and who had tried to ''lose himself'' in his work for many years, while drawing his Person, an elderly male invalid sitting in a bassinet-like chair and staring into the fireplace, spontaneously commented:

''Cartoon, or what?'' The S sighed while beginning to draw his Person's abdomen.. A few seconds later the examiner noticed the S apparently was drawing a bust only, and he repeated the original instructions to draw the entire Person. "Well, I'll see if I can make it all in, then." Sighing, the S drew the lower vest line. While drawing the collar, he commented, "Got the damned thing out of proportion. I'll make him a little runt like Carter Glass." (laughing.) The S coughed and hummed while he was drawing the eye and the eyebrows. While he was drawing the mouth, he exclaimed, "Did you see that atrocious thing in Time? Somebody dug up a mummy 100 years old!" While he was shading the tie, he remarked, "I reckon this is an old man sitting in his chair with his bathrobe or blanket, or something on." The S then hummed and whistled a bit. During his drawing of the back of the fireplace, he remarked, "Can't you be any warmer than that looking at *my* fireplace?" His final comment, made while he was shading the hearth material, was "Convalescent."

Initially the S expressed hostility by: (1) suggesting that he would like to caricature his Person, and (2) ignoring the instructions to draw the whole Person. By the time the Person was half-completed, he was trying to make it appear that the proceeding was of no import and might be merely an unpleasant joke. At the end, the drawn Person was in the S's living-room, almost acknowledged to be a self-portrait. His prognostic comment, "Convalescent," was later borne out clinically.

These comments were made at intervals during the fifty minutes he consumed in drawing his Person.

A possible explanation of the dynamics of the "pencil-release" factor is: When an element of the personality, which had been engaged previously in defending the ego by suppressing verbalization of certain material, becomes occupied in the act of drawing, previously suppressed material is released for expression.

(2) *Relevance:* This continuum here is from superfluous, through irrelevant, to bizarre.

A superfluous, relevant, spontaneous comment, for example, is the defining of a part which needs no definition, such as, "I'll put this necktie on him." In many instances this is: (1) a manifestation of a need to structure a situation with meticulosity, thus representing an underlying insecurity; (2) an attempt to ease test-situation tension through verbalization.

Irrelevant comments have nothing to do with the task at hand. For example, one S, while drawing his House, queried, "You say this is your first day here?" (Referring to a remark the examiner had made some time before while establishing rapport.)

Careful analysis of seemingly irrelevant remarks is worthwhile: one psychoneurotic young woman remarked in a peculiarly bitter tone, "I *always* draw a Tree like that." In the P—D—I the examiner questioned her closely concerning this remark and was rewarded with a vivid account of a painful traumatic experience, previously concealed, which the S had had while she was in art school.

Frankly bizarre were the following comments made by a catatonic schizophrenic woman while drawing her House: "Eight days instead of one--seconds though--eight--sixty seconds--leap year has sixty-five, I believe it does.--Twenty days in March--Imagine--Ingles." (These were made at varied intervals as the dashes indicate.) After she had completed her drawing she wrote "Has 60; Can't 820 in March" on the page. Such comments obviously are highly pathological.

(3) *Range:* A wide range of topics is not necessarily unhealthy, for all topics may be relevant to the drawing or drawings, but a wide range of irrelevant topics is to be regarded as highly suspicious..A hypochondriacal psychoneurotic woman, for example, gave a rather complete, but very disconnected, autobiographical sketch while she was drawing.

(4) *Subjectivity:* Ideas of reference and persecution often are freely expressed (apparently because of the "pencil-release" factor) and they speak for themselves..

(5) *Emotionality:* Many Ss become highly emotional while they are drawing or while they are being questioned in the P—D—I phase, presumably because of their expression (through drawing, verbalization, or both) of hitherto suppressed material. It is imperative for the examiner to make a careful and complete record of any emotion exhibited, no matter how minor.

Any S, regardless of his personality adjustment, may exhibit symptoms of test-situation fright. However, neither persistent minor emotional expressions, nor major emotional expressions, nor a marked flattening of affect is to be expected in the absence of personality imbalance or maladjustment. Assignment of the degree of probable pathology depends on the intensity, duration, and type of the S's emotions.

(6) *Point of Occurrence:* It is postulated that spontaneous comments never occur without a reason; that the most important factor provoking a spontaneous comment is the part of the whole which the S has just completed, is then working on, or is about to draw.

Closer investigation may reveal that a spontaneous remark, which at first appeared innocuous, is actually pathoformic. Spontaneous remarks, of course, often are significant by themselves, but usually they are more meaningful when evaluated relative to their points of occurrence. The examiner must remember that a given comment may have more than one implication.

(2)   POST – DRAWING PHASE

I. Achromatic

The P—D—I is designed to provide an S with the opportunity to define, describe, modify, elaborate and interpret his graphic productions and to associate concerning them. Evaluation of the S's P—D—I responses is perhaps the most difficult step in qualitative analysis. It is difficult, too, for the author to discuss this step adequately because of the myriad answer-possibilities. The following brief question-by-question analysis with sample answers and their probable implications may be helpful. However, the student should carefully study the P—D—I's of the illustrative cases in Chapter 7 and also the examples in the cases in Appendix A

P1. *Is that a man or a woman (boy or girl)?* (R)

An S who states that a definitely feminine figure in man's clothing (not simply in slacks) is a man, or that an obviously masculine figure in a dress is a woman, confirms verbally the impression already created by the drawing: that is, that the S manifests sexual role confusion and indecision which may be pathological.

Markedly withdrawn or highly disturbed Ss not infrequently state that a drawn Person is of the sex opposite to the one presented. Such a reality-testing flaw always is pathological.

P2. *How old is he?* (R)

The primary purpose of P2 is to find how closely the apparent age of the drawn Person approximates the age assigned him by the S.

Occasionally the age stated represents the S's "felt age" rather than his chronological age.

P3. *Who is he?* (A)

This blunt attempt to determine the identity of the Person often is answered by, "I don't know"..Frequently at this stage of the P—D—I the Person may suggest no one to the S; but later, as the result of less direct questioning, the S can make a positive identification.

In a number of instances the Person ultimately will be found to be some one other than the individual named in response to the question. It is qualitatively useful, however, to pursue here a line of interrogation designed to reveal whether the Person represents one or many personalities.

P4. *Is he a relation, a friend, or what?* (A)

If the Person has been identified (in reply to P3) as someone other than the S, this question may help to establish the positive or negative valence which that person has for the S. When P3 has been answered "I don't know," P4 may elicit more positive indentification.

P5. *Whom were you thinking about while you were drawing?* (A)

In certain cases the individual named here is not the one named in answer to P3. The answer "No one," does not necessarily represent evasion or falsification, for the S may not have thought of anyone consciously while he was producing his Person.

P6. *What is he doing? (and where is he doing it?)* (R & P)

The primary purpose is to see how closely the apparent action of the drawn Person approximates the S's verbal designation. The secondary purpose is to test for feelings of pressure, as of compulsion.

The motion designated by the S (voluntary, pleasant, fluid), the force and the degree to which they conform to the graphic presentation, may be highly significant. An absence of motion is not regarded as pathoformic unless it is of a rigid, over-controlled, essentially crippling type.

A young male adult with a severe character neurosis answered P6, "He's telling people to get on his trolley (the streetcar named *Desire,* Ed.). This is the world. Everyone gets on the streetcar to satisfy their desire. The streetcar goes 'ding-dong', then starts off. When it makes the first stop, people get off. Everyone gets off at a different stop, but the street) car goes the same place every day. Just goes to show you that you never get anywhere!''

P7. *What is he thinking about?* (A ℞ P)

Evidence of obsessive and/or delusional thinking by the S may be elicited by P7. If the S regards the drawn Person as a self-portrait, he will often reveal at this point well-developed feelings of guilt, anger, bewilderment, resentment, etc. If the S sees his drawn Person as someone else, he may express what he feels is the opinion that the other person has of him.

P8. *How does he feel?* (P) *(Why?)* (P)

The answer to this question usually appears to express the feeling that the S has toward the situation involving the drawn Person. The question also may provide sufficient stimulus to produce direct comments concerning the S's feeling about his present condition or about matters which he has not been able to discuss.

T1. *What kind of Tree is that?* (R)

Ss usually draw Trees of the kind most common in the vicinity of their homes. However, this is a matter of manifest content only, for apparently the Tree has the same latent meaning for all Ss: That is, it is a living, or once living thing, in an elemental, dynamic environment.

The S who calls an obvious *pine* a *maple* suffers from a gross reality-testing flaw

T2. *Where is that Tree actually located?* (A)

Most frequently the S draws a Tree situated near his present or past home or in a place which he associates with a past experience of high positive or negative valence.

If he says that his Tree is in a forest, his definition of *forest* may be revealing: For some, it is a place of peace, quiet, and solitude; for others, a place of dread and threat, promising strongly felt danger. The answer, "In a group of Trees," suggests that the S needs (and enjoys) companionshipl

T3. *About how old is that Tree?* (R ℞ P)

Most often the age is (1) the *chronological* age or *felt* age of the S; (2) the number of the years the S has lived past puberty; (3) the number of years S has felt his environment to be unsatisfying or (4) the age of the person other than the S who is represented or symbolized by the Tree.

T4. *Is that Tree alive?* (R & P)

No completely well-adjusted S ever answers, "No". A negative answer usually indicates that the S feels physiologically inferior or psychologically inadequate, guilty, deeply depressed or some combination of of those feelings. Occasionally further questioning will reveal that the S see the Tree as *dormant* rather than dead; this is a hopeful sign.

T5. *I (If* the S says that the Tree is alive.)

(a) *What is there about that Tree that gives you the impression that it's alive?* (R & A)

The answer to this question may be the first indication to the examiner that the S sees the Tree in motion, a motion that may range from a mild tremor of the leaves to a frank swaying of the trunk. Other responses indicate that such qualities as strength, vigor, etc., create the impression of life in the Tree for the S. The most obvious reply is that the Tree must be alive because it has foliage.

One would expect deciduous Trees to be drawn more often as leafless in winter than in summer. Drs. Judson and MacCasland, of Marcy State Hospital, New York, wrote the author that they had found that women tended to draw more barren Trees in winter than in the summer, but that this tendency was not shown by men. As was to be expected also, they found that older patients drew barren Trees more often than younger patients.

(b) *Is any part of the Tree dead?* (P) *What part?* (P)

It has not been proven conclusively that the concept of a wholly dead Tree indicates greater maladjustment than the concept of a *partially* dead Tree; but thus far this has seemed to be the case. Most commonly, the branches or the roots are regarded as the dead or dying part. Dead branches appear to express the S's belief that his great frustration has been produced solely by extra-personal factors within his environment. Dead roots, on the other hand, imply an intra-personal imbalance or dissolution with the start of a serious loss of contact with reality.

(c) *What do you think caused it to die?* (P)

When worms, insects, parasites, blight, lightning, wind, or occasionally maliciously aggressive actions by children or adult are said by the S to be the cause, the S expresses his conviction that something extra-personal is to blame. If, however, death is said to be due to rotting of some part or of the entire Tree, he indicates a feeling that something within himself was at fault.

(d) *How long has it been dead?* (P)

The attempt here is to determine the S's impression of the duration of his disability or maladjustment. This "time" will not often coincide with the date derived from the anamnesis, as January, 1952. But when an S specifies a date, the examiner should attempt to determine the event which fixed that date so firmly in the S's memory.

    T5. II (If the S says that the Tree is dead.)

        (a) *What do you think caused it to die?* (P)

        (b) *How long has it been dead?* (P)

    The import of both questions is the sàme as (c) and (d) in the preceding subdivision of T5.

    T6. *Which does that Tree look more like to you: a man or a woman?* (A & R)

    The S's responses to T6 and T7 often provide valuable information concerning his psychosexual level of maturation.

    In general, pines and fir trees are seen as males; maples and fruit trees as females.

    A middle-aged, temporarily sexually impotent male stated that his Tree was a soft maple.

    T7. *What is there about it that gives you that impression?* (R & A)

    The sex ascribed to the Tree usually seems determined by characteristics such as shape, strength, ruggedness, grace, slimness, etc. Not infrequently, however, certain aspects of the Tree are seen as specific counterparts of the human figure. The long hanging branches of an evergreen reminded one S of his mother's hair. A maladjusted little girl explosively stated she saw ner father's fist in the middle of the branch structure of a maple Tree! "'Just as he used to raise it to strike my mother!''

    At times the sex will be determined by the person the S has associated with the Tree. One S associated his Tree with his father because the father chopped down trees. Another saw his Tree as feminine because it reminded him of his mother with whom he would sit under such a Tree while she told him stories. Whenever the gender of the Tree appears to have been determined by association only, the examiner should interrogate further to try to elicit some more direct sex-determinant.

    A woman of above average intelligence stated that her Tree made her think of a woman, "Because it is deciduous". Further questioning revealed that she felt that all deciduous trees were feminine because, "They change their purpose periodically." The dropping of the leaves symbolized the menstrual function for her. For this same patient "ornamental" trees were feminine and "wild" trees were masculine.

    T8. *If that were a person instead of a Tree, which way would the person be facing?* (P)

    Since a tree has neither front, side, nor back except as so seen by the viewer, the S's response to this question is a projection of (1) his view of his own stance toward his environment, or (2) his view of the attitude toward him adopted by the person symbolized for him by the Tree. A nostalgic, small boy saw his Tree as a motherly figure facing him. A neurotic, male adult saw his Tree as a rugged, rejecting father figure with his back turned to the S.

One obsessive-compulsive, paranoid young man of superior intelligence said, "I really couldn't say. It looks like it's facing upward. That's the way it grows, that's the way it'd face. At least I *think* it grows up." At that time he faced a possible death sentence.

T9. *Is that Tree by itself, or is it in a group of trees?* (P)

Answers to this question are not too significant unless they are strongly emotional, since a Tree must be either by itself or with other Trees, even though the other Trees are not drawn because the H—T—P instructions require only *a* Tree. However, feelings of isolation and/or a need for association with others frequently are elicited by T9.

T10. *As you look at that Tree, do you get the impression that it is above you, below you, or about on a level with you?* (R)

The S's reality-testing ability is dangerouls weak if he states, "Above me," when obviously the Tree was drawn from a "bird's-eye" view.

To some Ss a Tree drawn growing on a hilltop is symbolic of tense striving toward a distant and perhaps unattainable goal; for others it re-- flects needs for autonomy and dominance. For many, a Tree drawn as partly sheltered by a hill indicates a need for protection and succor. A Tree drawn as clearly below the viewer almost invariably connotes a depression of mood as well as of position.

T11. *What is the weather like in this picture? (Time of day and year; sky; temperature)* (P & R)

It is postulated that the Tree expresses an individual's conscious or subconscious feeling of himself in relation to his environment. Since external forces affecting a living tree are largely meteorological, it is not surprising that many Ss are able to express symbolically through their answers to T11 their feeling that their environments are supportive and friendly, or oppressive and hostile. Ss may describe minutely unpleasant weather conditions, despite the absence of anything in the drawing to indicate the presence of such conditions.

T12. *Is there any wind blowing in this picture?* (R & P)

Wind symbolizes feelings of pressure by environmental, personal, or situational forces.

One young adult male with a severe character neurosis answered, "It's the calm before the storm." The the examiner's, "Will the storm damage the Tree?" He replied, "No, I don't think so. It's the calm before the atomic war..It will not destroy the Tree, just the dog." The S reiterated time and again that his Tree (obviously a self-portrait) represented "Beauty"--and the dog that was sniffing at the Tree's trunk stood for "Man".

T13. *Show me in what direction it is blowing.* (R)

Usually the wind is said to be blowing from left to right horizontally. This is interpreted as revealing, in the absence of unusual intensity, the psychological field tendency of locomotion from past (left) to future (right).

Winds which are more than mild in intensity and which deviate from the more or less conventional direction appear to be significant. One acutely disturbed individual stated that the wind was blowing in all directions simultaneously! One rigid neurotic pictured the Tree as his paramour and described his feelings in detail when she first disrobed before him: He said that the wind was blowing from behind the Tree toward him, implying narcissistically his belief that he was so irresistible that his paramour was impelled to come to him.

Wind "seen" as blowing from the ground's level to the Tree's top, diagonally upward and across the page, symbolizes a strong desire to escape from reality into phantasy; the reverse applies for winds said to be blowing from an upper to a diagonally opposite lower corner (and the temporal connotations, left for *past,* right for *future,* appear to hold).

T14. *What sort of wind is it?* (P & R)

The S's description of the velocity, humidity, and temperature of the wind can be revealing. A wind said to be blowing with great force, to be very damp or very dry, or to be very hot or very cold, or some combination thereof, is presumed to symbolize the fact that the S feels painful pressure from one or more environmental sources, with the degree of felt pressure presumably corresponding to the degree of variance from a calm weather state; tnis assumes, of course, that the response is not merely a parrot-like description of the weather at the time of examination.

H1. *How many stories does that House have?* (R)

This is a reality-testing question. Also, in a sense, it is a measure of attention, for withdrawn or highly disturbed Ss sometimes answer here without looking at their drawings.

H2. *What is that House made of?* (R & A)

In certain sections of the country a brick house has prestige which a frame house lacks. In other parts, the stone house is socially most desirable, and so on. It is well to determine what the specified material of of the House means to the S. *Brick,* for instance, might represent stability for one S and economy of maintenance for another.

H3. *Is that your own House?* (A) *Whose House is it?* (A)

Most frequently Ss attempt to draw their homes, but they seldom reproduce them accurately for several reasons besides the fact that most people do not draw with architectural exactitude. For example: (1) because the House is a self-portrait of the S as he functions in a setting involving the most intimate of interpersonal relationships; (2) because Ss tend to emphasize aspects of the home which have had the most pleasant or unpleasant meanings to them: This emphasis may include exaggeration or diminution of detailing, and/or a distortion of proportion and/or perspective; (3) because the House, in part, sometimes represents several dwelling of the past, present, and future.

H4. *Whose House were you thinking about while you were drawing?* (A)

This question, like P5, attempts to elicit information leading to a more accurate identification. The drawn House, like the drawn Tree or Person, may have a multiplicity of identities.

H5. *Would you like to own that House yourself?* (P & A) *Why?* (P & A)

The S's replies to the first part of this question and particularly to the "Why?", may reveal his attitudes toward his home and those who share it. It may show what sort of House he would like to own, the strength of his desire to own it, and the likelihood that his "goal-setting" will produce further frustration for him.

H6. *If you did own that House and you could do whatever you liked with it:* (a) *Which room would you take for your own?* (P) *Why?* (P)

The expressed desire of withdrawn Ss to seek refuge in a back room of an upper story is striking at times; suspicious individuals tend to take rooms allowing them full observation of the approaches to the doors.

H   (b) *Whom would you like to have live in that House with you?* (P) *Why?* (P)

Maladjusted children may indicate strong needs for paternal affection and approval by stating that they want their parents to live with them but not their siblings. Strongly paranoid Ss usually prefer to live alone or with one other person whom they can dominate. An unhappily married physician said that he wished to have only his voluptuous blond receptionist live with him---no one else. He stated that she had been a most cooperative bedfellow and added, "She offers no intellectual threat!"

Patients at times quickly detect implications behind this question and evade direct replies: The attempt at evasion may be more revealing than a frank response.

H7. *As you look at that House, does it seem to be close by or far away?* (R)

This is another "reality question" and responses flatly contradicting reality are significant. Usually *proximity* appears to equate attainability or feelings of warmth and welcome, or both; *distance* suggests striving or feelings of rejection or rejecting, or both.

H8. *As you look at that House, do you get the impression that it is above you, below you, or about on a level with you?* (R)

Answers to this question appear to have approximately the same significance as answers T10, but here they refer to the more specific area of inter-personal relationships, with emphasis upon home and family.

H9. *What does that House make you think of, or remind you of?* (A)

The associative possibilities here are too numerous to be illustrated adequately. The examiner is interested in the quality of the association and its valence for the S.

    H10. *What else?* (A)

    H11. *Is that a happy, friendly sort of House?* (A & P)

The emotional tone accompanying a negative answer may tell much of the S's view of his home and those in it. Highly evasive answers may indicate strongly negative valence.

    H12. *What is there about it that gives you that impression?* (A & P)

Occasionally an S will attempt to justify his response to H11 by describing superficial physical details of the House; stating, for example, that it is a happy House because it has curtains, smoke coming from the chimney, and so on. In the main, answers to this question presumably will be a direct expression of the S's feelings about the people who occupy the drawn House and his opinion of them and/or their feelings toward him.

A psychoneurotic artist with many paranoid tendencies answered H11, "I would think so," then sighed deeply. To question H12, he replied, "Well, I don't know that anything about the drawing gives me that impression, I've associated my own self and family living in that home and I think ours *could----is* a friendly, happy place in which to live." The *could* together with the definite pause following it showed clearly that he had grave doubts about the happiness of his home.

    H13. *Are most Houses that way?* (P & A) *Why do you think so?* (P & A)

Here the attempt is to see to what extent the S's friendly or hostile feelings toward the House and its occupants have been generalized. H13 may produce elaborations of the responses to H12 and thus clarify the S's attitude toward home and interpersonal relationships.

    H14. *What is weather like in this picture? (Time of day and year; sky; temperature)* (P & R)

One need not be surprised to hear the S describing weather that has little resemblance to his reply to T11, for the House and the Tree offer different approaches to personality projection, and not infrequently produce widely different reactions.

    T15. *What does that Tree make you think of, or remind you of?* (A)

Although most Ss associate with the House easily, since a dwelling place readily arouses many memory traces, associations with a Tree are less easy. Perhaps for this reason, associations with the Tree, when they are restricted to such things as "Men---because they chop down trees," etc., tend to be less superficial and thus more revealing.

    T16. *What else?* (A)

A paranoid, schizoid male answered this question, "It's badly out of proportion because the paper wasn't tall enough. I guess I started out at the right point, but the paper made it too broad." Even the paper persecuted him!

T17. *Is it a healthy Tree?* (R & P)

At least 25 questions have been asked since the S first commented upon the health of his Tree. Therefore, it should not be surprising to find that an S's answer to T17 is inconsistent with his reply to T4. A deeply anxious or depressed S may have indicated anxiety or depression by answering T4 with, "It's dead." By the time T17 is reached, however, he may say merely that the Tree is not well. This might indicate that (1) he does not feel that everything is hopeless (regarding the Tree as a self-portrait), (2) he feels guilt over expressing overt hostility, albeit symbolically (regarding the Tree as a Person -- not himself --whom he disliked).

T18. *What is there about it that gives you that impression?* (R & P)

Ss have expressed body feeling, feelings of inadequacy, isolation, environmental pressure, and so forth, more easily through comments about the Tree than about the Person, apparently because the Tree does not arouse as strong feelings of identification or as many conscious or near-conscious-level associations as does the Person.

T19. *Is it a strong Tree?* (R & P)

Health and *strength* are two different qualities to most people; the presence of health does not necessarily imply the concomitant presence of strength, or vice versa.

T20. *What is there about it that gives you that impression?* (R&P)

In justification of his affirmative response to T19, one epileptic S said, with pride: "Yes, it *must* be strong to have stood all the punishment that it's gone through."

This is another "reality" question, for though a frail or bent Tree may be healthy, it scarcely can be regarded as strong. Disparity between objective reality (the drawn Tree) and the S's answer to T20 might indicate: (1) a vacillant view of his ability to cope with life; (2) pathoformic inattention; (3) a vacillant attitude toward the person other than himself whom the Tree symbolizes.

The examiner should ask the S to draw his concept of the Tree's root structure (this should *not* be scored quantitatively). There is reason to suspect that the root structure may represent the S's view of the strength and quality of those personality aspects theorized as being below the conscious level.

P9. *What does that Person make you think of, or remind you of?* (A).

P10. *What else?* (A)

Here are sought associations about the drawn Person specifically and interpersonal relationships generally.

P11. Is that Person well? (P & R)

For Ss who have indulged in flights into illness, P11 at times is a sufficient stimulus to produce detailed accounts of somatic complaints.

In some cases P11 releases hostility (previously suppressed) against the individual, other than the S, represented by the drawn Person.

       P12. *What is there about him that gives you that impression?* (P&R)

       It is not unusual for Ss of limited or temporarily impaired intelligence to reply negatively, "He looks well, because he doesn't look sick."

       P13. *Is that Person happy?* (P & R)

       This question often precipitates expressions of complaints, fears, anxieties, etc., which had been supressed partially or wholly. On occasion, it brings forth hostile comments concerning the individual other than the S represented by the Person.

       P14. *What is there about him that gives you that impression?* (P & R)

       Most Ss are compelled to draw upon their feelings about themselves to answer this question satisfactorily.

       P15. *Are most people that way?* (P & R) *Why?* (P & A)

       The attempt is to see whether or not the S's expressed feelings about the Person, particularly if they are unpleasant or hostile, are generalized in interpersonal relationships. From the S's reply to P15 and the subsequent "Why?" much can be learned concerning his sympathy and empathy.

       P16. *Do you think you would like that Person?* (A & P) *Why?* (A & P)

       An S who feels sorely mistreated may launch into a vigorous defense of the drawn Person. The narcissist is unlikely to reply negatively to this question.

       P17. *What is the weather like in this picture? (Time of day and year; sky; temperature)* (P & R)

       It is rare for the S to draw details indicative of the weather such as raindrops, snowflakes, etc., in the picture of the Person. Graphic depiction of weather, therefore, demands careful Post-drawing interrogation and is presumed to be highly significant.

       P18. *Whom does that Person remind you of?* (A) *Why?* (A & P)

       This question may bring the first frank identification of the Person. On the other hand, the individual named here actually may be the 5th named by the S as his Person. While such a multiplicity of identification is rare, it is not uncommon for the Person to represent at least two people; the S himself and someone else of particular significance to him in his environment The S's explanation of why the drawn Person reminds the S of someone other than the one first named as the Person often is revealing.

       P19. *What does that Person need most?* (P&A) *Why?* (P&A)

       Not infrequently the S uses the first person singular pronoun in reply to this question. The "need" questions are among the most productive of the P–D–I. Needs may be expressed directly or symbolically, or both, and may range from the grossly physical to the most abstract psychological.

T21. *Whom does that Tree remind you of?* (A) *Why?* (A & P)

One psychoneurotic S so convinced himself that his Tree was a picture of his paramour, that when the P–D–I was over and certain aspects of the Tree which were obviously *self-portraiture,* were being interpreted to him, he agreed wholeheartedly, but then said, "Yes, that's just like Helen. Yes, that's just like Helen. She's exactly that way," demonstrating his gross lack of insight..

One mildly neurotic, pregnant S who had said in answer to T1 that her Tree was a maple now stated "The fool thing's trying to be an apple tree--," thus symbolizing her longing to look like the slim maple that she had drawn but revealing a concomitant fear of the responsibility of childbearing.

T22. *What does that Tree need most?* (P & A) *Why?* (P & A)

Definite answers most commonly express symbolically the S's needs for affection, shelter, security, good health, etc.

H15. *Whom does that House make you think of?* (A) *Why?* (A&P)

This is the most freely answered of the three "Whom does that make you think of" questions. Ordinarily the person named is an intimate member of the S's family.

H16. *What does that House need most* (P & A) *Why?* (P & A)

Again definitive answers usually are symbolic: for example, the reply of a woman violently jealous of her husband who, she thought, was breaking up their home, "It needs a good foundation."

H17. *If this were a Person instead of a Tree (or a shrub, or a windmill, or any other object not a part of the House itself) who might it be?* (A)

Not infrequently the seemingly irrelevant objects drawn about the House represent members of the family or persons with whom the S is intimately associated in his daily life. Their geographic relationship to the House on the form page symbolizes the closeness or distance of these personal relationships.

T23. *If this were a Person instead of a bird, (or another Tree, or anything else not a part of the originally drawn Tree), who might it be?* (A)

To repeat: Interpersonal relationships occasionally are symbolized by the drawn objects, especially when the S draws more than one Tree. Several maladjusted children have drawn two Trees (one feminine, one masculine) which they readily identified as mother and father, respectively.

In some instances, the character of the symbolized person is savagely caricatured by the animal which is used to represent this person.

For example, a mildly neurotic male drew a rabbit, then identified it as his father whom he held in contempt because the father was dominated by the S's mother.

P20. *What kind of clothing does this Person have on?* (R)

The greater the disparity between the objective appearance of the Person and the S's account of the clothing worn by that Person, presumably the less effective is the S's grasp of reality.

The type of clothing of the Person may provide insight into the S's needs. For example, the uniform of a general would suggest needs for status and power.

A complete lack of clothing might indicate (1) a feeling of crippling helplessness and exposure or (2) strong narcissistic and exhibitionistic tendencies (as a self-portrait). It might also express a desire (1) to degrade and/or (2) to place some other person in an embarrassing position (as the picture of some person other than the S).

HOUSE

The examiner records (in the space provided on the folder) the plan of each floor of the drawn House, noting the location and type, as living-room, etc., of each room and the customary occupant of that room, if any.

The S's production of the floor plan of his House may express through proportional distortions, difficulty of presentation, or the frank omission of one or more rooms, the presence of conflicts with occupants of the House or the customary functional use of one or more of the rooms.

SUPPLEMENTARY QUESTIONS

The examiner records the answers to questions asked to ascertain the significance of: the absence of essential details; the presence of unusual or bizarre details; any unusual proportional or positional relationships.

The number of possible Supplementary Questions and their possible answers is almost infinite and makes adequate specific illustration impossible. The discussion of the qualitative points under Details, Proportion and Perspective indicated why such Supplementary Questioning is imperative.

II. CHROMATIC

Each of the 22 questions for the chromatic P—D—I (except P6) is a duplicate of a question in the achromatic P—D—I. P6 (chromatic) attempts to combine several achromatic P—D—I questions to save time.

To recapitulate: The intent of the P—D—I phases is two-fold: (1) to afford the S with every opportunity to project his feelings, needs, goals, attitudes, etc., through his verbal description of and his comments on his pencil and crayon drawings of a dwelling-place, a living or once-living thing, and a living or once-living human being, respectively, and (2) to provide the examiner with an opportunity to clarify aspects of the drawn wholes which are not clear to him.

The higher the intelligence level of the S, usually the easier he can verbalize freely, and the more productive will the P—D—I be diagnostically and prognostically.

III. ANALYSIS

Until one is thoroughly experienced in the administration and interpretation of the H—T—P, it is best for him to analyze each P—D—I, point by point, as follows:

(1) *Volume:* The S's refusal to comment at all in the P—D—I is pathological, for here the examiner asks direct questions. The answer, "I don't know," is not to be construed as *no answer;* neither is it a satis-factory answer. Since the questions are specific, and restrictive at times, that which constitutes a terse or a verbose answer is not the same for all 60 questions in the achromatic P—D—I and the 22 questions in the chromatic P—D—I. One might be surprised to receive a more lengthy answer than,"Man," or, "Woman," to the question, "Is that a man or a woman?" But it would be strange if one received less than several words in a positive response to the question, "What is he thinking about?" In short, the interpretation of volume to a great extent is relative to many factors.

The longest spontaneously produced series of comments that the author has experienced was made by a psychoneurotic male, who, after answering T20, went into a trance-like state and free-associated thousands of words concerning his Tree and several other Trees (none of which resembled the Tree he drew) which were in a picture hanging on the wall of the examining room.

(2) *Relevance:* An irrelevant response to P2 was a prepsychotic's comment, "He's 100, but I'm 27 myself."

Examples of bizarre replies are: (1) a manic patient's excited answer to H14, "All kinds of weather. It's snow, summer, fall, rain, dry, everything! *(2)* a psychotic patient's reply to T5. I (b), *"Is any part of the Tree Dead?"* "I can't hardly hear you much on account of the people talking so much!" The startled examiner asked, "What people?" The patient replied,"Oh, God and Dr. R." (Dr. R had died several weeks before.)

(3) *Pressure:* appraisal of the S's replies to all P—D—I questions (particularly those that have the letter *P* as one of the letters or the only

letter following them in brackets) often will provide insight into the people, situations, physiological and/or psychological needs, etc., which the S feels produce strains and stresses for him.

(4) *Reality:* As was suggested in the discussion of the administration of the P—D—I in Chapter Three and the appraisal of P—D—I responses in this chapter, the S's replies often provide information concerning his grasp of reality which, in turn, aids greatly in the appraisal of his personality balance and his functioning level of intelligence.

Very helpful in this connection are answers to P1, P2, P6, T1, T3, T4, T5, T6, T7, T10, T11, T12, T13, T14, H1, H2, H7, H8, H14, T17, T18, T19, T20, P11, P12, P13, P14, P15, P17, and P20.

(5) *Associations:*

(a) *Number:* Wide individual differences appear among well-adjusted people in the number of associations produced in reply to P—D—I questions in general, and to questions H9, H10, T15, T16, P9, P10, P18, T21, and H15, in particular.

(b) *Relevance:* A mildly irrelevant association to P9 is: "It reminds me of a fourth-grader trying to draw."

A bizarre association to H9 was given by a chronic schizophrenic, "Well, it makes you think of a picture, silver pictures," Examiner: "Why do you say that?" Patient: "Kite flying, mosquitoes." Examiner: "What do you think of when you think of *House?*" Patient: "Cinnamon, I taste it." Examiner: "Do you like the taste?" Patient: "Man, children."

(c) *Conventionality:* Of 38 medical students, 21 indicated that to them *House* meant *home.* For *Tree,* their most frequent response was a specific type of tree, with "shade" closely following. For *Person* the greatest number of responses, 16, might be grouped under "opposite sex," (which would include girl, fiancee, and woman).

A significant response would be for H9: "A place to live (indicating a feeling of non-belonging); for T15: "Lumber" (only dead or destroyed Trees become lumber); "Shelter" (need for protection); "Forest" (the interpretation of this response depends upon further interrogation to determine whether *forest* implies a need for the company of contemporaries, or if it had a fearful or oppressive feeling-connotation.. A pathological response to P15 by a strongly paranoid S was, in part, ". . .Most people are natural enemies through a mistake or error. Well, I'd better skip that. Just keep rubbing you the wrong way -- to be simple".

(d) *Subjectivity:* primarily the examiner is interested here in determining the degree of self-reference exhibited by the S in his associations. One maladjusted S replied to H9, "The future!" At first sight this did not seem to be an unusual reply, for the examiner assumed she meant she wished in the future to own such a House, but realizing that in the P—D—I nothing should be taken for granted, the examiner continued "Why?" The S made no reply. The examiner then asked, "What ideas come to your mind? Tell me anything at all, even if they are vague.'' The S replied indignantly. "They are not vague; not at all! I think of writing as well as possible all the books I want to write. I don't care if they sell; I don't care if they are popular -- as long as I know they're good. .Whether they appeal to the average reader or not is *irreverent!*"

Another subjective and revealing response was the one made by a chronic alcoholic male to P9, "Well, I told you, Mr. Buck, he's waiting for his father to go over for the mail so he can get a bottle of beer. And the fence is over here. You can't see *me*, but I'm waiting for a bottle of beer too!"

One psychopathic adolescent male drew a Tree with many masculine characteristics; protruding from the trunk was a short branch resembling an erect penis. Considering the Tree as a self-portrait, it appeared that the S was placing great emphasis on his presumed object of preoccupation. In answer to T10, he responded immediately: "I'm looking down at it," emphasizing the *it*.

(e) *Feeling Tone:* Bitterness, hate, fear, and other negatively-toned cathectic reactions speak for themselves and are pathoformic or pathological in accordance with their adjudged severity.

(6) *"Life:"* The average, well-adjusted person sees his House as occupied and containing a living being; he also sees the Tree and Person as living. Responses on the P–D–I which indicate that the S sees the House as temporarily unoccupied or deserted, the Tree as dying or dead, and the Person as ill, dying or dead, appear as indications of maladjustment; the lesser the degree of "life" ascribed to a whole, and the greater the number of wholes which deviate from a "normal" state of "life", the greater is the maladjustment.

(7) *Movement:* In the discussion of movement as depicted by the drawings (see subhead E under *Perspective* in this chapter), it was suggested that the House and the Tree had to be distorted markedly in order for graphic movement to be expressed, and that such expressions implied a major disturbance of personality. It was pointed out, however, that the drawn Person's movement need not necessarily involve distortion; that its diagnostic significance depended on the quality of the movement, and this at times could be determined only by the S's responses on the P–D–I which would define the characteristics thereof. For example, the examiner cannot assume the S to be relaxed and comfortable in most interpersonal relationships simply because he draws a smiling Person and justifies his affirmative answer to P13 by calling attention to the smile, for follow-up interrogation may reveal that the Person is smiling, "Because he's just killed his father whom he hates."

In his responses to T11, T12, T14, and H14, the S can express feelings of "induced" motion in the House and Tree, and assign values which may indicate clearly whether he feels the motion as unpleasant or pleasant, compulsive or voluntary, destructive or stimulating, etc. From the characteristics assigned by the S to the motion and his description of causative agents, deductions can be made concerning the S's feelings of pressure, rigidity, flexibility, etc., and the probable sources thereof in the areas tapped by the whole.

For example, a well-adjusted adult of average intelligence said in answer to T11, that it was clear and warm; to T12, that a mild breeze was blowing; to T14, that the breeze was gentle and balmy. In sharp contrast are the replies to the same questions of a deteriorated organic: he said that a March gale was blowing; the wind was bitter cold; and it would probably damage the Tree.

A catatonic schizophrenic who had drawn as her Person an erect penis in process of ejaculation, stated that she saw it moving in all directions and found it most exciting.

In general, the examiner views with suspicion responses indicating extremes of weather in the drawings of the six wholes.

(8) *Consistency:* Consistency is least likely to be found in the P—D—I responses. The well-integrated individual, as a rule, presents in the P—D—I, as in life in general, a reasonably consistent picture; at times, so does the grossly maladjusted individual, but the examiner should not be misled thereby.

NOTE: In attempting to assay the significance of certain responses in the P—D—I, the examiner must bear in mind that if it has been necessary to rephrase a question several times and/or prod the S to reply, the S's response should be appraised carefully before credence is given it, because the response may be (1) the result of a direct suggestion, or (2) a sort of desperation answer to ward off further questioning along that particular line.

In passing, note that in a sense the P—D—I phases of the H—T—P are somewhat comparable to the Thematic Apperception Test, *but* the pictures in the H—T—P are created by the S himself.

One must be careful not to become too dependent upon the S's responses in the P—D—I and thereby overlook the wealth of diagnostic and prognostic material to be derived from the drawing alone. Ss who have difficulty verbalizing or who reject the P—D—I must *not* be assumed to have sterile H—T—P's.

Until the student becomes thoroughly familiar with the system of qualitative analysis, he will find it helpful to use the outline* designed by Dr. George Mursell, formerly of Rainier School, Buckley, Washington (see Appendix B). Dr. Mursell's original outline has been modified somewhat by the author to conform to this edition of the Manual.

---

* Also Isaac Jolles' "A Catalogue For The Qualitative Interpretation of The House-Tree-Person (H—T—P)" is of great help, provided it is used with the caution which sound clinical practice demands and Jolles counsels.

XI. CONCEPTS

Once the examiner completes his analysis of the S's freehand drawings of the Houses, Trees, and Persons and the S's comments upon them, both spontaneous and examiner-induced, he synthesizes these materials and draws deductions concerning the S's concepts from the following standpoints.

A. CONTENT

1. HOUSE

Viewed as a self-portrait, the S's House can provide the examiner with insightful material concerning:

(a) *The S's psychosexual maturity and adjustment:* A woman college professor, whose sexual maladjustment was made patent by her history and facts derived from other sources, exhibited difficulty dealing with sex symbols in her drawing of the House (her home, incidentally). For example, she could not permit the triangular window (female sex symbol) which she originally drew, to remain as it was, but later felt compelled to obscure it with lattice work. While she was drawing this triangular window, she remarked, "That damned window!" She was unable to draw the chimney (male sex symbol). And she expressed anxiety, through line-quality, in drawing the window of her bedroom.

(b) *The S's accessibility:* A psychoneurotic woman drew her House high up on a hill far from the road, reached by a winding pathway. She placed a high picket fence with a closed gate about the yard. The House's tiny steps made poor contact with the small door which was one of the last items drawn.

(c) *The S's contact at the level of reality:* Detail sequence, emphasis upon the groundline, ground floor windows, doors, and so on, appear to be highly correlated with the degree of permeability of the peripheral boundaries of the self or the S's grasp of and interaction with reality. The more closely the detail sequence, the line quality, and the proportional and positional relationship of the details approach the average, presumably the better adjusted the S is at the reality level.

(d) *The S's intra-personal balance:* An adult male pre-psychotic indicated his feelings of personality disorganization by his markedly atypical detail presentation sequence, a deviation which was wholly obscured in the completed whole. By his overemphasis of the peripheral lines (the endwall lines, the roof lines, and the baseline) of the House, he showed feelings of anxiety concomitant with a striving to maintain personality integrity.

A schizophrenic expressed his personality disorganization by a House consisting of windows, a door, a chimney, a roof, and so on, but with these details having no connected relationship.

(e) *The degree of rigidity of the S's personality:* An anxious psychoneurotic man indicated his great rigidity by: (1) drawing his House framed absolutely by the page's borders; (2) the over-meticulosity of his his drawing; and (3) the definitive "hair-splitting" of his spontaneous comments..

(f) *The relative roles of the psychological past and future in the S's psychological field:* Viewing the *right* side of the page as the future, and the *left* side as the past, at times it is possible from an analysis of detail volume, sequence, emphasis, perspective, and so on, to secure worthwhile information concerning "temporal dominance". Evidence which indicates that the psychological past plays a major role in the psychological field suggests that past events may be creating crippling fixations; dominance by the psychological future suggests unhealthy striving toward possibly fictive goals.

(g) *The S's attitude toward his family and/or his interpretation of his family's feeling toward him:* For example, (1) a maladjusted man expressed his hostility toward and rejection of his mother by greatly reducing the size of the window of her bedroom and by stating that he would take the room in the House farthest from hers, (2) an epileptic male indicated his feeling of being rejected by his family by drawing a garage for a House, (3) a psychopath indicated his feelings of being rejected by his family and his willingness to forgive by drawing a small figure (which he said was himself) in the doorway of the House with his arms outstretched toward four persons on the walkway who had their backs turned toward him. He identified the four as his sister, mother, father, and brother (the brother, incidentally was dead).

The second approach is to consider each House in the light of the quality of the concept evolved by the S as a solution of the problem presented him by the drawing.

The House, a dwelling place, is regarded by most Ss as the scene of very intimate and satisfying or stressful and conflictual inter-personal contacts.

(a) *Home as it is now:* Actually, this is as the S "feels" it to be, for the S almost never reproduces his home exactly as it is.

(b) *Home as the S would like it to be:* Medical students, for example, frequently draw "mansions.." These appear to be an expression of their recognition of the social status usually still conceded to physicians in the American scene, as well as their feelings of superiority..

Since the S's drawn House frequently is a composite of several houses, it may represent:

(c) *An unsatisfying past home:* A psychoneurotic male drew a log cabin in which his father, toward whom he had ambivalent feelings, had been born. This patient was incensed by the fact that his father had been born in a cabin instead of the large brick house that the family owned. The S felt that this humble place of birth was degrading to him.

(d) *A satisfying past home:* A mildly schizoid physician drew his childhood home with great care; he made spontaneous comments expressing a strong desire to be able to return to that home (and his boyhood status) where he had been happy and secure.

2. *TREE*

The Tree appears always to represent the S.

(a) *The S's subconscious picture of himself in relation to his psychological field in general:* It is believed that the Tree is well adapted for such projection since malformation and distortions of its growth and form, which would be seen conventionally as crippling in the drawing of a Person and presumably would arouse defensive reactions in the S, serve to lend realism to the drawing of the Tree.

To recapitulate briefly: The trunk seems to represent the S's feeling of basic power; the branches by their size and positional relationship to the trunk and the form page appear to indicate the S's satisfaction-seeking resources; the inter-relationship of the branches seems to express the the flexibility and the organization of the modes of satisfaction-seeking available to the S.

For most S's the root structure appears to represent at a more superficial level: (1) sources of elemental satisfaction; (2) stabilizing strength within the personality. At a deeper interpretative level, the root structure represents basic, elemental drives.

A young psychoneurotic woman drew a Tree which was a shattered, jagged trunk only, and had no branch structure. Later she stated that this seemed to symbolize her own unfulfilled and undeveloped life.

A profoundly paranoid male, of high intelligence, who correctly felt that he might need institutionalization, drew a Tree that had a solid, sturdy trunk, powerful roots, huge branches that stretched out defiantly and rigidly but were not well drawn proportionally: this indicated his strong feelings of environmental pressure. At the end, he contaminated his Tree by resorting to a very poor use of shading: his employment of shading clearly expressed strong anxiety. Two weeks later, when his institutionalization was necessary, he drew a tremendous (in proportion to the page) weeping willow with only the trunk lines closest to the ground showing definite force insofar as line quality was concerned. The full Tree created the impression of something limp, hopeless, and defeated in striking contrast to the Tree of two weeks before which had expressed rugged defiance. Seldom does a set of drawings exhibit such marked personality changes occurring in so brief a time.

Organics tend to draw 1-dimensional stereotyped Trees which appear to express graphically the S's feelings of inadequacy, incompetency, and progressive loss of efficiency.

(b) *The S's subconscious picture of his development:* Scars, broken branches, and the like, seem always to symbolize traumatic episodes which the S feels were scarring to him. Variations in growth indicated by by unusual trunk size fluctuations, variations in branch symmetry, and so on, represent periods in the past when the environment was psychologically rich or poor in affording satisfaction and stimulation to the S.

(c) *The S's psychosexual level:* A male patient with strong homosexual impulses indicated his bisexuality by drawing a Tree with an unusual admixture of feminine and masculine characteristics; in the P–D–I he verbalized his bisexual attitudes freely.

A young woman with a character neurosis first drew a sturdy trunk which appeard to be almost a photographic reproduction of a penis. After a brief pause, during which she exhibited signs of tension, she hastily covered the upper portion of the trunk with curving, hair-like lines. The final production strongly suggested "penetration"..

It is the author's conviction that the Tree usually provides a deeper and more accurate picture of the S's psychosexual maturity than the drawn Person.

(d) *The S's contact with reality:* A markedly withdrawn S indicated his preference for phantasy and his rejection of reality as a source of satisfaction by drawing his Tree with the trunk suspended above the groundline, tiny 1-dimensional roots providing the Tree's only contact with the ground, and the Tree's top extending beyond the upper edge of the page.

(e) *The S's feeling of intra-personal balance:* A young woman, who shortly afterward developed a schizophrenic psychosis, indicated her feeling of her impending personality disorganization by her Tree, which was an unusual mixture of diverse types of branch-structure depiction, 1-dimensional, 2-dimensional, and implication -- all without any real interrelationship.

The examiner can learn much concerning the S's level of concept formation from both a quantitative and a qualitative standpoint by appraising the Tree as representing other things besides a self-portrait of the S.

The Tree may also be:

(a) *Some person other than the S:* A psychoneurotic man free-associated at great length concerning his Tree which so resembled his paramour as to be almost her portrait. In his verbalization he exhibited the intense guilt feelings which this extra-marital sexual affair had aroused within him.

A deteriorated, epileptic man who had difficulty, at times, differentiating his clergyman father from God, symbolized his feeling of inadequacy by first drawing a towering fir Tree, representing his father, and then a shadow cast upon the ground by the Tree. In the P–D–I the shadow was found to represent the S.

A young man who felt completely rejected by his mother, stated that his oak Tree looked like a woman with her back to him.

A maladjusted young boy drew two Trees; a deciduous one to the left, a fir to the right. Then he reversed the conventional sexuality of the Trees by saying that the deciduous Tree was his father and the fir Tree his mother. In this reversal of sexuality he expressed cynically his view of the masculinity of his parents; later his view was found to be correct.

3. *PERSON*

The Person as a living, or recently living, human being lends itself well to direct self-portraiture, to projection of body-feeling, and so on; but since it is a person, at times it arouses such intense feelings in certain paranoid and/or psychopathic Ss that they refuse to draw it.

Viewed as a portrait of the S, as it always must be, the Person may represent:

(a) *The S as he is now:* Cosmetic flaws, physiological distortions, and so on, often are reproduced faithfully and exactly. *But* the S usually reproduces them in his drawing of the Person as if the Person were his mirror-image. For example, if the S has a finger missing from his *left* hand, the drawn Person will have a finger missing from his *right* hand.

A woman college professor who was badly maladjusted sexually, drew her Person as a small girl holding a doll. In the P—D—I she first said that her Person was a child in a fashion magazine. Soon she amended this by saying that it was an artist's portrait of his daughter. It would have been difficult to find a more accurate, though hypercritical, self-portrait. Dynamically it meant that if the S could again be a small child, she would be free from the threat of sexual intercourse; she also could rule her dolls as dictatorially as once she had ruled her children. In addition, she would be free from adult responsibilities. Her fondness for social exhibitionism was indicated by her "posing" child. .

(b) *The S as he now feels:* An adult epileptic illustrated with clarity his feeling of being "possessed" by his disease by drawing a Person, a recognizable likeness of himself though not so to the S, depicted as a marionette.

(c) *The S as he would like to be:* A young, pregnant, unmarried woman who recently had passed through a .period of reactive depression, drew an assured and graceful dancer in the center of the stage, a marked contrast to the state of the S at that time.

An adolescent boy, who was reacting with strong hostility toward parental rejection and environmental pressure, drew a large, muscular male adorned with a badge and armed with pistols. He described his Person as a sheriff about to shoot a band of robbers. In this way he expressed his feeling of hostility, yet indicated his awareness of social norms by having the aggression-by-proxy assume a socially-acceptable form.

(d) *The S's concept of his sexual role:* A post-encephalitic man, who had engaged in uninhibited sexual activities at several levels, drew a man with unshaven face, hairy chest, broad shoulders, huge penis and testicles; this was a stereotype of the rugged, "dominant male."

A sexually maladjusted, married woman expressed her feeling of sexual inadequacy by drawing an unattractive female (thus denying her femininity) with her hands clasped apprehensively in the "pelvic defense" position (protecting herself against sexual approach).

A manic woman indicated her ambivalent attitude toward "sex" by drawing a Person with eyes and mouth that were emphatically feminine; nose and chin that were obviously masculine; a Person whom she ultimately and laughingly identified as a hermaphrodite.

(e) *The S's attitude toward inter-personal relationships in general:* An advanced paranoid male drew his Person in absolute profile, with his body rigid and the broad brim of the hat lowered over his face so that visual contact could be made only with the consent of the Person. In this way he depicted his own rigid unadaptiveness and reluctance to make contact with others.

A psychoneurotic woman drew a female Person whose face looked apprehensive, whose hands were held out hesitantly as if warding-off a threatening figure, and whose feet were turned to facilitate flight. She thus expressed her feelings of guilt and anxiety in reaction to a recent illegitimate pregnancy.

An obsessive-compulsive woman drew an obvious self-portrait but omitted the hands, which she regarded as the source of most of her difficulty. To her, her hands were so contaminated that she did not dare to put out milk bottles unless she wore rubber gloves, for fear that she would poison anyone who touched the bottles.

(f) *The S's attitude toward a specific inter-personal relationship:* A deeply nostalgic, borderline defective drew an elderly woman with arms outstretched toward the viewer. She said that this was her mother welcoming her.

A psychoneurotic male drew a picture of a young woman clad only in a slip. He expressed disgust at his inability to draw a better picture of his beautiful mistress. This S's emotionality, his vacillation, and the relatively inferior quality of his Person indicated his ambivalent feelings toward his relationship with his mistress.

(g) *Certain specific fears, obsessive beliefs, etc.:* An obsessive-compulsive, elderly woman, several weeks after a prefrontal lobotomy, drew a young boy identified as, "so and so Junior." She identified him as the son of her husband and a servant. Then, with almost uncontrollable laughter, she said she knew that there was no such child and that her husband would want to kill her if he heard what she had said, and so on. In this manner, she expressed her rigid, obsessive jealousy, but without the bitter effect which had accompanied it prior to the lobotomy.

Viewed as a picture of someone other than the S, the drawn Person may represent:

(a) *The Person in the S's environment whom the S most likes:* A well-adjusted young psychiatrist drew a recognizable picture of his fiancee.

(b) *The Person in the S's environment whom the S most dislikes:* A psychopathic adolescent girl drew an excellent likeness of a ward attendant whom she hated. She expressed her hostility frankly by her gross and degrading graphic caricature and by making highly insulting remarks about the attendant in the P-D-I.

(c) *A Person toward whom the S has ambivalent feelings:* A young man with a character neurosis drew a picture of his stepfather, whom he hated with good reason because of the ill-treatment that he had received at his hands; yet the S felt and expressed admiration for his stepfather's bravado and ruthless ability to dominate the family.

To sum up, consideration of the content of the disparate wholes can be revealing. However, content alone should not be expected to provide a diagnosis any more than a careful inspection of any of the other analytic points. But content often furnishes insightful clues into the S's attitudes, needs, fears, and so on, which can help clarify the dynamics operating in the case.

B. *CONVENTIONALITY*

By *conventionality* is meant conformity to the average from the standpoint of originality of the whole. This subhead bears a resemblance to "originality" in the Rorschach; in view of the restricting limitations of the items House, Tree, and Person, however, it is more difficult for the S to be as original on the H-T-P as on the Rorschach.

In discussing variations from the average, the concept produced may be considered to diverge from the average on a 3-item continuum: ranging from *unusual* through *unconventional* to *pathological.*

(1) An *unusual* concept is the drawing by a physician of a British tar of sailing-vessel days, stooping to pick up a scented handkerchief, while a weather-beaten parrot hovers in the background. Such a concept is pathoformic because it is a first degree variation from the average. The concept reasonably may be interpreted as a desire by the S to escape from the artificialities of his scientific prosaic life to a materially-oriented world more exciting and earthy. It is noted that the censor in the physician-S's personality attempted to disguise his expression of these hitherto suppressed desires by compelling him to draw a Person of another day,

who by the nature of his work and custom would be expected to "pick up" the owner of the handkerchief,as well as the handkerchief, itself, without anyone's raising an eyebrow.

(2) An *unconventional* concept is a House which looked like a barn and was so identified by the middle-aged woman who drew it. It expressed her bitter feeling that she was regarded by her family as a mere beast of burden to be granted lodging and food as recompense for her work.

(3) *Pathological* concepts often express originality but are not thereby "healthy." Examples are: (a) the transparent "glass box" House, drawn by a markedly narcissistic, paranoid woman which expressed simultaneously her feeling of being watched by everyone and her willingness to exhibit herself but in an enclosure which would, however, limit contact to the visual mode; (b) a schizophrenic woman drew a House which consisted of three objects which were identified by the S as a pillow, a chimney, and the torrid zone; (c) the Tree drawn by an elderly schizophrenic woman with less than half of the Tree shown on the page. The trunk was drawn as if it were bisected by the left lateral margin of the page; the branch structure was presented by a thin, deeply shaded area which touched the the page's top margin. In the P–D–I the S said that the "best" part of her Tree could not be seen (the part which did not make contact with reality presumably; the part which symbolized her phantasy world; (d) another Tree, drawn by a deteriorated organic, resembled the vaginal orifice; (e) the Person drawn by a young woman patient of above average intelligence. This Person, a male, was wired to a wooden cross; his head was bloody, but bandaged; he was clad in trunks only; his right hand was bandaged; his left arm was crudely amputated just below the elbow; his left foot was missing; his body was emaciated; his face was haggard and hollow-eyed. The interpretation was that the S was thus expressing her savage and total rejection of "man." Clinical evidence indicated that she never had made any satisfactory heterosexual adjustments. The scoring of this concept as pathological was soon justified, for shortly thereafter she rejected reality as fully as she had rejected "man" in her drawing; (f) another pathological production was the Person of a schizophrenic which consisted of a head, a leg, and a foot only.

C. *SUBJECTIVITY*

Here the attempt is made to determine the consciously recognized and expressed degree of relationship of the S to the Houses, Trees, and Persons which he has produced. In determining the degree of subjectivity, from the standpoint of pathology, the examiner must bear in mind that subjectivity may range from some evidence of a narrowing of the psychological horizon to obvious and convincing evidence of extreme ideas of self-reference.

D. *MULTIPLICITY*

A given whole may represent, in one way or another, a number of people besides the S. Ss of average adjustment usually restrict the "multiplicity" of persons represented by a whole to two, one being the S. If the identity of a whole is restricted to self-portraiture, or if it is multiplied to represent four or more persons, maladjustment is to be suspected.

E. *VALENCE*

One index of maladjustment is the intensity of the negative valence ascribed to the wholes by the S.

F. *ORGANIZATION*

This is a qualitative appraisal of the proportional and spatial relationships of the details within a whole. Ss with organic deterioration tend to produce wholes in which the details appear to have little relationship to each other or to the whole, and the relationships expressed in drawings by advanced schizophrenics are often even more dilapidated. In general, except for the mechanical difficulties presented by the act of drawing, a plan once formulated will be executed by the S without much hesitancy and/or vacillation. Marked "detail-conflict," such as inability to complete the pelvic region, or marked preoccupation with the pelvic region, or marked vacillation, such as inability to permit an arm to remain in its initial or some subsequent position, is at least second-degree variation from the average and is pathological.

Organizational ability may be interfered with by functional factors or organic factors, or both.

It appears that: (1) If organizational difficulty is shown in all six drawings, a major organic disability or a major emotional disturbance, or both, must be suspected. (2) If organizational difficulty is shown in several drawings but not in all six drawings, the disturbance is more likely to be functional than organic. (3) If the organizational difficulty is confined to the drawings of only one of three figures (as only the Houses, for example) the disturbance almost certainly is functional. (4) If the organization of all six wholes is good, the S's personality may be assumed to be reasonably well-integrated even in the presence of many pathoformic signs.

G. *CONSISTENCY*

While it has been found that it is rare for the House, the Tree, and the Person (achromatic and/or chromatic) to be of exactly the same quantitative level, there should not be too much difference in the qualitative level of the disparate wholes.

Greater consistency may be expected in the vertical dimension (achromatic House to chromatic House, etc.) than in the horizontal dimension (achromatic House to Tree to Person, for example). Any considerable variance (that is, more than one classification level either way) demands explanation.

Perfect consistency may well be pathoformic. It has been seen clinically that the S who has several D1's in his quantitative scoring probably is better adjusted than the S who has no D1's. So it may be expected that the better adjusted individual will not exhibit a picture wholly uniform as to concept-quality. It seems unreasonable to assume that all six drawings, (the two Houses, two Trees, and two Persons) should have complete or approximately complete equality of value from any S's point of view.

It also can be expected that any S, regardless of his adjustment and integration, and no matter how slight the environmental pressures which may be or have been exerted on him, will show at least several pathoformic signs. Complete absence of pathoformicity is suspicious, since it suggests rigid hypercriticality.

Personality maladjustment may be revealed by: (1) many pathoformic signs; (2) two or three highly pathological signs; (3) perseverated deviations even if they are of one type only; (4) many deviations from the "normal" of varying degrees of magnitude.

XII. SUMMARY

After the examiner completes his analysis of the S's productions and his synthesis of the analytic points, he should be in a position to draw specific deductions concerning the S's total personality and its interaction with its environment. To facilitate and systematize the recording of these deductions and to express them in conventional clinical terminology, the following outline is suggested.

A. Test Situation Observations

(1) Cooperativeness; (2) stress symptoms; (3) physical disabilities; (4) mannerisms; (5) attention span; (6) empathy; (7) reaction time; (8) orientation; (9) other.

B. Intelligence

(1) H—T—P derived I.Q.s (the examiner should comment briefly upon the consistency or disparity of these I.Q.s; and if they are markedly

disparate to attempt to account therefor; (2) present functional level as indicated by the H—T—P and an analysis of the factors of internal construction; (3) H—T—P I.Q.s vs. I.Q.s derived from standard intelligence tests; (4) artifacts possibly affecting the H—T—P I.Q. scores, such as physical disability, artistic training, etc., (5) evidences of concreteness or fluidity of thinking.

C. *Affect*

(1) Tone (depressed, elated, etc.); (2) intensity; (3) appropriateness; (4) control; (5) consistency.

D. *Verbalizations*

(1) Flow (scant, free, etc.); (2) spontaniety; (3) modulation (monotonous, dual, etc.); (4) idea content (perseverative, bizarre, inferior).

E. *Drive*
(1) level; (2) control; (3) consistency (fatigability, etc.).

F. *Psychosexual*

(1) Satisfaction levels and their relative dominance; (2) conflicts and their probable sources (for example, S is unable to adjust satisfactorily at the heterosexual level because of a fixation at the oral level, or religious beliefs, or physical disability, etc.).

G. *Inter-environmental*

Under this broad heading the examiner comments concerning aspects of the S's general behavior from the following standpoints: (1) *satisfaction sources:* (a) reality-phantasy; (b) extratensive-intratensive, does the S tend to *respond* more to external (extra) or internal (intra) stimulation; (c) extracathection-intracathection, does the S tend to *seek* external or internal sources of satisfaction (a paranoid S, for example, presumably would exhibit ·extratensivity and intracathection); (d) range (are satisfaction sources, for instance, restricted to the home, to the reality level, etc.); (2) *goal attainability* (are the S's goals realistic or fictive) and *intensity* (how avidly are they sought); (3) *temporal dominance* (here the relative roles of the psychological past, present, and future are considered); (4) *adaptability* (is the S generally flexible, or stereotyped and rigid); (5) *accessibility* (is the S relaxed, friendly, sociable or is he tense, hostile, withdrawn).

H. *Inter-Personal Relationships*

(a) Intra-familial: (1) affective tone; (2) intensity; (3) permanence; (4) flexibility; (5) identification; (6) felt-role (S's conception of his position within his family, including his sexual role). (b) Extra-familial (1) Affective tone, (2) Intensity, (3) Permanence, (4) Flexibility, (5) Parental-substitute reaction, (6) Felt-role (The S's conception of his position in society in general, including his sexual role).

I. Intra-Personal Balance

The S's view of the balance of the factors making up his personality as expressed in his drawings and by his verbal comments.

J. Major Needs

(Such as autonomy, achievement, sexual satisfaction, etc.).

K. Major Assets

(Above average intelligence, flexibility, accessibility, etc.) *A word of caution:* In his zealous efforts to identify the factors of actual or potential weakness in the S's personality, the examiner must be careful not to lose sight of the factors of strength within that personality; the positive factors which determine the potential-danger weight that may be assigned to the negative or weak factors.

L. Impression

Within the present inadequate classificatory systems, the examiner must express his impression (as psychoneurosis, mixed type; average intelligence, etc.). Perhaps the most satisfactory method is to list the principal dynamic elements noted in the S's personality picture together with an evaluation thereof.

M. Prognosis

Hammer (4) has concluded (and, there seems good reason to think, correctly) that if:

1. The Tree conveys a "healthier" impression than the Person, or
2. The chromatic House, Tree and Person indicate a better adjustment level than the achromatic House, Tree, and Person, or
3. The H—T—P presents a "healthier" personality picture than the Rorschach, the clinician is probably justified in assuming that the S's chances for recovery under therapy are good.

However, if:

1. The chromatic H—T—P shows more and deeper signs of psychopathology than the achromatic H—T—P, or
2. The Tree conveys a "sicker" impression than the Person, or
3. The H—T—P presents a picture of greater personality maladjustment than the Rorschach, the clinician is probably justified in predicting a poor prognosis for the S.

If both the H—T—P and the Rorschach have many indications of pathology, the prognosis is very poor.

Patterns like these are valuable aids to the therapist; it is hoped ᴛᴛᴀt other patterns can be identified and tentatively validated. Ultimately a prognosis must depend upon a careful analysis of the relative weights of (1) the assets and liabilities within the S's personality and (2) the advantages and disadvantages of the S's current environment.

Any prognosis must be offered with the greatest caution. At best, accurate diagnoses are difficult to make. But because of the many intangible unknowns which can emerge in the future, valid prognoses are vastly more difficult to make.

CONCLUSION

At this point the clinician or student trained in the scientific method logically may remark, "This certainly is an interesting approach to the appraisal of personality. It is persuasive, but what statistical proof is there that the H—T—P is a valid and reliable instrument?"

The answer is: There is almost no statistical proof* of the validity of the qualitative scoring points and their interpretations which would satisfy in the words of Brown (2) "The nomothetically-minded experimentalist. . .who is indoctrinated in the tenets of research design and scientific method. . . ." And it appears unlikely, in fact, that such evidence ever will be available for several reasons, two of which are:

1. The fact that almost no H—T—P scoring point has a single implication. For example, take the simple detail *brick,* in the drawing of the House.

A might use bricks for the wall material of his House because of his lifelong feeling that a brick House stands for prestige and power.

B might draw a brick House because for him a brick structure is stronger and more stable than a frame one.

C might wish to have a brick dwelling because bricks required less maintenance expense than wooden siding.

D might draw bricks because they satisfy his obsessive-compulsive need to demonstrate his grasp of minutiae.

2. The fact that a given characteristic or trait may be expressed in the H—T—P in many ways. The S might express his hostility: (1) by rejecting the task outright; (2) by turning the form page so that the axis of original presentation no longer pertains; (3) by drawing a tiny House with one window only; (4) by producing a Tree with spike-like branches and talon-like roots; (5) by drawing a Person in absolute profile, etc.

The almost completely unstructured character of the H—T—P and the multitude of opportunities it affords the S to express his dominant behavioral traits, his major needs, his emotional reactions, the pressures both intra-personal and extra-personal which beset him, which almost auto-

---

* For a review of the literature see The House-Tree-Person Research Review by V. J. Bieliauskas, published and distributed by Western Psychological Services.

matically preclude the development of statistical proof of validity on a on a point-by-point basis.

There is, however, a wealth of empirical evidence that the H–T–P technique is valid and this evidence has satisfied many dynamically oriented clinical psychologists and psychiatrists who believe that the conventional experimantal approaches to test validation are over-simplified and ignore what Brown (2) terms "the constellative" aspects of projective techniques.

This empirical evidence was compiled by: (1) comparing the conclusions and diagnoses made by professional hospital staffs; (2) comparing the H–T–P conclusions and diagnoses with conclusions derived from Rorschach examinations made upon the same Ss by skilled Rorschach examiners; (3) comparing the conclusions arrived at through *blind analyses* of H–T–P productions with (a) the opinions of psychiatrists or psychologists intimately acquainted with the Ss; (b) the opinions of insightful Ss concerning the accuracy of the deductions made from their H–T–Ps, and (c) staff diagnoses; (4) comparing the conclusions and diagnoses based on H–T–P productions with staff-reported changes in Ss based on longitudinal studies; (5) checking the H–T–P interpretations against historical data and observed behavior.

It is the author's belief that the validity of the principle of the H–T–P method as a whole has been satisfactorily established (although the evidence is almost wholly clinical). The evidence of the validity of the individual differential items and their interpretations is less well-established but is certainly sufficient to justify the conclusion that the H–T–P is a mature clinical instrument.

As for reliability, no significant data are offered at this time. However, it has been well established empirically that as the S's clinical picture deteriorates, his H–T–P productions do likewise, but usually at a more rapid rate. Studies by Hammer (4) and Meyer, Brown , and Levine (6) indicate this finding strikingly.

Also, it has been shown that as the S's clinical picture improves, his H–T–P productions also improve (but usually much more slowly).

In brief, the S's H–T–P productions tend to *anticipate* his clinical breakdown and to *lag* his clinical recovery.

It is apparent that as the S matures intellectually, his concept formation, as appraised by the H–T–P, likewise matures, but not always at a similar pace.

The basic aspects of the personality remain fairly constant as they appear in the H–T–P (in the absence of some gross disturbance). but specific characteristics contributing to the total personality picture may change radically from time to time.

It is believed that the H–T–P as a procedure which attempts to evaluate the total personality must necessarily reflect these relatively minor changes in the total configuration if it is to be of any clinical value, and that, therefore, *reliability* in the sense in which the term is used in evaluating formal measures of intelligence is not desirable.

The H–T–P does notpossess a high order of statistically defined reliability and, as a projective technique, it should not.

Chapter Bibliography

1.   Anastasi, A., and Foley, J. P., Jr. "An Experimental Study of the Drawing Behavior of Adult Psychotics in Comparison With That of a Normal Control Group." *Journal of Experimental Psychology,* XXXIV, (1944), 169-194.

2.   Brown, Fred, "House-Tree-Person and Human Figure Drawings." *Progress in Clinical Psychology,* I (1952), 173-184.

3.   Hammer, E. F. "An Investigation of Sexual Symbolism: A Study of The H—T—P's of Eugenically Sterilized Subjects. *"Journal of Projective Techniques,* (1953), XVII, 401-413.

4.   Hammer, E. F. "The Role of the H—T—P in the Prognostic Battery." *Journal of Clinical Psychology,* IX (1953), 371-374.

5.   Machover, Karen. *Personality Projection in the Drawing of the Human Figure.* Springfield, Illinois: Charles C. Thomas, Publisher, 1949.

6.   Meyer, B. C., Brown, Fred, and Levine, Abraham. "Observations on the House-Tree-Person Drawing Test Before and After Surgery." *Psychosomatic Medicine,* VI (1955), 428-454.

Chapter 7   Illustrative Cases

In the first edition of the H—T—P Manual, ten sample cases were presented to demonstrate what might be expected from the H—T—P in clinical use. Ten different syndromes were represented. The protocols in question illustrated most of the quantitative and qualitative points of analysis. These ten cases appear in Appendix A of this edition of the Manual: the student is urged to give them his careful attention and study.

The five additional cases which are presented in this chapter were selected because the relationship of the chromatic drawings to the achromatic drawings varies considerably from case to case. In *Case B* the the two H—T—P sets are almost identical; in *Case D* they are incredibly different. The student should study each of these five cases with care, particularly noting the points of similarity and/or difference between the two sets of drawings which affect the diagnostic and prognostic conclusions in each case.

Case A and *Case B* are from the author's collection and have been analyzed on a point-by-point basis in efforts to present thoroughly the orthodox system of the quantitative and qualitative analysis of the H—T—P. *Case C, Case D,* and *Case E* were contributed by three clinical experts who have used the H—T—P skillfully for many years. These clinicians have not followed the methodical, step-by-step approach of analysis which the author employed in *Case A* and *Case B*.

As an aid to the H—T—P novitiate attempting to master the fine points of qualitative analysis, the author has appended brief comments after *Case C, Case D* and *Case E* to call attention to certain points which the contributors carefully weighed in their analyses but did not refer to specifically.

It is the author's belief that *Cases A, B, C, D,* and *E* offer strong evidence that the chromatic series of drawings adds greatly to the breadth and depth (and to the objectivity of the quantitative and qualitative analyses of the H—T—P and provides useful data upon which clinicians may base a cautious and hopefully valid prognosis, in addition to the diagnosis.

CASE A

By J. N. Buck

"A" was born in 1934 at full term. Delivery was uncomplicated and there was no birth injury. He was the seventh of eight children. His family history is rife with mental disease: his father and one brother are paranoid schizophrenics. Two maternal great-aunts, two maternal aunts, three maternal cousins and two nephews are, or have been, psychotic.

When "A" was 13 months of age he was walking well and had a surprisingly good vocabulary. He had the usual diseases of childhood: none was serious, none left complications. He has never been seriously injured.

He began school at 7 years of age. According to his teachers, he made slow progress, except in reading; found completion of tasks difficult; participated in group activities but seldom and only with reluctance. His adjustment in school slowly but surely became less satisfactory as time went on. Shortly after his eleventh birthday, he exhibited vague somatic complaints. From time to time, he had unexplained periods of depression. His mother took him to a physician, but he refused to allow the doctor to examine him. Finally he stopped school at the age of 13 years because he could no longer endure the children who teased him and picked on him. When he was 15 years old, he was committed to the custody of the State Department of Public Welfare as incorrigible after he had flatly refused to live at home, had thrown rocks through the windows of his home, and had fought with and threatened to kill an older brother.

"A" adjusted badly in two boarding homes and finally was referred to a clinic for psychological and psychiatric examination. The psychologist reported that although "A" appeared to be at least of borderline intelligence, he was not functioning at that level because of interference by a possible schizophrenic disturbance with obsessive features. "A" was committed to the Colony as mentally deficient, however.

On admission at 14 years, 9 months of age, his Wechsler-Bellevue I.Q.s were: verbal, 69; performance, 83, full scale, 73. His Wide Range Achievement scores were: reading grade, 5.0; spelling grade, 5.1; arithmetic grade, 3.3.

The achromatic-chromatic H—T—P was administered. See Figures 5A and 5B.

Quantitative scoring of the achromatic productions showed a per cent Raw G I.Q. of 108; a Net Weighted score of 106; a Good I.Q. of 109; and a Flaw I.Q. of 98.

HOUSE

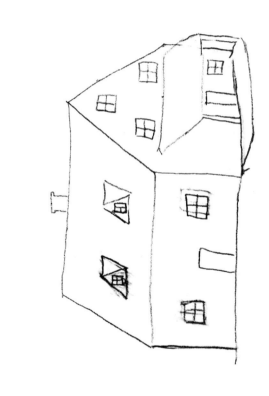

Figure 5 A

Figure 5 A

PERSON

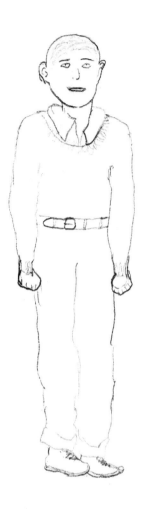

Figure 5 A

HOUSE

Figure 5 B

Figure 5 B

PERSON

Figure 5 B

Appraisal of the "quality of the quantity" of "A's" achromatic drawings provides a number of diagnostic "leads". To begin with, since all the I.Q.s are in the average range, "A's" clinical picture of inadequate intellectual function is not due to mental deficiency.

The Raw G, Net Weighted and Good I.Q.s are definitely constricted in range. The Flaw I.Q. score would be above the Good I.Q. but for a single D3 factor.

The relatively low number of the D-scores and the S-scores in the presence of many A-scores connotes overstriving into reality, not infrequently seen in patients fighting to overcome powerful withdrawal tendencies.

Appraisal of the raw "means score" scatter suggests the presence of a disturbance of at least pre-psychotic proportions, since the classification swing involves at least six areas. It is not yet psychotic, however, because of too few D2s and D3s and too many A-scores.

The high level Perspective scores offer further evidence, if more is needed, that "A" is not mentally defective. The fact that the Proportion scores are lower than the Perspective scores, and the Detail scores are the lowest of the three, suggests that insight still is present but judgment has been affected mildly, and there is a definite beginning loss of adequate reality contact.

Of the House, Tree and Person, the most adversely affected from a quantitative standpoint is the House, with both the Good and the Flaw scores falling well below "A's" mean. This implies that one of his major sources of conflict is his relationship with his home and those in it. His Good score for the Person also is depressed, but his Flaw score for the Person remains high. This is interpreted as representing an inability. to function smoothly in interpersonal relationships in general with a concomitant highly critical and suspicious view of others and their motives.

Quantitative scoring of his chromatic productions indicates that under the stimulus of color and the depressing effects of fatigue and emotion-enhancement, the I.Q. disparities are enhanced; that although "A's" productivity is stimulated, his insight is affected adversely and his judgment is sharply reduced. Color and fatigue, in short, enhance the previously expressed disturbances in interpersonal relationships.

Post—Drawing Interrogation

P1. *Is that a man or a woman (boy or girl)?*
    A. Boy.
P2. *How old is he?*
    A. About 13.
P3. *Who is he?*

A. Ain't nobody. I drawed him.

P4. *Is he a relation, a friend, or what?*
 A. O.K. about that.

P5. *Whom were you thinking about while you were drawing?*
 A. Not thinking about anybody.

P6. *What is he doing?*
 A. Standing up.
 Where?
 A. I don't know; just drawed him.
 Why did you draw fists?
 A. Ready to fight. Reason I drawed it that way, because I couldn't draw fingers.

P7. *What is he thinking about?*
 A. Paper can't think.
 Question repeated.
 A. (laughs) I don't know.

P8. *How does he feel?*
 A. I don't know; feels crazy if he was in this place.
 Why?
 A. Like to be home.

* * * * * * *

T1. *What kind of Tree is that?*
 A. Cedar tree.

T2. *Where is that Tree actually located?*
 A. Don't know.

T3. *About how old is that Tree?*
 A. About 14 years.

T4. *Is that Tree alive?*
 A. Yeah.

T5. (a) *What is there about that Tree that gives you the impression that it's alive?*
 A. I don' know; because it's not cut down.

T6. *Which does that Tree look more like to you: A man or woman?*
 A. Woman.

T7. *What is there about it that gives you that impression?*
 A. Like a dress skirt.

T8. *If that were a person instead of a Tree, which way would the person be facing?*
 A. Side.
 Why?
 A. I don't know; got two lives; feet going both ways, ain't that crazy to think trees look like people.

T9. *Is that Tree by itself, or is it in a group of trees?*
   A. By itself.

T10. *As you look at that Tree, do you get the impression that it is above you, below you, or about on a level with you?*
   A. Above me.

T11. *What is the weather like in this picture?*
   A. Pretty weather.

T12. *Is there any wind blowing in this picture?*
   A. No.

T13. *Show me in what direction it is blowing.*
   A. From the east.

****

H1. *How many stories does that House have?*
   A. Three.

H2. *What is the House made of?*
   A. Wood.

H3. *Is that your own house?*
   A. No.
   Whose House is it?
   A. Ain't nobody's I know of.

H4. *Whose House were you thinking about while you were drawing?*
   A. Nobody's.

H5. *Would you like to own that House yourself?*
   A. No.
   Why?
   A. Made out of paper.
   Question repeated.
   A. Windows crooked; door's crooked.

H6. *If you did own that House and you could do whatever you liked with it:*
   (a) *Which room would you take for your own?*
   A. (indicated window opening onto porch)
   Why?
   A. Cause it's got a porch to it.
   (b) *Whom would you like to have live in that House with you?*
   A. Nobody--except my people.
   Which ones?
   A. All of them!
   Why?
   A. So I would not be by myself.

H7. *As you look at that House, does it seem to be close by or far away?*

A. Close.

H8.   *As you look at that House, do you get the impression that it is above you, below you, or about on a level with you?*

A. Up on a hill.

H9.   *What does that House make you think of, or remind you of?*

A. Don't make me think of nothing, only a house.

H10.   *What else?*

A. Barn.

Why?

A. Built like one.

H11.   *Is that a happy, friendly sort of House?*

A. Never did live in it, I don't know.

H12.   (Question not asked in this case.)

H13.   *Are most Houses that way?*

A. Yeah.

Why do you think so?

A. But not these houses up here; old brick houses; Colony.

H14.   *What is the weather like in this picture?*

A. Rainy weather.

****

T15.   *What does that Tree make you think of, or remind you of*

A. I don't know what to think of it. Looks like a tree

T16.   *What else?*

A. Yeah; a house; shaped like one.

T17.   *Is it a healthy Tree?*

A. Yes, ma'am.

T18.   *What is there about it that gives you that impression?*

A. I don't know.

T19.   *Is it a strong Tree?*

A. Wish I'd never drawn it; have to answer so many questions I don't know about.

T20.   *What is there about it that gives you that impression?*

A. 'Cause it's straight.

****

P9.   *What does that Person make you think of, or remind you of*

A. Nothing.

P10.   *What else?*

A. Nothing.

P11.   *Is that Person well?*

A. Yes.

P12. *What is there about him that gives you that impression?*

A. (No response).

P13. *Is that Person happy?*

A. Yes, ma'am.

At this point the patient flatly refused to answer any more questions. A few minutes later, however, the following two questions were asked and they were quickly and willingly answered.

Which is the "good" side of this House and which is the "bad" side? (the S smiled and his expression seemed to say: "Now for the first time you ask a sensible question.")

A. (pointing) The right side is the good side, the left the bad.

Which is the female side of this House and which is the male side?

A. (again pointing) Right side female; left side male.

QUALITATIVE ANALYSIS

ACHROMATIC HOUSE

Details: All essentials are present; the nonessentials are relevant. The detail sequence is atypical. After the shell of the House (walls and roof) was completed, the first details drawn were the dormer windows in the sidewall's roof. Each window was drawn with a triangular frame and not tied into the roof in dormer fashion until everything else, except the ground floor window in the endwall, had been drawn. No door was drawn until the porch roof and pillars were produced, indicating at best a reluctance to make contact. The chimney was added late in the drawing and no attempt was made to show depth (suggesting a sexual conflict). The last items drawn were the windows and door in the ground floor of the sidewall. "A" found all detailing within this sidewall disturbing and difficult to produce. (See his answer to the second supplementary question at the conclusion of his achromatic P—D—I).

The peripheral lines of the walls were emphasized, as were those for all the windows in the sidewall, indicating that he feels a strong need to maintain control.

Proportion: The achromatic House is about average in size. The windows in the conflictual wall were drawn large at first, then erased, and redrawn smaller.

Perspective: The House was placed slightly to the left of center. The reversed profile ("A" is dextral) is significant: The reversed profile for a House or Person is interpreted as representing a conscious attempt to maintain acceptable relationships with reality in the face of strong withdrawal tendencies. Note, too, that the left porch pillar has its base against the wall despite the fact that the base line angulation is good. This is a most unusual combination of Good and Flaw points, but even more striking is the great disparity as to the floors between the sidewall and the endwall. This highly inferior endwall and sidewall relationship in the presence of the excellent endwall and sidewall presentation, together with the mentioned unusual Good-Flaw combination, makes one strongly suspect that a serious personality breakdown of the schizophrenic type is imminent.

Time: "A's" time consumption of 8 minutes is excessive. There was a 40-second latency period after the shell of the House was completed and the attic windows were partially produced in the sidewall. Then the porch roof, the pillars and the floor were drawn. "A" still conforms to reality, but only after exerting much effort. He would like very much to maintain himself inaccessible.

Line Quality: There is an almost pathological vacillation in the quality of the lines: some are forceful, some faint; some well controlled, others poorly controlled.

Criticality: There was much erasure. Evidence of some failure of critical function is seen in the fact that although "A" recognized the porch roof transparency (the far right wall of the endwall could be seen through the porch roof) and attempted to correct it, he did not notice that the base of the left porch pillar was against the House.

Post-Drawing Comments: His statement that this is a three-story House is a serious reality-testing flaw.

"A" does not like this House because it is made of paper (he finds it difficult to abstract). Later, he stated that it reminded him of a barn (subjects whose home situations are sources of intense conflict often degrade the "home" in this or some similar fashion.)

The two most pathologically significant responses to questions about the achromatic drawings were (1) instant identification (by pointing) of the "good" side and the "bad" side of the House and (2) an equally prompt assignment of a gender. Such "normative" responses when made seriously by a reasonably cooperative adult, of at least dull average intelligence, are almost certain pathognomonic signs of schizophrenia.

CHROMATIC HOUSE

Details: All essential details are present. However, one important irrelevant detail, the tool shed to the lower left, badly contaminates the drawing.

Again there was an atypical detail sequence. As in the achromatic House, "A" completed the porch before drawing openings in the endwall. Then he drew the upper endwall window, the door, and the lower windows. Before any openings were drawn in the sidewall, however, he drew the tool shed (he is most reluctant to make contact with this environment in general and people in particular).

Emphasis was placed on the chimney which is deeply and heavily shaded (suggesting sexual conflict) and on the containing lines, particularly those of the doors and windows: "A's" control is as difficult to maintain, as is his contact with reality.

Here "A" makes an unusual use of vertical shading in the endwall. Most often wall shading is produced in horizontal fashion (vertical shading implies a lack of control over basic drives).

Proportion: The chromatic House is larger than the achromatic one, but not to the degree of being pathological. This enlargement, however, seems to signify the high degree of sensitivity he feels in intimate relations when his ego-defences are hampered by additional pressure plus fatigue.

Perspective: The House is placed to the left of and below center, showing a need for frank and free emotional expression, concomitant with a mild depression of mood.

As in the achromatic House, the chimney is drawn without any attempt to indicate depth. The House again is in reversed profile. There is an unusual porch perspective flaw here which gives the viewer the impression that the House is striving to leave its profile position and become full-face.

The disparity between the floors in the two walls is very marked and, in addition, there is a disparity between window placement from floor to floor within the same wall.

Time: The time consumption of ten minutes, fifty seconds is excessive.

Color: "A" selected his colors easily and quickly. His choice was conventional and he used color in all three ways: lines, dots and shading, with the shading predominating. However, he completed the House and the tool shed before using any color but black.

Spontaneous comments during drawing: When "A" began his House, although he had been specifically told he might use any or all colors, he asked: "Do you want me to color it, too?" When he was drawing the ground floor windows in the endwalls he remarked: "I got the windows a lot bigger than I did the door."

Concept: The contamination of the drawing by the tool shed (presumably representing "A" himself) which is both paper-based and paper-sided, speaks for itself. The organizational difficulty shown in the achromatic House is even greater in the chromatic House.

ACHROMATIC TREE

Details: All essentials are present in effect. The absence of a specific trunk base line and a branch system base line implies a lack of total personality organization.

From the standpoint of sequence, the drawing was atypical. First, tne so-called periphery of the branch structure was produced, except for the two straight horizontal lines, about an inch long, at the base of the branch envelope structure; then interior branches were drawn before an attempt was made to depict a trunk. The lack of unity between the elements of the personality is sharply pointed up by this unusual sequence.

Emphasis is upon the branch structure of the upper Tree ("A" undoubtedly seeks satisfaction in phantasy) and on the trunk edges ("A" apparently feels anxiety because of tne lessening of nis ego control). He had difficulty deciding how large a trunk he wished to draw (he is not sure just how strong he is any more). The sun was produced only after he had been asked where he would have put a sun if he had drawn one. The contrast in line quality between the sun and most of the Tree suggests some felt difficulty in relationships with authoritative figures.

Proportion: The Tree is rather large; apparently it expresses his consciousness of unpleasant external and internal pressures.

Perspective: Noteworthy is the almost perfect framing of the Tree indicative of the S's marked rigidity at this time. There is a striking disparity between the quality of the upper branches, which give excellent implication of depth, and the base of trunk, that part of the Tree closest to reality. Such extreme qualitative difference within a whole always makes one suspect the presence of a schizophrenic process. In passing, no mental deficient could convey the impression of depth as "A" did in the upper Tree.

The Tree appears to lean slightly to the right ("A" shies from free emotional expression which frightens him).

The beginning failure of critical function is pointed up by the inadequate.corrective measures "A" undertook in the left root area.

Post-Drawing Comments: He sees the Tree as live only because it has not been cut down (negative reasoning). One suspects that "A" has premonitions of a major emotional breakdown. The "cut down" aspect of this reply suggests strong feelings of an external threat (castration fear).

The Tree is feminine because its shape suggests a dress skirt; later it reminds "A" of a House because it is shaped like one. This shift from the reasonable to what might be called "an answer for the sake of answering only" is pathological.

The Tree would be facing to the side if it were a person ("A" shuns contact with others, but is not ready to turn his back on reality). When he was asked why the Tree (if it were a Person) would be facing to the side, he said, "I don't know; got two lives; feet going both ways. . ." The pull of reality on the one hand and the ever-growing lure of irreality on the other, place "A" in almost an intolerable tension state.

In answer to T12, "A" said that no wind was blowing in the picture. Yet wnen he was then asked in what direction the wind was blowing, not only did he not reject the question as ridiculous but he replied quickly and firmly, "From the east." This segmental treatment of questions and failure to see a continuing relationsnip from question to question is obviously pathological, particularly in one of his intelligence level.

Concept: The organization of details is inferior. It is unusual to see a fir Tree with so many feminine characteristics (psychosexual confusion is strongly suggested).

CHROMATIC TREE

Details: All essentials are present. The detail sequence was average. As far as emphasis is concerned, three things are noteworthy: (1) the shading is heavier in the left (emotional) area of the branch structure (his need for immediate satisfaction creates anxiety); (2) the union of the base of the tree trunk with the ground is tenuous (as is his grasp upon reality); (3) the branch structure is emphasized at the expense of the trunk (there is definite over-striving).

Proportion: Once again the whole is very large ("A" is painfully conscious of environmental pressures and his turmoil looms large in his thinking).

Perspective: There is a marked framing of the Tree on the page (which reflects his great need to maintain personality balance). "A" employs implication well but the impression of depth created in the achromatic Tree largely disappears in the chromatic.

Color: Color was chosen quickly and easily.

His use of color is conventional and conforms to reality. His shading of the Tree is inferior to that for the House since the color spills over the poorly defined peripheral lines (his overstriving is not well controlled).

Concept: "A" can produce a masculine Tree but only with difficulty. There is a tendency to lose progressively the masculinity shown in the achromatic Tree.

ACHROMATIC PERSON

Details: All essentials are present.

First the eyes were drawn as hollow ellipses without pupils; the the pupils were not added until the nose and mouth had been produced (A's withdrawal tendencies still are controllable).

The first hand drawn was the left, produced as a loop without fingers; after completing it "A" commented, "Hand doesn't look right" Several details later he asked "Can you rub any of it out?" This question, since "A" had erased extensively in the first two achromatic drawings, provides further evidence that "A" is seriously disturbed.

After "A" was told *again* that he could erase, he erased the hand which displeased him, redrew it and added the other hand, in each case inserting the fingers. Note that the left hand has *six* fingers and both hands are fists. Again there is extreme quality vacillation which is pathological.

Initially the legs were drawn as a skirt, and only later was differentiation made by the midline and cuffs ("A" is badly confused as to his sexual role).

The last detail drawn was the ear convolutions which, in part, differentiate the ear from the skull and correct the initial impression that the head had two handles.

Emphasis: Great emphasis is placed on the hands, which were drawn as fists, and on the peripheral lines of the head (the meaning of the former is obvious; the latter implies a felt need to control phantasy).

The feet are well drawn; ordinarily the feet are aesthetically the poorest of the Person details, but "A" is no ordinary Person.

Proportion: No significant malproportions are shown.

Perspective: The Person is almost perfectly framed upon the page (the rigidity that this implies is pathologically reinforced by the tension exhibited by the figure).

Again there is, at the least, a partially reversed profile. The eyes glance upward, as if to avoid contact with others.

Line Quality: The line quality is vacillant.

Post-Drawing Comments: When he was asked why he drew his Person with fists, he quickly replied: "Ready to fight" (clearly expressing his latent hostility and precarious control). Then he added, "Reason I drawed it that way, because I can't draw fingers" (he can still suppress his aggressive tendencies).

To P7 he replied scornfully, "Paper can't think". When this question was repeated, he laughed and said, "I don't know"

Concept: "A" drew a standing Person, ready to fight, who feels as if he is psychotic. Yet, says "A", his Person is well and happy. Quality vacillation is patent in the verbal area also.

CHROMATIC PERSON

Details: All essentials are present. The quality of the detailing, however, is inferior to that for the achromatic Person. The feet, by comparison, are ineptly drawn ("A" has almost lost the ability to function efficiently when additional pressure is placed on him).

Proportion: The arms and legs are disproportionate to the trunk (the elongation of the legs expresses, one suspects, his profound feelings of a need for autonomy; the arms, in turn, depict his great need to defend himself against external threat.

Perspective: Here, for the first time, in a whole easily presented in profile, there is no longer a reversal of the profile. The suggestion here is that at the end of this frustrating experience, he no longer wishes to struggle to maintain an acceptable facade. His Person is rigidly framed; the stance is less flexible and the figure less accessible than in the achromatic Person. Rather striking is the position of the hand to the left (as the observer sees it) which suggests subconscious self-destructive impulses.

Color: This was drawn first as a simple black figure and later shaded in. The shading is inferior, particularly for the upper body and arms. This combination of blue and black is used not infrequently by schizo-affective Ss, although here there is nothing unconventional in the use of these two colors.

Concept: Here is a Person with eyes closed, standing rigidly and awkwardly, with one hand at his throat, as if to shut off hostile verbal expression or even to throttle himself.

Diagnosis and Prognosis: "A" is not mentally deficient. Both the graphic and the verbal H–T–P material provide ample evidence for the conclusion that he is moving toward a frank schizophrenic breakdown. His prognosis seems poor.

Several weeks after this study was made, "A's" condition deteri- orated and he became catatonic.

CASE B

By J. N. Buck

This 23-year-old, white-woman was brought to the Colony to await transfer to a Virginia State Hospital for the insane. "B" had been diag- nosed by the committing physicians as having a manic-depressive psychosis, acutely depressed stage.

Upon being questioned by the author, "B" readily indicated expe- riencing frank hallucinations in five spheres: She "tasted" the poison that people were putting into her food; she "heard" women's voices making derogatory remarks about her, and at times she "saw" those who made these statements; she "smelled" evil and harmful odors; and she "felt" electricity around her which from time to time entered her arms and legs, paralyzing them.

No unbiased history was available. The following, taken *cum grano salis,* came from "B" herself. She completed the seventh grade and then left school. Later she ran away with a man whom she subsequently married and by whom she had two children. She had left her husband about two years prior to this interview and since then had been living with her parents, and supporting herself by working in a shoe factory. Her two children were living with her husband; she does not know their present

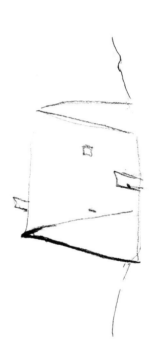

Figure 6 A

Figure 6 A

PERSON

Figure 6 A

HOUSE

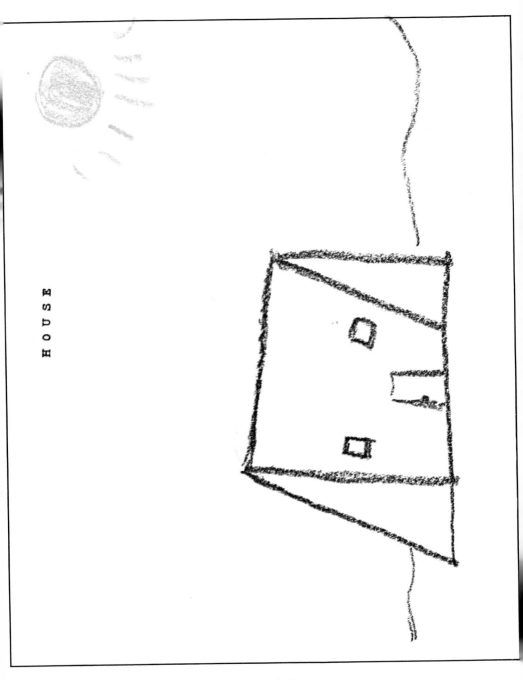

Figure 6 B

Figure 6 B

P E R S O N

Figure 6 B

whereabouts.

"B" claimed to have had syphilis three years before and to have been treated therefor with "needles!" However, physical examination revealed no evidence that she had ever had lues.

QUANTITATIVE SCORING

On the achromatic H–T–P there were the following I.Q. scores: Per cent Raw G 67, Net Weighted 48, Good 57, Flaw 44. The 19-point disparity between the Net Weighted and the Per Cent Raw G., in favor of the Raw G, suggests that she has a quantity necessity; and the quality of what she does (Net Weighted I.Q. 48) is so far below the amount of what she does (Raw G I.Q. 67) that it implies the presence of an acute disintegrative personality disturbance. The further finding that the Good I.Q. score is not the highest of her four scores also is not a favorable sign.

Analysis of the Means score pattern shows the typical "Psychotic V". She has no less than 6 D3 scores. An unusual characteristic of her Means score pattern is that the D1 and the A1 scores are at the average and the dull average levels, respectively. This offers further quantitative evidence that there is definite quantity striving which appears to represent a last ditch effort to maintain contact with reality: the inferior calibre of this effort indicates the degree of her pathology.

Inspection of the scores for Details, Proportion and Perspective shows that the scores for Proportion are depressed far below those for the other two areas which still range from borderline to dull average: the suggestion is that her judgment is being interfered with catastrophically.

From the standpoint of the areas of sensitivity, her scores for the House are the lowest with her Tree scores not much higher. Her scores for the Person remain relatively high. This implies: (1) a crippling conflict in the home; (2) a well-advanced *intra*-personal conflict. The fact that her scores for the Person still are relatively high suggests that in the field of *inter*-personal relations she does not feel so acutely threatened.

The quantitative scores for the chromatic set of drawings, however, reveal a marked constriction, with a Per cent Raw G I.Q. of 52, a Net Weighted I.Q. of 47, a Good I.Q. of 46 and a Flaw I.Q. of 47, from which it may be assumed that as "B" is subjected to increased pressure she becomes more rigid and functions even less efficiently. The Means score pattern (if the D3 score, still of psychotic proportions, is discounted) reveals a spread of only two adjacent classification levels which provides further evidence that as pressure increases, she reacts by becoming more rigid.

The most striking thing, however, is to find the Detail scores lower than the scores for Proportion and Perspective which suggests a pathological abandonment of reality. Under additional pressures her grip on reality becomes even more tenuous.

The scores for the House, Tree, and Person maintain about the same ratio as pertained for the achromatic set, so it may be assumed that the points of sensitivity revealed here are basic.

QUALITATIVE ANALYSIS

ACHROMATIC HOUSE

Details: An important essential detail is missing: there are no walls. The House is essentially composed of roofs only.

Smoke is depicted as a tiny one-dimensional wisp, the base of which has left the chimney. This type of smoke usually is drawn by those who have assumed a more or less "there is little or no hope" attitude.

The absence of window panes for the single window expresses hostility.

From the standpoint of detail sequence, there is nothing significant to report except that there were a number of spontaneous comments during the drawing phase. Initially she said: "I don't know how I used to draw; I don't know how to start". After making the short vertical line, above and to the left of the door, which looked like a half-hearted attempt to depict a window, she remarked, "It won't be a House, it will be a barn'". After drawing the vertical line at the left end of the House (the one heavily reinforced) she remarked: "I don't know how a House goes". At the end she commented, with deep feeling," Everything you do comes back to you".

The emphasis on the left end of the House is obvious. One might postulate that "B" feels a strong need to erect defenses against emotional experiences and unhappy memories.

Proportion: The House is pathoformically small and seems to express her feelings of impotence in intimate inter-personal relationships.

Perspective: Placement of the House on the horizontal axis is about average, but on the vertical axis it is below average, and a depression of mood is connoted thereby.

The double-perspective presentation of the roofs, which are, in effect, walls, indicates sharp concept regression.

Time: The time consumption, 12 minutes, 30 seconds, is pathological. An initial latency of a minute and a half occured before the first response was made and that was verbal only; 3 minutes elapsed before she drew her first tentative line (new tasks are almost too difficult for her).

Line Quality: The line quality is widely vacillant.

Post-Drawing Comments: "B" flatly refused to answer any of the questions asked her when Post-Drawing **Interrogation** was attempted.

Concept: Here is a House whose disorganization suggests great confusion and anxiety. It is postulated that the roof area represents the life phases most remote from *concrete* reality. Her House, in a sense, is a roof only. It may be concluded, therefore, that this patient lives largely in phantasy.

CHROMATIC HOUSE

Details: Again there are no true walls. Here "B's" oppositional tendencies are more clearly expressed than in the achromatic House by the absence of window panes and the concomitant accentuation of the enclosed white space.

There is nothing atypical about the detail sequence for the chromatic House.

All peripheral lines are emphasized heavily, expressing a strong need to maintain ego control.

Proportion: Although this House is larger than the achromatic House, its size is not atypical.

Perspective: Tne chromatic House is lower on the vertical axis than the achromatic House (as frustration increases, "B" appears to become more depressed).

The double-perspective presentation speaks for itself. In tne chromatic House, however, the double-perspective is not as inferior as that for the achromatic House: there both the inner line of the endwall and the external line of the right endwall are perpendicular to the baseline.

The most striking diagnostic point, and perhaps the most pathological prognostic point as well, is that the House is drawn as if it were toppling.

Time: The time consumption of one minute, fifty-three seconds, while slightly excessive in the circumstances, contrasts sharply with the time consumed for the first House. In this drawing, "B" is more frustrated and draws more rapidly, decisively, and aggressively (she speedily leaves reality as represented by the test situation).

Color: Color is used for lines only. Essentially this is color avoidance. The choice of brown is mildly atypical; the black crayon is usually employed if the crayon is to be used as a pencil only. One might make the cautious interpretation that this use of brown represents a regressive tendency.

Concept: When "B" is pressed, she becomes more expansive and hostile, and her grasp upon reality becomes still more tenuous.

ACHROMATIC TREE

Details: All essential details are present.

Proportion: The Tree is not atypical as to size. From a segmental standpoint, however, the visible tip of the trunk is somewhat broader than the base.

Perspective: The 1-dimensional branches not only do not join the trunk but do not even join each other. This dramatically expresses her futile, disorganized, poorly associated, almost explosive striving to obtain satisfaction.

Despite the fact that this Tree is paper-based (expressing insecurity), it is a Tree which seems almost pathognomonic for schizophrenia. The tilting of the Tree to the left implies: (1) a strong need for frank, free, immediate emotional satisfaction; (2) a regressive narcissism; (3) a longing for the past which was presumably more satisfying than the present.

Time: The time consumption of 40 seconds is pathoformic.

Criticality: The critical function failure is obvious.

Concept: The toppling, exploding Tree speaks for itself and portrays vividly her feeling of imminent personality disintegration.

CHROMATIC TREE

Details: All essentials are present. Emphasis is placed on the trunk border lines (this points up "B's" feeling of a need to exercise careful and great control to prevent complete ego disintegration).

In this picture the irrelevant details, sun and groundline, were produced spontaneously. While she was drawing the sun, "B" commented, "This represents the sun---yellow gold". It is interesting to note that the sun's rays are directed at the Tree only. Since the rays are not seen by "B" as threatening, this is interpreted as representing a very strong need for warmth.

Proportion: The chromatic Tree is larger than the achromatic Tree. The disparity between the width of the trunk at its base and at its tip is more marked than was the same disparity in the achromatic Tree.

Perspective: This Tree, also, is paper-based (feelings of insecurity are basic). It is very poorly organized. One forms the impression that the Tree, too, is exploding (this H—T—P may well have been secured during the most acute stage of the early phase of her emotional breakdown).

Time: The time consumption of 53 seconds is pathoformic.

Concept: The concept here is a duplicate of the achromatic concept.

ACHROMATIC PERSON

Details: Two essential details are missing: (1) the lowest portion of the trunk and (2) the legs. Severe neurotics occasionally omit the hands and the feet but they do not omit part of the trunk and the entire legs. These omissions provide convincing proof of the magnitude of the personality disorder in this case.

Strong emphasis is placed on the facial characteristics and the containing lines of that portion of the body which is drawn. This points up, once again, "B's" pathetic attempts to maintain contact despite her profound intellectual confusion and obvious sexual difficulties.

This is the first of the *achromatic* drawings in which the sun's rays point toward the central figure only.

The details sequence was atypical. No facial characteristics were inserted until the head, the hair, the neck and the shoulders had been drawn. The pupils of the eyes were the next to the last items drawn ("B" wished to delay identification and was reluctant to portray a receptive organ).

Her failure to complete the trunk and her inability to close the pelvis strongly suggest sexual conflict.

Proportion: The mouth is too large and obviously sensual.

Perspective: That portion of the figure which *is* drawn is placed below the average midpoint on the page; the figure is seen toppling to the right ("B's" attempts to avoid emotional relationships are overwhelming her).

Time: The total time consumption of one minute, forty seconds, is almost pathologically fast when one recalls that there was an initial latency of one minute and ten seconds.

Line Quality: The line quality is highly vacillant.

Concept: The pathology of this concept is obvious. The quality of such details as the shoulder and the neck indicate that this is *not* the drawing of a chronic mental deficient, incidentally.

CHROMATIC PERSON

Details: Less of the Person is shown than in the achromatic drawing. The intensity of the body conflict is pointed up even more sharply. The detail sequence was not as pathological as for the achromatic Person, but again the presentation of the facial characteristics was delayed.

Emphasis is on the unusual hair formation which creates the distinct impression that the formation is a nutcracker, which expresses symbolically the crushing affect upon "B" of her sexual phantasy.

Emphasized are the rays from the oversized sun ("B's" need for emotional warmth is pathetic).

Proportion: The head of the chromatic Person is longer and still more disproportionate than the head of the achromatic Person.

Perspective: This figure seems, in a sense, to be in a state of dissolution. It makes one think, and not in a happy vein, of the Cheshire cat, whose face was the last thing seen before it vanished.

The figure, at least the visible part, is almost perfectly framed on the page, slightly down from center. Under additional pressure, "B" becomes more rigid and withdrawn.

Line Quality: The line quality here is more decisive and consistent than in her other drawings.

Color: From the standpoint of color "B" uses the black crayon in lieu of a pencil. She attempts no shading. This is not unconventional, but does not conform strictly to reality.

Concept: The concept patently is pathological.

Conclusion: This is an extremely striking H—T—P protocol of an acute schizophrenic. The marked similarity between the achromatic and the chromatic sets, with all drawings loaded with pathology, makes for a most unhappy prognosis.

Postscript: The student will note that the fact that "B" flatly refused to respond to the P—D—I did not emasculate the protocol. It is highly desirable to obtain a full P—D—I whenever possible, but the achromatic and chromatic drawings by themselves in all cases can stand on their own merits.

CASE C

Masculine Character Posturing: A Man in the Clothes of a Clown,
in the Clothes of a Man [1]

By Emanuel F. Hammer, Ph.D.
New York City

The following case was seen in response to a challenge made over the telephone by a rather skeptical psychiatrist-colleague, who had been treating a 37-year-old man and wished to obtain a psychological evaluation. But he wanted the evaluation done "blindly", as he put it, so that he could be sure that the results came solely from the psychological examination and were in no way the result of constituted inferences made from data otherwise known about the patient. By "blind" analysis the psychiatrist meant that he did not want the writer to know anything about the patient or his symptoms other than what came through the projective examination. He had no objection to the writer's conducting the projective-technique-restricted examination, however.

The psychiatrist was putting projective techniques to the test, to determine whether or not anything of importance could be learned about a person from the way in which he drew a House, a Tree, and a Person, composed stories related to pictures, and interpreted inkblots.

The writer explained to the psychiatrist that the soundest and

1. Appreciative thanks are extended to Drs. Joy Roy and Robert Wolk for their helpful comments and editorial suggestions.

most effective use of projective technique evaluation is not one in which the procedure is attempted blindly. However, the psychiatrist remained firm. And a challenge is a challenge.

When the man appeared for the psychological examination, he was well-dressed and had an air of assurance and poise. He was pleasant and cooperative, and readily participated in the psychological examination.

H−T−P Projective Drawings

The writer ordinarily follows up the achromatic H−T−P with a supplementary drawing of another Person, of the sex *opposite* to that of the first Person drawn. Thus one House, one Tree, and *two* Persons (one of each sex) are elicited. Then the pencil and the finished drawings are taken away. The patient is given new sheets of paper and a set of crayons and one House, one Tree, and two Persons, (one of each sex) again are obtained.

In this case, however, the patient had already given a relatively full and extensive Rorschach and T−A−T; time was running out, and "C" had to catch a train. So after "C" had completed the achromatic House, Tree and a Person of each sex, no P−D−I was attempted, and the chromatic drawing phase was abbreviated to merely a Tree and one Person. See Figures 7A and 7B.

"C's" first drawing, that of a House, was drawn in a slow, meticulous manner. Compared to his other drawings, the House is small, constricted, and set way back from the viewer. Feelings of inadequacy, inferiority, constriction, and withdrawal in the home situation, past and present, are suggested.

The wide and conspicuous driveway implies a need to present himself as interested in social and interpersonal contacts, in relatedness to others. But since the driveway does not reach the House and is U-shaped rather than merely leading *to* the House, it conveys the impression that this man's emotional accessibility is more apparent than real. The roadway leads people past him, rather than to him. We may then *hypothesize,* but not yet *deduce,* that a seemingly cordial and friendly exterior is used to conceal an underlying detachment and a need for retreat from others. In keeping with the merely token acceptance of the fact that society expects him to be reasonably accessible, the windows on the ground floor are placed well above the usual level in relation to the door, and all the windows have the shades half-lowered.

His drawings of Trees, both achromatic and chromatic, emphasize the bark, a finding frequent in people hypochondriacally oriented with feelings of physical disjointedness and inadequacy.

Both the chromatic Tree and the achromatic Male Person have the top of the drawing sliced away, as it were. Thus, the suggestion is offered

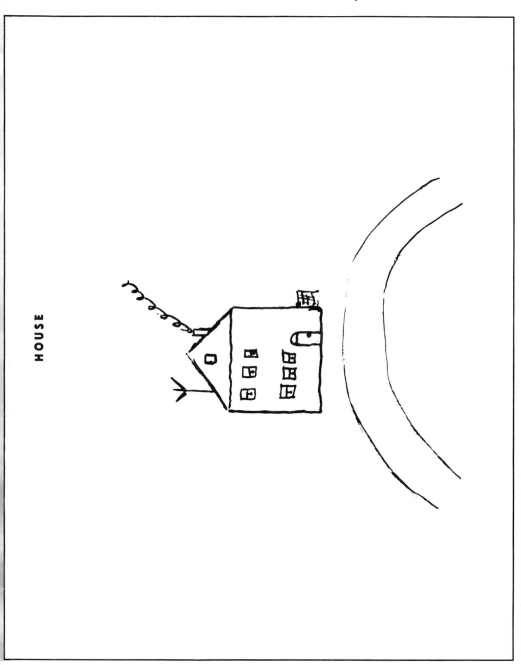

HOUSE

Figure 7 A

Figure 7 A

PERSON

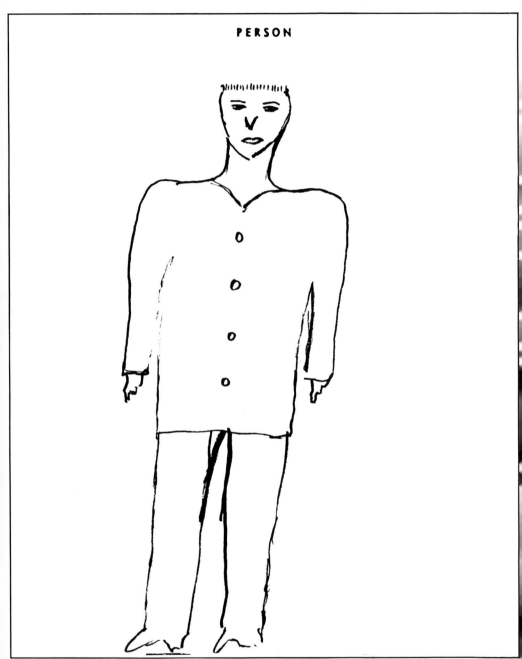

Figure 7 A

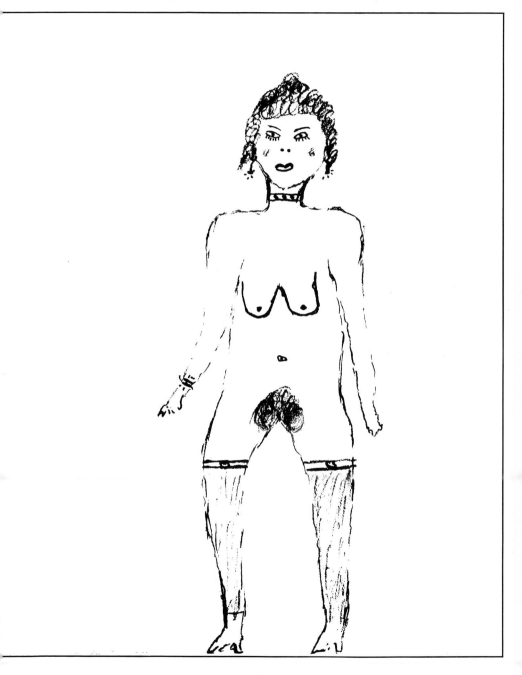

Figure 7 A

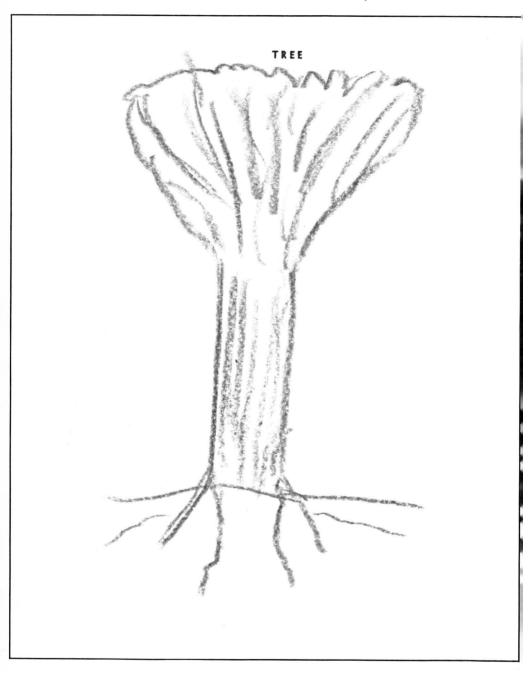

Figure 7 B

Figure 7 B

that "C" attempts to deny that phantasy area, presumably because of the unacceptable content of his phantasy and the guilt it produces.

The first male drawing attempts to give an impression of virility and masculine prowess: The crew-cut hair, the bull neck, and the broadened shoulders. However, these are belied by the anxiety-indicating difficulty that "C" experienced with the crotch area, the flaccid droop of the toes, and the apparently withered hands. As in his drawing of the House with his withdrawal tendencies tucked away behind superficially cordial front, reaction-formation again is used, this time combined with compensation in an effort to conceal his feelings of sexual impotency behind a characterological parade of masculinity.

Following this less than successful attempt to present a virile front convincingly, "C's" next drawing is of a provocatively-posed, nude female. His attempt to present the female as sexually exciting also does not quite succeed. She has a cold, doll-like, immobile, uninviting expression made only superficially attractive with dabs of rouge and the absence of clothing. The body lacks feminine shape and grace with no hip curve or waist delineation The breasts appear shapeless, drooped, and devoid of youth and appeal, at least as defined in Western culture.

Despite the profuse hair at the vaginal area, erotic emphasis actually is shifted to the legs. This is consistent with "C's" many eroticized Rorschach responses involving legs (and is discussed more fully later under the Rorschach section of this report).

Following the attempt to draw a sexualized woman, "C's" next drawing of a Person (chromatic) is a male clown. Here "C" portrays graphically his major need to play a role which will amuse and disarm rather than antagonize. Thus, he attempts to indicate the harmlessness of of his drives. On top of that, following his transgression of contemplating a female in raw sexual terms, he draws a skirt on the male clown and then places a cross-hatching of lines across the pelvic area as if to protect the genitals. Hence, two defensive maneuvers are used by "C" to protect himself against genital damage: (1) harmless lack of assertion, and (2) effeminacy

In addition, a depressed and resigned quality comes through beneath the clown paint---*i.e.* shows through his unsuccessful attempts to use the reaction formations of cheerfulness, gaiety and carefreeness:

Following "C's" stream of associations through his three Persons, we find that a particularly virile facade and an ambivalently-perceived sex object produce massive fear within him and result in his presenting himself as an innocuous, passive and female-like character.

Excerpts from Rorschach Section of Report

As both confirmation and elaboration of the H—T—P picture, the following excerpts from the Rorschach section of the report are of interest:

> The patient's intrinsic definition of the Rorschach situation was in compulsively-toned competitive terms.
> This led to fully twelve responses on the first Rorschach card, where the average is closer to four or five. Thus, the subject attempted to compete with previous subjects or with an imaginary standard by trying to show that his imagination, his astuteness of observation, or his diligence was inexhaustible.
> His resigned submissiveness has its deepest roots in a fear of assuming the active male role. One of the patient's Rorschach responses offers a parallel to the H−T−P drawing sequence from virile male to clown. To Card VIII the patient projects, "Here's a bull; no, it's a a rat, it's a rat, or it might be a hyena." On the positive side, we see that the patient can project an image of virility, a bull, but this rapidly gives way (with increasing conviction) to a symbol which retreats to stealth rather than assertion (the rat), and ends up with the hyena which is, in spite of its wily and insidious qualities, in some ways an animal-equivalent of his drawn clown. In addition, the hyena may connote the feeling that the patient may take over only the leavings that more assertive competitors no longer want..
> A similar sequence occurs on another Rorschach card. First, the patient sees "Moose standing up with horns," but then offers as his next response, "A big tree without any branches." He doesn't dare be masculinely assertive for long and retreats into a "castrated" position out of fear of terrible damage ("Rips in a piece of material," "Wounds, raw skin," and "Poodles with bloody paws.") He then ends up not knowing which way to turn (*i.e.* "A dog with two heads running either way"). The quantitative Rorschach picture (high *W*, reduced *M* and *FM*) suggests reduced buoyancy and vitality as personality assets, consistent with the above qualitative indications.
> On still another card, the patient once more dares be assertive for only a little time, retreating rapidly to a position in which he gives up his masculine prerogatives. The response, "Animal, light and fast with long legs," is immediately followed with the projection, "Body of a chicken, without the wings."

The patient's entire performance on Card V deserves mention in this regard. He opens with the response, "Woman's legs, in old-fashioned days," (we are reminded of the eroticized leg treatment on the drawn female, with the perception of them in an old-fashioned setting being consistent with the Oedipal indications on the T—A—T). His next two responses, "Mouth of a big bird of prey," and "Mouth of a crocodile"--both "ready to bite"--reveal his massive fear of bodily damage as retribution for his tabooed sexual interest. He then retreats for security into a safe and innocent response, "A butterfly." He has the capacity to experience security, however, for he then comes out of this response with a return to the percept, "Legs." Although to some degree culturally-endorsed, the patient's *continual* shift of erotic focus to the legs may be linked with his "castration" anxiety by the formulation that seeing a person without his penis is too anxiety-producing as an example that he might lose his own. Thus, by focusing on the legs as a symbol of a penis in a woman, he attempts to shut out his fear and permit himself sexual arousal. His fetishistic leanings thus serve as a defense against his "castration" anxiety.

In an attempt to avoid the threat of "castration" the patient has given up both the use of his penis and his masculine assertiveness. The implications of this unconsciously-motivated switch to femininity are far-reaching. He probably could not usurp any of the father's strength through the normal identification process. He could not pattern his ego-ideal along male lines. And finally, he probably could not adequately engage in heterosexual activity.

Follow—Up

After receiving the report, the psychiatrist called the writer to tell him something about the patient. It turned out that the patient had been married for six years but had never had intercourse. Impotency problems were at the core of his reasons for seeking psychiatric treatment. Along with this, he had frequent masturbatory fantasies of half-undressed women in which his attention was focussed upon their legs and high heels.

The psychiatrist knew little about the etiological or developmental influences in this case, since he had had only the initial interview with "C". The psychiatrist's impression, however, was consistent with the title of this chapter: that "C" was a man who hid under the protective disguise of a clown over which, on a secondary level, he then placed the superficial varnish of being a virile, impressive male.

Postscript to Case C

By John N. Buck

General Comments

This case is of major interest for several reasons: (1) Dr. Hammer offers a masterly illustration of content analysis; (2) it demonstrates how the H—T—P and the Rorschach frequently corroborate and complement one another; (3) it shows that rich diagnostic and prognostic material may be derived from an H—T—P protocol even though no historical material is available (there is no P—D—I) and the chromatic House is missing.

Specific Comments

Details: "C" identified the small hatched rectangle attached to the right side of the House, (from the point of view of the observer) as a woodshed. Ss for whom intimate interpersonal relationships present almost insoluble problems frequently degrade their Houses in this or in similar ways.

The vine-like lines implying the presence of bark on the chromatic Tree are sometimes seen in the drawings of Ss plagued by obsessive drives which they feel are obvious to others.

The relatively sturdy Tree trunks imply the "C" does not believe that his adjustment problems are due to innate flaws.

Proportion: The branch structure of each Tree is inadequate in size when compared to the trunk: "C's." satisfaction-seeking resources are limited and produce frustration and tension.

The contrast in size between the shoulders and the hands and feet of the achromatic Person is striking and pathetic. "C" feels painfully inadequate in his attempts to make satisfying psycho-social relationships.

The huge chromatic Person strikingly points up "C's" feelings of frustration and ineptness: his unsatisfied needs and drives seem to balloon within him. The reversed leg taper drawn by one of "C's" known intelligence reveals the degree to which his emotions inhibit his functions as a man.

Perspective: The House is a facade only, serving as a prim, precise mask to cloak his feelings of inadequacy in the home.

The hands and feet of the achromatic Person create the impression that "C's" approach to psycho-social relationships is on a diffident, tiptoe basis and not warm and sharing.

The arms of the chromatic Person are attached to the trunk well below the shoulder level: by the time "C" drew this last whole, he was fatigued and quite probably overwhelmed by the associations aroused by all the projective material that had preceded it.

Color: The chromatic Tree was produced with brown crayon only: this is not an unconventional use of color or a denial of reality. The Person first was outlined in black: then, suddenly, "C" went color wild, using no less than five additional colors for his clown (purple, red, orange, green, and yellow). Yet the brighter colors were used only as after-thoughts and as ornamentation. One cannot say that this is unconventional usage, since no standards for color use have been or could well be established for a clown's garb.

Neither can one say that "C's" use of color shows a loss of adequate reality testing. It does suggest, however, and strongly, that basically "C" is reserved and colorless, much as he would give almost anything to be a more dynamic and popular person.

Concepts: A comment concerning "C's" drawing of the female Person: psychosexually immature male Ss who cannot establish "normal" heterosexual relationships frequently draw females in a manner which degrades them; perhaps this is the "sour grapes" system of devaluing something which one cannot possess and/or enjoy.

"C's" Trees are of the type which is often identified as a strong but feminine figure: such Trees often are produced with Houses similar to "C's" by Ss who have identified strongly with their mothers; by Ss whose psychosexual development is inadequate. In the absence of the P—D—I, one can only assume that "C's" Trees were seen by him as feminine and powerful, but this assumption seems sound and affords a strong secondary confirmation of the validity of Dr. Hammer's content analysis of the drawn Persons.

In considering the chromatic Person, one should bear in mind that as a clown "C" would occupy a position of some prominence. Those watching him would regard his blunders and posturing with amused tolerance at the worst. He would have the close attention of a group with whom he need not attempt to make close, sharing relationships.

Conclusion: To assign a specific diagnostic category (which seems unnecessary in view of the wealth of dynamic material elicited), one might say "C" has a deep-seated character neurosis of long duration, which probably will not incapacitate him, but will handicap him rather severely and subject him to much frustration and dissatisfaction. The Prognosis does not seem too promising. Apparently only prolonged, intensive psychotherapy would offer much hope of improvement.

CASE D
Rebel with Cause
By Isaac Jolles, M.A., Psychologist
Thornton Township Special Education Association, Harvey, Illinois

"D" is 12 years and 7 months of age. At the time of this examination, he was on suspension in a private school because of his poor attitude toward his work. The school authorities had recommended that the parents seek consultation with a psychologist in order to make appropriate plans for their son. "D's" report cards indicated that he had been an above average pupil until this year. According to the parents the school staff had felt that "D" could do better work, because he had proven himself to be a bright pupil; therefore, the parents exerted strong pressure upon "D" to work harder in school. The boy greatly resents this attitude by the school and his parents because he feels that he has done as well as he could.

"D" comes from what appears to be basically a good home; however, there are factors which probably have contributed to some of "D's" emotional difficulties. The father easily shows irritation toward the boy on many occasions; the mother admits that she too, has not been blameless. It is conceivable that the mother, in spite of her good intentions, finds it difficult to provide "D" with the emotional warmth which he needs.

The Wechsler Intelligence Scale for Children revealed a verbal I. Q. of 124 and a performance I. Q. of 107. Analysis of this performance indicated that "D's" chief deficit was in the area of attention. In all other areas he performed at a superior level. See Figures 8A and 8B.

CASE D

JOLLES' CHILDREN'S REVISION OF THE H−T−P

Post−Drawing Interrogation

P1. *Is that a man, a woman, a boy, or a girl?*
    A. A boy.
P2. *How old is he (she)?*
    A. Eleven.
P3. *Who is he (she)?*
    A. I don't know.
P4. *Who is that?*
    A. (no reply)
P5. *What is he (she) doing?*
    A. Standing.
P6. *Where is he (she) doing it?*
    A. On the ground.

****

T1. *What kind of Tree is that?*
    A. Maple.
T2. *Where is that Tree?*
    A. Just came out of my imagination.

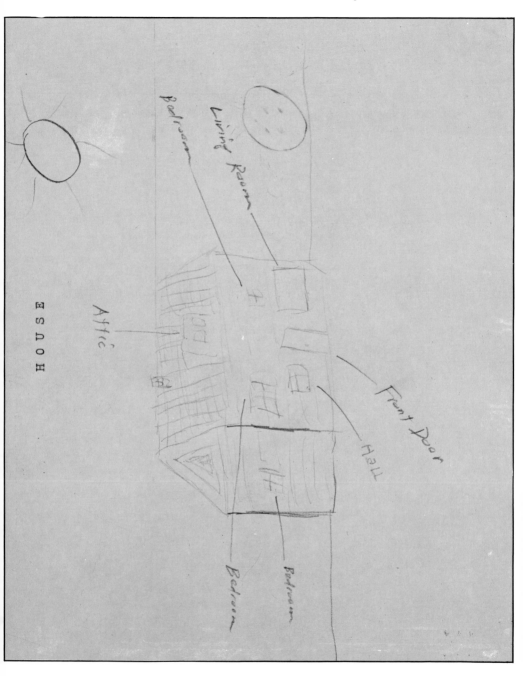

Figure 8 A

Figure 8 A

PERSON

Figure 8 A

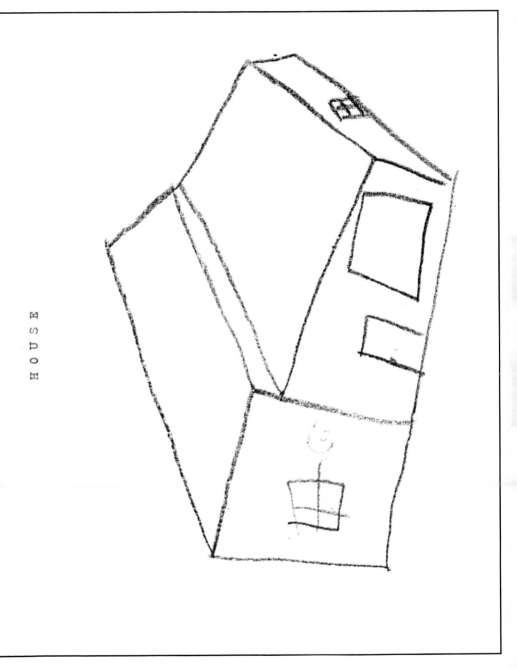

HOUSE

Figure 8 B

Figure 8 B

PERSON·

Figure 8 B

T3. *About how old is that Tree?*
    A. Fifteen years.
T4. *Is that Tree alive?*
    A. Yes.
T5. A (if subject says Tree is alive:)
    a. *What is there about that Tree which makes you think it's*
       alive?
    A. Got leaves.
    b. *Is any part of the Tree dead?*
    A. Yes.
    Which part?
    A. Outer bark.
    c. *What do you think caused it to die?*
    A. Weather.

* * * * * * *

H1. *Does that House have an upstairs?*
    A. Yes.
H2. *Is that your House?*
    A. No.
    (If not:) *Whose House is it?*
    A. Just made it up.
H3. *Would you like to own that House?*
    A. No.
    Why?
    A. It's shabby.
H4. *If you owned that House and could do whatever you liked*
    with it:
    a. *Which room would you take for your own?*
    A. I wouldn't take any; would sell the joint.
    (Urged)
    A. None in particular.
    b. *Whom would you like to have live in that House with*
       you?
    A. Nobody.
    (Urged)
    A. Mom and Dad and my brother.
H5. *As you look at that House, does it seem to be close by or*
    far away?
    A. Close by.
H6. *Does it seem above you, below you, or about even with you?*
    A. Even with me.

* * * * * * *

T6.   *Does that Tree look more like a man or a woman to you?*
      A. Nobody.

T7.   *If that Tree were a person, which way would that person be facing?*
      A. Towards me.

T8.   *Is that Tree by itself or in a group of trees?*
      A. By itself.
      (Would it like to be with other trees?)
      A. Not exactly.

T9.   *Looking at that Tree, does it seem above you, below you, or about even with you?*
      A. Below.

                    * * * * * * *

P7.   *What is he (she) thinking about?*
      A. Nothing.

P8.   *How does he (she) feel?*
      A. Down in the dumps.

P9.   *Of what does that Person make you think?*
      A. Art class.

P10. *Is that Person well?*
      A. Yes.

P11. *Is that Person happy?*
      A. (no reply).

P12. *What is the weather like in this picture?*
      A. Regular--sunny.

                    * * * * * * *

T10. *What is the weather like in this picture?*
      A. Plain, every day.

T11. *What kind of weather do you like best?*
      A. Warmer weather.

T12. *Is any wind blowing in this picture?*
      A. No.

                    * * * * * * *

H7.   *Of what does that House make you think?*
      A. Tenements in New York.

H8.   *Is that a happy, friendly sort of House?*
      A. No.

H9.   *What is the weather like in this picture?*

A. Every day.

H10. *Of which person you know does that House make you think?*
    A. Nobody.

H11. *Has anyone or anything ever hurt that House?*
    A. I guess so.
(If so) *How?*
    A. Kicking it, hitting it.

H12. (If sun is not drawn, have subject do so) *Suppose this sun were some person you know--who would it be?*
(Sun not drawn originally)
    A. I don't know. (Groundline induced)

****

T15. (If sun is not drawn, have subject do so) *Suppose this sun were some person you know--who would it be?*
(Sun not drawn originally)
    A. I don't know.

T16. *Of what does that Tree make you think?*
    A. Acorns.

T17. *Is it a healthy Tree?*
    A. Yes.

T18. *Is it a strong Tree?*
    A. Not too strong.

****

P13. *Of which person you know does this Person remind you?*
    A. No one.

P14. *What kind of clothing is this Person wearing?*
    A. (no reply).

P15. *What does that Person need most?*
    A. Something to do.

P16. *Has anyone ever hurt that Person?*
    A. Yes.
(If so:)
a. *How?*
    A. Couple of fights.
b. *How old was that Person when it happened?*
    A. (no reply).

****

T19. *Of which person you know does that Tree remind you?*

A. (no reply).

T20. *Has anyone or anything ever hurt that Tree?*
A. Yes.
(If so:) *How?*
A. Pulling on it.

T21. *What does that Tree need most?*
A. Water.
Why?
A. (no reply).

****

H14. *What does that House need most?*
A. New paint job.
Why?
A. (no reply).

H15. *Where does that chimney lead to in the House?*
A. Furnace.

ANALYSIS OF PROTOCOL

Examination of the achromatic drawings indicates that a reasonable effort was made by "D" to control his impulses (horizontal placement), but there also is considerable evidence of a weak ego having difficulty in maintaining control of his emotional energy, as indicated by excessive reinforcement of the wall lines on the left side of House and reinforcement of the outer limits of the Tree's trunk. This suggests that "D" is over-concerned with maintaining ego control.

In the remainder of the House and the Tree, the lines are weak, tending to indicate a rather weak ego. This assumption is substantiated by "D's" response to T18 in which he indicates that the Tree is not too strong. Also, on T5, he states that the outer bark is dead; this is certainly suggestive of a deterioration of ego control. "D" indicated that the bark died because of the weather. This suggests that "D" feels that environmental pressures are responsible for his difficulties.

Of further interest is the fact that the chromatic House is much larger than the achromatic House. This suggests that "D" may tend to over-react to excitable stimulation, a further indication of poor ego control. Furthermore, the chromatic Tree presents a picture of one striving hard for control, as is indicated by the leaning of the Tree from left to right. The use of blue-green for the chromatic Person suggests that "D" has a strong need to maintain control in order to hold on to the feelings of security that he still has. It is possible that the blue trousers also express "D's" need for control. However, one must interpret this cautiously because the use of blue in this instance is conventional. Finally, the rigid achromatic Person suggests that "D" employs constriction as a defense against his impulsiveness.

"D" evidently lacks adequate resources for deriving satisfactions from his environment. Although the branch structure of the Tree appears adequate in the achromatic drawing, its weak lines seem to reveal "D's" concern in this area. This assumption is confirmed by the chromatic Tree with its limited branch structure.

Certainly "D" indicates that he is concerned about the warmth in his environment. His responses to the P—D—I weather questions also imply this. "D" used heavy lines when depicting the sun in his drawings of the House and the Tree, again suggesting anxiety concerning his source of warmth. In inter-personal relationships he is much more responsive when warmth is experienced, as shown by the difference between the achromatic and chromatic Persons. On H8 he states that the House is not a happy, friendly home. This may express a feeling of a lack of warmth in intra-familial relationships which can contribute to his feelings of insecurity. There is an indication that he does not feel accepted in inter-personal relationships. See T8 in which "D" says that the Tree stands by itself: usually this reflects a feeling of social isolation among one's peers. Furthermore, "D" gives evidence of asocial tendencies by stating that the Tree is not interested in being with other trees. It is not surprising to find that "D" is somewhat depressed. His treatment of the sun in his drawing of the House (first drawing it on the horizon, then erasing it and redrawing it in the sky) graphically portrays his attempt to hide his depressive feelings.

Throughout the examination, "D" manifested hostility in various ways. Therefore, some P—D—I questions were omitted because the examiner sensed that these particular questions might stimulate withdrawal and thus damage rapport.

"D's" hostility is shown, in his chromatic House, by his using the black crayon only. Furthermore, for the exposed parts of the chromatic Person he used yellow-orange, a color that has been found to be a manifestation of hostility. The achromatic Person is presented in absolute profile; implying withdrawal and oppositional tendencies. Many of "D's" responses to the P—D—I were evasive and indicative of hostility. He expressed verbally his hostility towards his home. Note the responses to H3 and H4 which describe the House as shabby, something he rejects. He does not wish to consider the House as his; but if it were, he would not live in it, but would "sell the joint". In spite of his hostility towards his home, it is encouraging to note that when he was forced to select someone to live in the House with him he chose his parents and brother; conditions at home are not so completely bad that he would reject his family. On H5 he sees the House as close by, which tends to contraindicate a feeling of rejection. On H6 the House is seen even with him rather than below him; if it had been seen as below him, rejection would have been indicated.

From these findings one concludes that while the boy has considerable hostility towards his home, he also has some positive feelings which provide hope for his ultimately making a better adjustment in this area.

Finally, "D's" feelings of inferiority seem to have psycho-sexual implications. In the achromatic House the chimney is too small; in the chromatic House there is no chimney. Thus castration feelings seem present in "D".

Again, in response to T9 he states that the Tree is below him; sometimes this indicates feelings of inferiority. Indications are present that the intellectual aspects of "D's" experiences may have produced these feelings. In both the achromatic and the chromatic Persons, the heads are disproportionately small. This is especially true in the chromatic drawing. This strongly suggests that "D" tries to minimize the importance of intellectual activity. He has used this rationalization as a defense against his school difficulties.

Follow-up information revealed that "D's" adjustment improved considerably when he was entered into another school where adjustments were made to his problems in attention, and where excessive pressures to perform at high levels were removed.

Postscript to Case D

By John N. Buck

General Comments

This case merits serious attention because (1) the achromatic and the chromatic sets of drawings differ strikingly as to concept; (2) it demonstrates how great an aid to the interpretation of drawings the S's P–D–I responses can be, although the S is hostile and all P–D–I questions cannot be asked; (3) it illustrates how important the qualitative comparison of the two sets of drawings is to the formulation of a diagnosis and a prognosis.

Specific Comments

Details: Although almost all the details in the achromatic Person are drawn hesitantly and faintly, the ear is emphasized: "D" is acutely aware of and sensitive to criticism.

Perspective: The placement relationship of the windows in the two Houses (to the door in the achromatic and to the respective walls in the chromatic) gives "D" more difficulty than one would expect in a boy of his intelligence level. This suggests strongly that he is having equally great difficulty determining his true relationship to his family (presumably he alternates between withdrawal and over-accessibility). Obviously his home is a source of great frustration.

Line Quality: Almost the only lines drawn with force and assurance in the achromatic set are those for the trunk of the Tree: "D" (as yet) does not feel wholly inadequate to cope with the problems of living.

Concept: The change of concept from the achromatic drawings to the chromatic drawings merits discussion.

His achromatic House was produced hesitantly, anxiously and indecisively. However, his chromatic House, a much larger structure, was drawn quickly and carelessly; it appears about to topple.

His achromatic Tree has a comparatively sturdy erect trunk, but a cloud-like, nebulous branch structure. The chromatic Tree leans rather precariously and has only large fronds. One suspects that his chromatic Tree is a palm, a tree customarily associated with a warmer, more relaxed, and benevolent environment than that of his home state (Illinois). Note, too, that in the suggested South Seas environment of tne palm Tree, little emphasis is placed upon intellectual achievement.

His achromatic Person is small, tense, rigid, aloofly hostile. His chromatic Person is in almost violent motion, running and about to fall.

The achromatic series emphasizes anxiety, indecisiveness, and the S's need to maintain himself relatively inaccessible and under rigid control. The chromatic series stresses imminent collapse and poorly controlled flight.

Diagnosis and Prognosis: Qualitative analysis of the drawings and the P–D–I material makes it clear that "D" is an unhappy boy wno exhibits anxiety, confusion, dissatisfaction, and rebellion and is more than mildly paranoid about his situation. He is attempting to maintain personality integrity by holding himself inaccessible and under tense control. The chromatic drawings strongly suggest that his frustration tolerance threshold is dangerously low; that if he does not receive immediate relief, his defences will crumble.

A number of points argue for a relatively favorable prognosis, however: (1) "D's" basic intelligence is high; (2) he has not yet developed a deep-seated, well-ingrained maladjustment pattern; (3) his history indicates that his paranoid ideas are based on fact and not delusion; (4) he is fightIng hard to maintain his personality integrity; (5) his history indicates that pressures from family and faculty may well fully account for his present maladjustment.

To sum up: "D" is suffering from a severe maladjustment reaction to environmental pressures. These environmental pressures presumably can be removed or reduced.

CASE E

H−T−P of An Ambulatory Paranoid Schizophrenic

By *Selma Landisberg, M.A.*
New York City, N. Y.

"E", a 19-year-old male, in treatment for the past three months, was referred for study by his therapist. The question of psychosis was raised because of "E's" revelation of primitive, uncensored dreams, peculiar visual experiences, and latent homosexuality.

In the initial interview, "E" stated that his symptoms started when he was 12 or 13 years of age. He has difficulty in concentrating, meanders, lacks purpose, does not know what he wants to do in life, and dislikes working. He recently left X University, after attending for two years, because he did not like his course of study. He states that he is interested in business psychology but not the experimental psychology courses which he had to take. In the past, he has worked as a camp counselor, as an apprentice for two summers in his father's plant, and sold magazines. Currently he is working in a supply company, selling, buying, and packing. He says that he has never found satisfaction in any job he had. An older sister, age 21, is doing well in graduate school; a younger brother, age 10, is doing, "pretty well" in school. "E" describes his parents as distant toward one another and toward him; the mother shows concern for "E" only when he is in desperate straits; the father is stingy and critical of him..

"E" is slight in build, wears black frame glasses, sports a short-cropped beard and mustache, and is dapper in attire. He was detached and haughty in manner; spoke in a supercilious, blase manner; occasionally glanced at the examiner in a peering way, but generally did not look directly at her; often parried in a defensive and condescending style the questions put to him. For example, when he was asked if he had friends, he replied: "Oh, do you want their names and addresses? I go out with groups of boys; I go out with groups of girls; I go out with single people, girls alone, me and a girl."

He cooperated in the examination and seemed to enjoy the chance to display his prowess on the intelligence test and the opportunity to air his ideas and associations on the projective techniques.

See Figures 9A and 9B.

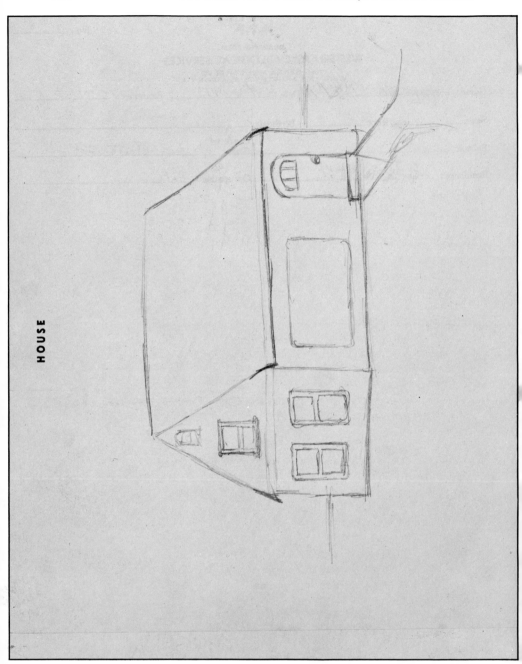

HOUSE

Figure 9 A

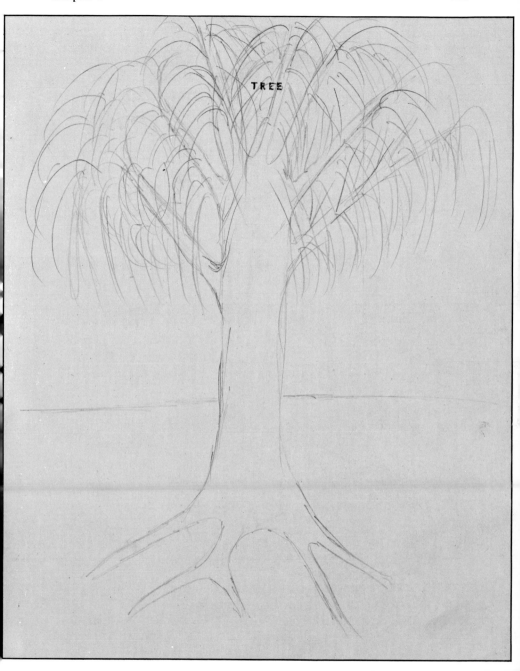

Figure 9 A

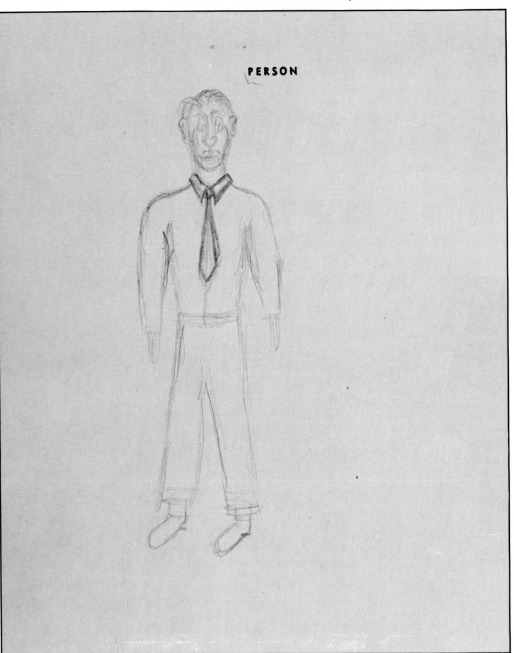

Figure 9 A

Figure 9 B

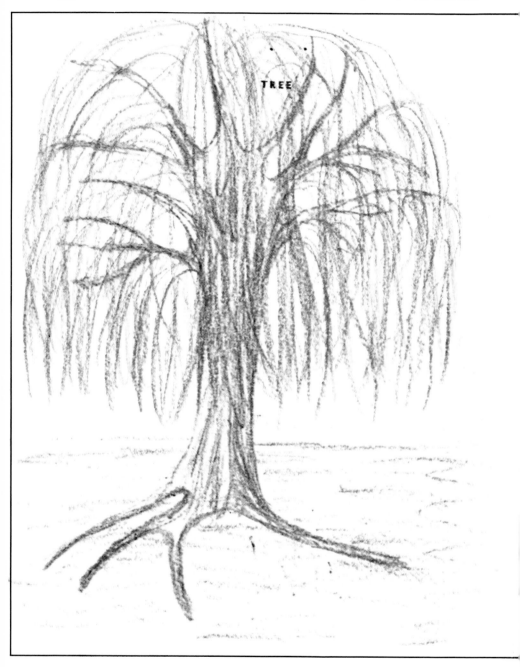

Figure 9 B

Figure 9 B

Achromatic H–T–P Drawing Phase:
Detail Sequence

HOUSE

1. Top roof area – Sketches in and reinforces.
2. "I'm not much of an artist."
3. Reinforces sides of roof.
4. Picture window.
5. Upper left wall windows.
6. Lower left wall windows.
7. Side lines – main wall and left sidewall.
8. Baselines – main wall.
9. Baseline – sidewall– reinforces.
10. Left sidewall windows – reinforced.
11. Door. Draws baseline first.
12. Door window with bars.
13. Door knob.
14. Groundline.
15. Reinforces base of wall.
16. Pathway.
17. Reinforces left wall windows.
18. "There you go."

Time: 5': 5''

TREE

1. Downward trunk lines.
2. Reinforcement of lower left side trunk lines.
3. Roots.
4. Background lines.
5. Alternating right then left branch depiction from bottom to top.
6. Center top branches.
7. Foliage lines--clockwise from lower left to lower right.
8. Covering foliage.

Time: 4': 10''

PERSON

1. "Uh-huh."
2. Head and face outline.
3. Hair.
4. Eyes.
5. Nose.
6. Mouth
7. Neck.
8. Left shoulder.
9. Right shoulder.
10. Upper trunk lines--shading.
11. Arm lines--off from trunk lines, with space in between.
12. Hands.
13. Left ankle.
14. Right ankle.
15. Left foot.
16. Right foot.
17. Joins arm lines to trunk area.

Time: 3': 15''

Achromatic P–D–I

P1. *Is that a man or a woman (or boy or girl)?*
  A. I really didn't think of either when I drew it. If I had anything particular in mind, I would have had to be a lot more careful about most of the dress. Would have had to be considerably more artistic. I'd say probably more like a boy.

P2. *How old is he?*
  A. (Pause) Oh--21–22.

P3. *Who is he?*
  A. I haven't got any idea. Just some sort of cartoon-like character. Not that I read comics. But it's a sketchy cartoon character.

P4. *Is he a relation, a friend, or what?*
  A. No.

P5. *Whom were you thinking about while you were drawing?*
  A. (Reinforces head area) Mostly I was thinking of putting to use my little knowledge of art, it didn't work out. When I really try, I can draw fairly decent likenesses, but that would take much too long.

P6. *What is he doing? (and where is he doing it?)*
  A. (S repeats the question) I don't know. Standing there. Staring at something that seems a little out of place to him. Sort of looks a little dismayed by what he sees.
  Where?
  A. I don't know. He might be down around 20th Street looking at some of these idiots who call themselves people who walk the street.
  What do you mean?
  A. Those people who think they're people but aren't--are out of place in the human race. There I go rhyming again. All sorts of people in this city who can be called people in the broadest definition. So foolhardy as not to realize their lot.
  Go on, please.
  A. They're not human but semi-human--culturally. Below level I consider human and intelligent as far as fulfillment goes. (Reinforces collar and tie.) They can't do very much. Most don't have an education. Mentally impossible. Not much chance of succeeding. Don't have inherent intelligence necessary to appreciate anything. Are far removed from their basic needs.

P7. *What is he thinking about?*
  A   Thinking how silly they must be not to realize their own lot.

P8. *How does he feel?*
  A. A little bit above the whole thing. A good deal above the

whole thing. I'm talking about myself.

What do you mean?

    A. This is a country where the majority are a shapeless mass. Some are close to it, in it, some are way below it.

Who are?

    A. Idiots.

****

T1. *What kind of Tree is that?*
       A. If I had taken more time---Don't know.

T2. *Where is that Tree actually located?*
       A. In my backyard where there is a weeping-willow.

T3. *About how old is that Tree?*
       A. 5 or 6 years old, I guess.

T4. *Is that Tree alive?*
       A. Most definitely.

T5. *I.* (If subject says that the Tree is alive:)
    a. *What is there about that Tree that gives you the impression that it's alive?*
       A. Nothing about the picture shows it. I'm picturing the leaves and roots. It's firmly planted in the ground.
    b. *Is any part of that Tree dead?*
       A. None whatsoever.

T6. *Which does that Tree look more like to you: a man or a woman?*
       A. For some reason I associate a weeping willow with women. A certain grace to the weeping willow. Certain grace and sweeping lines.

T7. *What is there about it that gives you that impression?*
       A. (See previous answer).

T8. *If that were a Person instead of a Tree, which way would the Person be facing?*
       A. Facing me, I guess.

T9. *Is that Tree by itself, or is it in a group of trees?*
       A. By itself.

T10. *As you look at that Tree, do you get the impression that it is above you, below you, or about on a level with you?*
       A. On a level with me.

T11. *What is the weather like in this picture? (Time of day and year; sky; temperature)*
       A. Sort of over-cast--mid-afternoon--fall--chilly.

T12. *Is there any wind blowing in this picture?*
       A. No.

****

H1.   *How many stories does that House have?*
      A. 1½ (Smiles)
H2.   *What is that House made of?*
      A. Clapboard, I guess.
H3.   *Is that your own House?*
      A. Resembles it to a minute degree. Ours is not clapboard
          and this is too small.
      How does it resemble yours?
      A. It's the central section. Picture window. Placement of door.
H4.   *Whose House were you thinking about while you were drawing?*
      A. No one's really. This was the quickest and best I could do.
H5.   *Would you like to own that House yourself?*
      A. Not particularly. I like things a little more extravagant.
      Why?
      A. It ties in with this idea of culture. A small house, a small in-
          come. On small incomes, there are certain things I like that
          can't be indulged.
      Such as?
      A. Like collecting art. Going to the theater regularly.
H6.   *If you owned that House and You could do whatever you liked with it:*
      a. *Which room would you take for your own?*
      A. I suppose the large upstairs room.
      Why?
      A. I don't know. It's too small to get much of a bedroom in down-
          stairs.
      b. *Whom would you like to have live in that House with you?*
      A. Various friends. My mother and father.
      Why?
      A. Because I feel most comfortable with people who have my in-
          terests and idiosyncracies.
      Why?
      A. I don't need an overwhelming amount of people..
H7.   *As you look at the House, does it seem to be close by or far away?*
      A. Close.
H8.   *As you look at that House, do you get the impression that it is
      above you, below you, or about on a level with you?*
      A. On a level.
H9.   *What does that House make you think of, or remind you of?*
      A. Reminds me of a group of houses similar to Leavittown. A great
          mass of nothing humanity. Nondescript mediocrity.
H10. *What else?*
      A. Of a place I wouldn't mind living in. But I aspire to things that
          are bigger. I wouldn't mind it though. (Parents?) They argue·
          Because my mother isn't practical.

H11. *Is that a happy, friendly sort of House?*
    A. It's sort of nondescript. Neither happy nor friendly.
H12. *What is there about it that gives you that impression?*
    A. It looks pretty empty.
H13. *Are most houses that way?*
    A. No.
    Why do you think so?
    A. Because most inhabitants of houses get along to a degree. It's rarely a situation where they exist with each other.
H14. *What is the weather like in this picture? (Time of day and year; sky; temperature.)*
    A. Again, overcast. Mid-afternoon. Fall. Chilly.

****

T15. *What does that Tree make you think of, or remind you of?*
    A. Of a weeping willow in our backyard.
T16. *What else?*
    A. I suppose it also brings to mind the sort of grace and beauty and freedom that I'd like to spend the rest of my life involved in if economically possible.
    What would you do?
    A. I paint a little. Build models. Spontaneously write a little-- short stories.
T17. *Is it a healthy Tree?*
    A. Not too robust. Foliage is a little scrawny. Neither is it sick.
T18. *What is there about it that gives you that impression?*
    A. (See previous answer).
T19. *Is it a strong Tree?*
    A. I think so.
T20. *What is there about it that gives you that impression?*
    A. Got pretty healthy roots.

****

P9. *What does that Person make you think of, or remind you of?*
    A. I guess it makes me think of sort of a cultured individual--a little too haughty as far as his own standing--compared to the standing of other people.
    Why?
    A. Tne look on his face is one of extreme arrogance.
    Why?
    A. One can be a little too arrogant, too.
P10. *What else?*

A. He's got a pretty bad tailor. His pants are too short; shirt is wrong; tie not tied right; collar completely out of style. I don't like pants with belts.

Why?

A. Serve no practical purpose.

P11. *Is that Person well?*

A. Yes, I think so.

P12. *What is there about him that gives you that impression?*

A. His general character. People who are sick don't have too much time to be arrogant--to worry about themselves.

P13. *Is that Person happy?*

A. Not particularly happy with the scene he's looking at.

What makes him happy?

A. In his own odd way of being, the greatest part comes from unusual pleasures--things off the beaten track. Parachute jumping, racing.

P14. *What is there about him that gives you that impression?*

A.. The way his eyes are. Looking down at what he sees. Heavy look in his face, coupled with disgust.

P15. *Are most people that way?*

A. No. Most are a little too insensitive.Most can't be in that position.

P16. *Do you think you would like that Person?*

A.. I don't know because I can never remember--decide whether I like someone. I have to see their actions a bit before I know.

P17. *What is the weather like in this picture? (Time of day and year; sky; temperature).*

A. Again--the same as before.

P18. *Whom does that Person remind you of?*

A. Me, to a degree?

Why?

A. Sometimes I'm a little too arrogant. My pleasures are the same as his.

P19. *What does that Person need most?*

A. The means to accomplish his end.

Why?

A. Basically economic.

What do you mean?

A. *He* has no idea and I have no idea. I have no vocational purpose. I like to indulge my own interests without means of self-support.

****

T21. *Whom does that Tree remind you of?*

A. I suppose to me a very graceful woman.

Why?

A. Weeping willow always brought to my mind a very graceful, beautiful woman.

T22. *What does that Tree need most?*

A. (S repeats the question). Not much of anything. I'd like to see more in the way of foliage.

Why?

A. Because there's not enough. It got clipped. People like Trees the way Trees should look.

****

H15. *Whom does that House make you think of?*

A. Nobody in particular.

Why?

A. Just nondescript mass. A great mediocre mass.

H16. *What does that House need most?*

A. *A fire.*

Why?

A. Well--moments of extreme danger tend to show people off at their best or their worst. Those who can get out, will; those who won't, won't. It's in the overall scheme of things. In a moment of extreme danger, a person acts purely on impulse and those are mediocre people. Those who act wisely stay alive and deserve to. Those who can't, won't.

But why a fire?

A. To show the difference between these two--get rid of what isn't needed. It is a way of deciding who is worthy of being called human and who is not. If you couldn't burn the House to the ground, it would be nice to separate the human race through tests like this.

****

Chromatic H–T–P Drawing Phase

Detail Sequence

House

1. Left side wall lines
2. Main wall lines.
3. Outer roof lines.
4. Bottom lines of main wall.
5. Door--Black outline with brown interior shading

HOUSE (Continued)

6. Picture window--main wall
7. Left wall window.
8. Black shading of roof with horizontal lines drawn across.
9. Vertical lines of roof area.
10. Reinforcement of wall boundary.
11. Reinforcement of wall lines.
12. Wall material across.
13. Reinforcement of wall lines.
14. Horizontal wall material lines.
15. Yellow wall material fill-in.
16. Reinforcement of main picture window.

17. Purple curtain lines.
18. Reinforces windows with black lines.
19. Left window red curtain fill-in.
20. Yellow wall fill-in.
21. Reinforces wall lines.
22. Chimney outlines.
23. Red fill-in of chimney.
24. Smoke
25. Black roof shading.
26. Yellow shading in left upper wall area.
27. "I guess that'll do."
    Time: 8':0"

TREE

1. Left trunk line downward to roots area.
2. Roots--left; toward center.
3. Roots--right.
4. Upward right trunk line.
5. Groundline--green fill-in.
6. Upper right branches.
7. Upper left branches.
8. Green foliage over branches.
9. Lower left branches.
10. Lower right branches

11. Upper center branches.
12. Green foliage downward from upper center and from lower branches.
13. Extends foliage lines downward toward ground.
14. Trunk fill-in with reinforcement.
15. Black bark shading.
16. Yellow foliage fill-in.
17. Green foliage fill-in.
    Time: 8':20"

PERSON

1. Profile lines.
2. Eyes, nose, mouth, detailing.
3. Ear detailing.
4. Neck.
5. Upper trunk.
6. Arm.
7. Trousers.
8. Hair.
9. Black shading of pants.
10. Pants pocket.
11. Red fill-in of shirt.

12. Reinforces arm outline.
13. Collar outline and red fill-in.
14. Reinforcement of back of neck and chin.
15. Reinforces mouth.
16. Reinforces eyes and shades in.
17. Ankles.
18. Shoes.
19. Extends arm further outward.
20. Hand and fingers with shading.
21. "All right."
    Time: 5':20"

Chromatic P—D—I

P1.   *Is that a man or a woman (or boy or girl)?*
      A. I don't know--whatever it is. His head's too big. I guess a boy.
P2.   *How old is he?*
      A. 14-15.
P3.   *Who is he?*
      A. Reminds me of some kid I saw shining shoes a couple of days
      ago. This kid's head looked too big, too.
P4.. *Is he a relation, a friend, or what?*
      A. (See previous answer).
P5.   *Whom were you thinking about when you were drawing?*
      A. Not anything but drawing.
P6.   *What is he doing? (And where is he doing it)?*
      A. I guess, accepting money for shining shoes.
      What is he looking at?
      A. The guy whose shoes he just shined.
      Where is he?
      A. Somewhere around Pennsylvania Station--outside. They don't
      let them inside.
P7.   *What is he thinking about?*
      A. How rotten it is to shine shoes. Not much of a way to make a
      buck--15 or 20 cents, I guess. I've never been a shoeshine boy.
      Why does he think it's rotten?
      A. Thinks it's a bother. Seems too young to worry about what
      he's doing. He'd rather not be just shining shoes but enjoying-
      himself.
      Then why is he doing it?
      A. He needs money.
P8.   *How does he feel?*
      A. Tired.
      Why?
      A. 'Cause he's been shining shoes all day long.

****

T1.   *What kind of Tree is that?.*
      A. Another weeping willow.
T2.   *Where is that Tree actually located?*
      A. Same place. Backyard.
T3.   *About how old is that Tree?*
      A. 5—6 years.
T4.   *Is that Tree alive?*
      A. Most definitely.

T5.   *I* (If subject says that the Tree is alive)

    a. *What is there about that Tree that gives you the impression that it's alive?*

    A. It's green.

    b. *Is any part of the Tree dead?*

    A. None at all.

T6.   *Which does that Tree look more like to you; a man or a woman?*

    A. A woman. Not a man or a woman.

T7.   *What is there about it that gives you that impression?*

    A. It isn't too graceful. It's supposed to be.

T8.   *If that were a Person instead of a Tree, which way would the Person be facing?*

    A. Facing me.

T11.   *What is the weather like in this picture? (Time of day and year; sky; temperature.)*

    A. Summer. About noon. Spring. A little warmish.

T12.   *Is there any wind blowing in this picture?*

    A. No.

****

H1.   *How many stories does that House have?*

    A. Just one.

H2.   *What is that House made of?*

    A. Clapboard and shingle.

H3.   *Is that your own House?*

    A. No.

    Whose House is it?

    A. Reminds me of some I see--where I went to school. Factory workers live in them.

H5.   *Would you like to own that House yourself?*

    A. Again, if it were a place to live in now, I wouldn't mind it. But not live in it long.

H6.   *If you did own that House and you could do whatever you liked with it:*

    a. *Which room would you take for your own?*

    A. Everybody's in the same room. Back of the front window.

    b. *Whom would you like to have live in that House with you?*

    A. Nobody. It would be too crowded. One or two friends--male and female. Wouldn't make much difference if a boy or girl.

H7.   *As you look at that House, does it seem to be close by or far away?*

    A. In middle distance.

H11.   *Is that a happy, friendly sort of House?*

    A. Not that it's so happy. Sort of lived in. Indifferent.

Why are the curtains drawn?
A. Whoever's inside doesn't care to have everyone looking in.

H12. *What is there about it that gives you that impression?*
A. Just live in it. Not big enough.

H13. *Are most Houses that way?*
A. No.
Why do you think so?
A. Most people can afford something better.

H14. *What is the weather like in this picture? (Time of day and year; sky; temperature.)*
A. Sort of bright-ɘnot sunny. Noon-ʳlate winter--chilly.

* * * * * * *

T15. *What does that Tree make you think of, or remind you of?*
A. Of a tree.

T17. *Is it a healthy Tree?*
A. Yes.

T18. *What is there about it that gives you that impression?*
A. It's got plenty of foliage.

T19. *Is it a strong Tree?*
A. Pretty.

T20. *What is there about it that gives you that impression?*
A. Pretty solid.

* * * * * * *

P9. *What does that Person make you think of, or remind you of?*
A. A shoe-shine boy.

P11. *Is that Person well?*
A. He came down with TB at an early age. He's not too healthy. He's just about to cough.

P13. *Is that Person happy?*
A. Not particularly.

P14. *What is there about him that gives you that impression?*
A. He doesn't like shining shoes. He'd rather do something else.

P15. *Are most people that way?*
A. No.
Why?
A. They don't have to grub along and don't want to improve their lot.

P16. *Do you think you would like that Person?*
A. I feel a little sorry for him--nothing more.
Why?

A. Sorry for anybody who's got to grub.

P17. *What is the weather like in this picture? (Time of day and year; sky; temperature.)*
A. Cold.

P18. *Whom does that Person remind you of?*
A. Some kid.

P19. *What does that Person need most?*
A. He needs a better job or no job at all.
Why?
A. I don't think a 14 or 15-year-old kid should spend time shining shoes.
Why not?
A. Wouldn't if he had enough money.

****

T21. *Whom does that Tree remind you of?*
A. Nobody.

T22. *What does that Tree need most?*
A. Water.
Why?
A. Tree's wilting.

****

H15. *Whom does that House make you think of?*
A. Waltham factory workers or homes down south..

H16. *What does that House need most?*
A. Needs less people in it..
Why?
A. Where you get 8, 10, 12 people living in two rooms, neither the House nor the people could be comfortable.

SUPPLEMENTARY QUESTIONS

Q. *Why is his hand black?*
A. He is wearing black gloves; it's cold outside.

Comparing the achromatic with the chromatic drawings, there is a marked similarity in the substantial size and placement of the drawings on the page. These factors and the overall relative stability of the drawings suggest that "E's" behavior is fairly predictable at this time and there is no immediate threat of further disintegration or disruptive acting-out.

Though there are noticeable signs of tension, and an ongoing struggle for emotional control is reflected in the sketchiness and reinforcement of the outer lines of the drawings and the highlighting of hostile and depressed colors (yellow, red, and black) which are compulsively bound by heavy peripheral lines, his conflict between control and eruption of impulses seems to be chronic. There is no sign of sweeping anxiety or bursts of feeling in the drawings.

One is alerted immediately by his Tree that "E" is a paranoid schizophrenic. While there is an overall tone of depression in the downward sweeping Weeping Willow foliage, the power orientation of "E's" fantasy and thinking is seen in the outspread spidery, claw-like branch structure and the talon-like roots which grandiosely encompass a large area of the ground. In "E's" reality contacts one would expect him to prey upon and attempt to dominate others. There is seen also a thinly-veiled delusional potential in the open-ended, vulnerable achromatic Tree branches, covered and slightly obscured by the compulsive downward strokes of the foliage. The lack of branch closure reflects a potential for ideas of reference, persecution, and power.

The liberal use of green in the foliage and ground areas suggests continued underlying vitality and awareness of nurturance possibilities in his environment. The Tree's dominating implantation on the ground indicates an egocentric demandingness and parasitic way of life. As he stated in his peculiar way on the achromatic P—D—I, "I like to indulge my own interests without means of self-support."

He likened the Tree to a "graceful, beautiful woman". Viewing the Tree as a basic self-portrait, it appears that he has a deep feminine identification which he expresses in an exhibitionist way, and he wishes to be admired and indulged on the basis of his physical attractiveness.

There is an empty, hostile, untrusting quality to his achromatic House shown in the highlighting of white space, the poverty of inner detailing, and the barring effect of the windows. While he shows movement into the environment, the pathway lines are rigid, with the sweeping out at the ends appearing to be forced, not naturally tied in with the wariness and restricted quality of the beginning pathway. There is also a barrier line crossing the pathway at an angle, veering off from the high doorstep, further depicting his fear of the environment. In the chromatic phase, under the impact of color or emotional stimuli, his House becomes more elemental (contains one room only) and draws back regressively toward the upper left quadrant of the page. The transparency of the chimney and the arbitrary and flamboyant use of yellow, red, and purple suggest impairment in judgment and in expression of affect. The drawn curtains ("Whoever's inside doesn't care to have everyone looking in.") and the peephole window in the door indicate suspiciousness.

He views the House condescendingly and sees it as a place of restriction. His rage toward the concept of home is not only brought into relief by his red chimney which obtrudes on the printed word "House" but blatantly comes to the fore in his response to "What does that House need most?" He replied with blandness, "A fire." Then added in reply to subsequent questioning, "Moments of extreme danger tend to show people off at their best or worst. It's in the overall scheme of things. It is a way of deciding who is worthy of being called human. Those who act wisely stay alive and deserve to .. Those who are mediocre won't get out. They are the idiots who call themselves people. They're not human but semi-human. Below the level I consider human and intelligent as far as fulfillment goes. The majority are a shapeless mass. If you couldn't burn the House to the ground, it would be nice to separate the human race through tests like this." He experiences himself at one time as sub-human and worthy of complete destruction, and at another as superior to all, capable of coming out on top under the most stressful situations.

Though his achromatic Person suggests (1) depersonalization symptoms in the blurring face-shading and the inhuman quality of the features; (2) castration feeling in the foreshortened arms and stump-like hands; (3) anxiety and withdrawal tendencies in the extremely light, sketchy limb and body lines, "E" views him in his verbal description as superior to the masses of people around him, and says of him, "He's a good deal above the mass."

He sees his Person as seeking excitement in offbeat pleasures (parachute jumping, racing) and seems determined to prove his masculinity in a competitive, exhibitionistic, masochistic way. His concern about his phallic adequacy is highlighted by his prominent tie depiction, with the marked heaviness of the outline shading contrasting with the light lines of the rest of the drawing. By comparison with this troubled, important aspect of himself, everything else in the direct social scene is dim. He needs to degrade and deprecate others to bolster his fragile ego and weak sense of manliness.

Using the color drawings as a prognostic indicator, it appears that his unconscious outlook on his future is quite grim. From the Tree, one would expect continued compensatory self-inflation. In general his drawings and P—D—I responses show a potential for increased turning of his hostility against himself, a growing apathy toward life, and increasing indifference about his sexual identification. The Tree is seen as "wilting"-the House is described as "indifferent"; and he stated that "it wouldn't make much difference if a boy or a girl lived in the House with him. The Person is seen as an outcast, grubbing away at a living: 'He needs a better job or no job at all," Without treatment, one would expect "E" to drift, live in a purposeless, occasionally thrill-seeking way, relating to people asexually, leaning on others to help him, and expecting very little sustenance from them. On the positive side, are noted: the extended arm of the Person; the implied movement of the legs and feet; the substantial size of the drawings; the elements of control; and the use of some vibrant color. These indicate some latent energy and optimism, and make one suspect that if "E" does extend himself with control and good use of his resources, there is the chance that he could receive gratification.

The overall impression is that "E" is an ambulatory schizophrenic with paranoid tendencies. 'Though he is still subject to phobic reactions toward people and fear, his own volatile affects during periods of outer stress, his feelings of deadness, morbidity and detachment long have been operative, and so have been his suspiciousness, his ideas of self-reference and persecution, and his compensatory narcissism and grandiosity. While retaining superior intellectual resources as reflected in his language use and concept formation, at times he shows marked breaks in judgment by fabulated, arbitrary, *non-sequitur* thinking, and extravagant flights of fantasy. His style of thinking seems comfortably established and is used blandly and confidently.

At this time he feels extremely isolated, full of despair, blocked and uncertain of his future; he feels helpless in an environment which he experiences as threatening and affording him no real support and nurturance.. Yet despite his grandiose compensations, his distrustfullness and fear of being overpowered, he still shows a desire for a nurturing, protective relationship and a willingness to struggle along.

Postscript to Case E

By John N. Buck

General Comments

Case E rounds out this quintet of illustrative cases well. This H–T–P protocol is one of a seriously maladjusted young man, who is still able to function in society albeit at a level well below his potential. This case demonstrates that: (1) it is worthwhile to use as extensive a chromatic P–D–I as time permits with an S who verbalizes as freely and fluently as "E"; (2) on occasion a comparison of the achromatic and the chromatic P–D–Is can be as richly rewarding as a comparison of the two sets of drawings; (3) there can be a wide difference in the degree of similarity (achromatic to chromatic) of the graphic production of the three wholes.

Specific Comments

Details: In the achromatic House, the windows in the endwall are framed and defined distinctly and carefully; by contrast, the "picture window" in the main wall barely is outlined. "E" can maintain himself relatively accessible in intimate interpersonal relationships only if he can set the terms.

In connection with the "picture window", (as Miss Landisberg pointed out in correspondence with the author) since that is the window closest to the door and is the largest window, it is postulated that "E" has a continuing interest in and hope for gratification from the environment. However, the lightness of the window lines implies a simultaneous fear of and tendency to withdraw from close contact with others.

The slab separating the first and second floors of the achromatic House implies an equivalent and rather serious separation of thinking and acting within "E's" behavior.

The absence of a chimney from the achromatic House, quite aside from its obvious psychosexual implication, points up "E's" feeling of a lack of warmth in his home.

The open-ended branches for both Trees (the shading only partly neutralizes their implications) suggest that at times "E" is given to frank, free, and relatively uncontrolled expression of his basic drives. Fortunately there are few such branches.

For each Tree (see detail sequence), "E" found it necessary to tie the trunk into the environment before drawing any branches. He is very insecure and hesitates to seek satisfaction in and from his environment until he reduces environmental threats.

By what may be called "graphic parapraxis", his chromatic Person was adorned witn an earring. All six drawings contain evidence of psychosexual immaturity and confusion.

The author concurs with Miss Landisberg's comment concerning the black gloves which the chromatic Person is said to be wearing: "I assume the blackening could mean his guilt about forbidden manual impulses. The gloves could refer to his need to insulate himself in the midst of a perceived cold environment."

Proportion: The large, unbroken roof space on the achromatic House would be broken by at least two dormer windows in most 1½ story Houses: one strongly suspects that "E" indulges in much hostile thinking and phantasy.

His satisfaction-seeking resources (Trees' branch structures) are not small, but in comparison to his needs and drives (Trees' trunks) they do not appear to be adequate and frustration seems inevitable.

His comment, "The head's too big," about his cnromatic Person indicates an awareness of the dominant role that hostile thinking and phantasy play in his life.

Perspective: The transparency of his sidewall roof overhang (permitting the slab separating the ground floor from the upper floor of the achromatic House to be seen) shows how much his emotional imbalance interferes with his critical ability.

The topmost branch of each Tree juts above the page's uppermost margin. "E" has a tendency, albeit still mild, to seek in irreality the satisfaction denied him in reality.

Time: Although his chromatic Tree is almost a photographic reproduction of his achromatic Tree, he took twice as long to draw it. By the time he reached this whole, fatigue, the presumed impact of color, and the multitude of associations aroused by the previous drawings and the achromatic P–D–I had taken their toll.

Color: "E's" use of color for the chromatic House is unconventional. His extensive use of yellow points up his rejection of the popular concept of "home". Any use of purple is highly suspect: its use for a detail of the House is deviant and probably pathological. Male Ss, as a rule, do not draw window drapes, much less draw them in red and purple.

"E's" use of the sequence green, then yellow, then green in shading the foliage of his Tree is more than merely atypical.. Apparently he recognized that he was behaving in an unconventional fashion, for he attempted to account for it by commenting (P–D–I) that the foliage was wilting. He apparently forgot that he had said that it was late in winter in that picture, and that in that season, willows would have no foliage.

P–D–I: "E" was almost logorrheaic in his achromatic P–D–I, which was characterized by numerous attempts to impress the examiner with his independence, wide range of interests, and intellectual superiority (he does have a Full I.Q. on the WAIS of 129).. His responses to the chromatic P–D–I, on the contrary, were relatively sparse and colored strongly by deep feelings of inadequacy, isolation, and rejection by an essentially hostile world, which he cannot understand and which does not understand him.

Much of the time "E's" projection was thinly veiled. At times he gave frank evidence that he recognized that the drawing about which he was speaking was a self-portrait. Such insight is a hopeful prognostic sign.

Concept: At first glance one might think that "E's" achromatic House presented the same organizational confusion as did that of "A" (q.v.); this is not the case, however.

"E's" chromatic House is the classical one-room dwelling of the well-advanced paranoid individual. With a House of this size, he cannot be considered inhospitable or anti-social if he invites no one to live with him. As he stated in the P–D–I, "It needs less people!"

For both Trees he drew what he called a weeping willow, a Tree usually regarded as feminine. Popularly, the willow is also thought to be a delicate Tree with an emotional connotation (at best) of sadness. These Trees, except for their foliage, do not closely resemble living willows.

"E's" achromatic Person is a "cartoon character" (compare this with the Person of Case 1 in Appendix A, and the chromatic Person of Case "C". As a cartoon character, "E" can expect others to view him (at best) as an entertaining individual; or (at worst) as not very amusing. Deviant behavior on the part of a cartoon character is expected and condoned, not condemned. Such a character offers no threat to anyone and, therefore, might be presumed to be relatively immune from threat himself.

"E's" chromatic Person is engaged in what "E" feels is a debasing, unrewarding, dirty, menial occupation.

"E" apparently believes that in psycho-social relationships he must remain aloof and rigidly defensive or those whom he contacts will detect his inadequacies and, even worse, will know how "E" feels about them.

Chapter 8   Summary

SUMMARY

The H−T−P attempts to appraise the total personality by presenting the subject with stimuli which are so familiar to him that in drawing his concepts of them, he must project. In a sense, therefore, each drawn whole (House, Tree, and Person) always is a self-portrait.

Because of the conventional definition and connotation assigned to each of the three wholes in Western culture, the *House*, as a dwelling place, may be assumed to arouse associations concerning the S's home-life and intra-familial relationships; the *Tree*, as a living or once-living thing in a stressful, elemental environment, may be presumed to arouse associations concerning the basic and elemental relationships which the S experiences within his environment, and the *Person*, as a living or once-living human being, may be expected to arouse associations concerning the S's interpersonal relationships, both specific and general.

From a qualitative appraisal of the aspects of the drawings which the S indicates are significant to him, much can be learned concerning the non-intellective factors of his personality.

The examiner with limited clinical experience will do well to restrict himself, in qualitative appraisal, to the identification and enumeration of the factors which seemed to have been significant to the S. However, the experienced clinician, through interpretation, can frequently obtain a surprisingly clear picture of the underlying dynamics of a person. But interpretation always must be made with the following in mind: (1) no qualitative point of analysis means the same to all individuals. Its meaning and weight can be determined only by a careful consideration of the part that it plays in the entire H−T−P configuration presented; (2) in all instances the S must have every opportunity to offer his own interpretation; (3) all interpretations must be made in the context of as full a knowledge as possible of (a) the S's present milieu, (b) the S's past history, and (c) the S himself.

From a quantitative appraisal of the H−T−P drawings much can be learned concerning the S's level and methods of thinking. The H−T−P, however, is not intended to be an intelligence test *per se*. The greatest value of the quantitative scoring lies in the differential diagnostic information that can be acquired by (a) comparing the H—T—P I.Q. scores with the I.Q. scores obtained by the S on tests specifically designed to measure intelligence, and (b) by appraising the "quality of the quantity."

In evaluating the H—T—P I.Q. s the examiner must bear in mind: (1) the nonverbal, primitive method of expression, drawing; (2) that the stimuli presented are almost completely unstructured and believed to accentuate (through associations aroused) the production of emotional factors which, in turn, stimulate or depress intellectual function; (3) that there is no age-correction factor for H—T—P I.Q. s.

The question has been raised: "Can one be sure the H—T—P reaches below the superficial levels of the personality?" This important question is difficult to resolve with other than empirical proof. An affirmative answer is apparently justified, however, in view of the following; (1) a very large number of Ss have exhibited strong overt emotional reactions during the H—T—P drawing phases, the P—D—Is, or both, indicating that areas of sensitivity have been tapped; and the strength of the emotional responses suggests that they were more than superficial; (2) during a P—D—I phase, or in subsequent interviews, some Ss have recognized spontaneously the signficance of certain details, proportional distortions, perspective flaws, and so on, and have then verbalized materials which previously they had been unable to express; (3) a number of Ss have reported that for several nights following their H—T—Ps they have dreamed more frequently, more vividly, and more disturbingly than before the H—T—Ps were administered; and (4) the dynamic material elicited by the H—T—P is often of the type which is produced (during psychotherapy) only after many hours of free association.

Another question frequently asked is, "How long does it take to administer, score and interpret the H—T—P?" The answer is, "It depends on several conditions." These include the S's degree of adjustment and level of intelligence, and the experience and skill of the examiner. The author has worked with deteriorated epileptics, "old" schizophrenics, and obsessive-compulsives who took hours for the achromatic drawing phase alone, and he has examined mental deficients and schizophrenics who completed all six drawings in less than five minutes. Some deteriorated epileptics and schizophrenics, and some manics, have taken hours with their P—D—Is, while some schizophrenics and psychopaths have rejected the P—D—Is entirely. The amount of time consumed by "normal" adults, as a general thing, is between 5 and 30 minutes for the drawing of one H—T—P series and a similar amount of time may be consumed in discussing the drawings in the P—D—I. An experienced examiner usually can score and interpret a full achromatic–chromatic H—T—P in one hour and a half or less.

CONCLUSIONS

Evidence indicates that the H—T—P appraises the individual by affording him an opportunity to reveal, through the mechanism of projection, the structural relationships of the elements of his personality, the areas of sensitivity within that personality, and the cause or causes of such sensitivities. The H—T—P also serves as a measure of the efficiency of function of an adult's intelligence by appraising the qualitative level of his concept formation and his understanding of proportional and spatial relationships.

The H—T—P is not presented as a diagnostic and prognostic method *per se*. The author believes that no single psychological procedure can or should be expected to provide full and sufficient evidence on which to base a conclusive diagnosis and prognosis, because no single test can be all-inclusive in its sampling of behavior. Psychological maladjustment often leaves areas of the personality relatively intact; appraisal of the personality by any procedure, therefore, may produce a picture that is neither wholly adequate nor complete.

However, the H—T—P provides the clinician with (1) an examining procedure which can produce rich and valuable information concerning the S's total personality and the interaction of that personality with its environment, both specific and general; (2) an examining opportunity to observe the S while he is under direct and indirect stress, which enables the clinician to acquire insightful information concerning the Ss reactive behavior.

Tne H—T—P, in short, is a procedure designed to facilitate the clinician's acquisition of diagnostically and prognostically significant data.

Factors which favor the use of the H—T—P are:

(1) The H—T—P has both verbal and non-verbal phases which provide a more complete sampling of behavior since both types of behavior are produced by the same stimuli.

(2) The non-verbal phase of the H—T—P is sufficiently productive to be used to good advantage with patients who cannot or will not verbalize and to whom the Rorschach or T—A—T cannot be administered.

(3) The H—T—P provides six graphic samples of the S's concept formation; three produced at one level of frustration and three at another level; a comparison of the two H—T—P sets, therefore, offers diagnostic and prognostic advantages. In effect, the H—T—P provides a miniature longitudinal study in psychological time. Empirical evidence supports the postulate that defense mechanisms, attitudes, etc., which are exhibited in the *achromatic* drawings and repeated in the chromatic drawings may be presumed to be more *basic* to the personality than characteristics which are not so repeated. If the characteristics shown in the achromatic series

are accentuated in the chromatic series, there is an even greater likelihood that they are well-ingrained in the personality. Wnere the character. istics exhibited in the *achromatic* series are not repeated or exaggerated in the *chromatic,* the assumption is that they represent a facade.

(4) The H–T–P provides the S with an opportunity, as he draws, to indicate *positively* or *negatively,* that a given detail, detail-complex, or method of presentation, is of significance to him. This does not necessarily aid in the interpretation but it does indicate that consciously, subconsciously, or unconsciously the S is disturbed by what the detail or detail-complex, or method of presentation represents for him actually or symbolically. And it is the S, not the examiner, who makes this determination.

(5) The drawings provide a relatively rare thing: a tangible and permanent sample of the S's behavior the recording of which is free from distortion by the examiner. This is of great importance in longitudinal studies.

(6) The H–T–P measures functional intelligence in a setting deliberately designed to be emotion-arousing; a setting in which the non-intellective factors within the personality,   which play important roles in the determination of the level of efficiency of function, have every opportunity to manifest themselves. In short, the attempt is to appraise intellectual efficiency as it functions in everyday life as a facet of the total personality. Perhaps the H–T–P's greatest contribution to the *intellectual* aspect of the clinical picture is that it affords the examiner an opportunity to compare the four H–T–P I.Q.s with I.Q.s derived from more stable and formal intelligence tests.. This can add greatly to the understanding of the S's level of intellectual function.

(7) The P–D–I phases provides the S with the opportunity to express verbally, directly and/or symbolically his feelings of environmenmental stresses and pressures; to indicate his grasp on reality; to associate concerning his two graphic phases each of which contains three specific drawings which bave been found to arouse associations at somewnat different levels of consciousness and to involve different areas of experience.

In the P–D–Is, the meaning verbally assigned to a qualitative point by the S may vary sharply from the examiner's interpretation or from the point's inherent symbolic meaning, and even from the S's previously assigned meaning. This does not invalidate any of the other interpretations, but it does serve to broaden the entire interpretative picture.

(8) Analysis of the content of the S's responses of the P–D–Is can be made with a relatively high degree of assurance, since the S is commenting on his own productions of three very familiar objects. Analysis of content serves to provide the examiner with answers to the important question, "Why does this S behave as his drawings indicate he be-

haves?'' Analysis of content places substance upon the skeletal framework of the personality.

(9)   The primitive method of expression (drawing) in the non-verbal phase allows disturbed and withdrawn Ss to demonstrate more effectively their existing potentials for more efficient function than do techniques which depend wholly upon verbalization.

(10)   Analysis of the S's organization of a concept contributes greatly to a more accurate evaluation of his "concept formation ability." In the H—T—P the S demonstrates to the examiner, as he draws his Houses, Trees, and Persons, his precise methods of organizing his concepts. The question, "How was each concept developed?" is answered by observing its creation.

(11) Both the quantitative and the qualitative systems of analysis are based largely upon analytic points whose maturational levels are rather well known.   This means that the patterning of the scores can be rich in diagnostic significance.

Experience indicates that the H—T—P can be used to good advantage in ways other than as a clinical diagnostic tool. For example it may used: (1) as an aid in establishing rapport with highly suspicious and/or negativistic Ss; (2) to take advantage of the "pencil-release" factor and to facilitate responses to general interrogation; (3) therapeutically* to produce association, either free, or partially or fully directed; (4) in industry to predict job success; (5) in cross-cultural studies, etc.

The H—T—P, however, as was said before, is not an all-inclusive psychological instrument. Clinicians have noted certain shortcomings: (1) the reluctance of adults, and particularly older adults, to attempt to draw; (2) the fact that as yet no specific quantitative or qualitative scoring points or patterns have proved to have universal or absolute meanings; (3) the fact that the influence of cultural differences on the productions of Houses, Trees and Persons has not been evaluated adequately; (4) the restriction of content to Houses, Trees, and Persons, and associations with those three concepts; (5) the fact that for many Ss the H—T—P is an emotional and rather disturbing experience; (6) the fact that administration and adequate evaluation of the H—T—P can be time-consuming and fatiguing to examiners as well as to Ss; (7) the lack of adequate statistical validation of the quantitative and qualitative points of analysis; (8) the lack of established norms for children. In the author's judgment, item 8 is the greatest of these shortcomings. It is his hope that norms for children will be developed in the near future.

Despite the lack of experimental statistical verification, and the above shortcomings, the H—T—P is warmly recommended to clinicians,

---

*   It is the author's belief that in the future the H—T—P will be increasingly employed as an adjunct to psychotherapy; that this will prove to be one of the most rewarding methods of employment of the technique.

whether clinical psychologist or psychiatrist, because its value as a technique for the appraisal of the total personality has been demonstrated rather convincingly in extensive clinical practice over the past twenty-five years.

Appendix A Illustrative Cases *

The ten following cases were in the original H−T−P Manual; at that time only achromatic drawings were sought. It is recommended that the student (and the experienced clinician who feels the need of a refresher course in the H−T−P) go over these cases carefully; the quantitative and the qualitative analyses are presented in detail and at considerable depth.

These cases represent as many diffierent syndromes as it is possible to present in the space available; they illustrate most of the quantitative and qualitative scoring points; the only major approaches missing from the present orthodox H−T−P are: (1) the chromatic drawings and the chromatic P−D−I; (2) the analysis of the S's use of color; (3) the comparison of the achromatic and the chromatic sets. These ten cases are not atypical of what the examiner can reasonably expect to derive from an H−T−P Protocol; more extreme examples could have been used.

In each case there is given, in addition to the drawings, (1) a brief biographical sketch; (2) the quantitative scoring, point by point, and a summary of the quantitative scores; (3) the main qualitative scoring points with the interpretation in each point following it in parentheses** (the interpretation in each instance is the one believed to be justified best on the basis of all known concerning the S); (4) a summary containing a discussion of the quantitative and the qualitative analyses, and the final impression.

The space available allows only the presentation of brief extracts from each P−D−I. The absence of the full P−D−I is *not* to be construed as indicating its lack of diagnostic value.

In the discussion of certain of the cases, diagnostic patterns will be suggested. The reader should view these with great caution, however, for: (1) no score pattern has been found to be presented by all patients of a specific diagnostic category; (2) whenever the drawings of Ss in the same classification-diagnosis have been analyzed carefully, marked differences have been discovered. It is the author's belief that score patterns always should be regarded as aiding diagnosis, not as providing it.

---

* For Case 7 the author is indebted to Mrs: Katherine Wilcox, then Chief Psychologist, Traverse City State Hospital, Michigan. Cases 5 and 9 first were reported in less detailed fashion by Miss Selma Landisberg, and Case 10 by Miss Catherine Hatley..

** To conserve space, the probable degree of deviation of each point is indicated by the letter P and a number. P1 = pathoformic; P2 = pathological; P3 = pathognomonic.

Case 1. K. N.

History

K. N., a 26-year-old white, male, native Virginian, came to one of the Colony's mental hygiene clinics in 1946. Although he was a high school graduate with a Wechsler-Bellevue Form I, full I.Q. of 121, he had never maintained himself much above a marginal economic level until shortly before this examination when he began to sell life insurance. Once the threat of a supervisor, presumably a father substitute, was removed, Mr. N. did well.

Although he was married, he had never made a satisfactory sexual adjustment, attributing this to his wife's physical incapacity.

He complained of chronic fatigue, diffuse anxiety, low frustration and satiation thresholds, and many minor somatic complaints. On psychological examination it was found that he had become prone to seek in phantasy the satisfactions denied him in reality.

See Figure 10. The quantitative scoring is shown in Figure 1 on page 39, q. v.

QUALITATIVE ANALYSIS

I. Details

House: (1) There is no chimney ⌈this omission, which cannot be explained on the grounds of intellectual inferiority, suggests (a) a lack of warmth in the home, P2, (b) difficulty in dealing with a male sex symbol, P2̄⌉. (2) The steps are of inferior quality ⌈the S is somewhat inaccessible, P1̄⌉. (3) A bar is drawn across the porch ⌈relative inaccessibility, P1; rejection of the House as an unpleasant dwelling of both the past and the present, P2̄⌉. (4) The walkway is incomplete, tentative only ⌈relative inaccessibility, P1̄⌉. (5) Two trees and a shrub are drawn beside the House ⌈they represent symbolically and actually, from left to right, the patient's father, brother, and mother. The mother is the farthest away, P2̄⌉. (6) The windows were drawn in an unusual sequence; the second from the left in the second story was drawn last ⌈strongly unpleasant associations resulted first in a temporary refusal to portray this room, and then in its devaluation when it was drawn, P2̄⌉; this room's window has bar-like window panes ⌈S felt imprisoned in it, P2̄⌉.

Tree: (1) Two scars are drawn on the trunk ⌈for *Mr. N.* the scar nearest the trunk's base symbolized the death of a playmate when Mr. N. was four; the scar farther up the trunk symbolized the psychic trauma which he experienced at 15 years of age when his brother died, P2̄⌉. (2) There is a prominent but not emphasized baseline ⌈basic insecurity, P1̄⌉.

Person: (1) The mouth and the cigar are emphasized ⌈strong oral preoc-

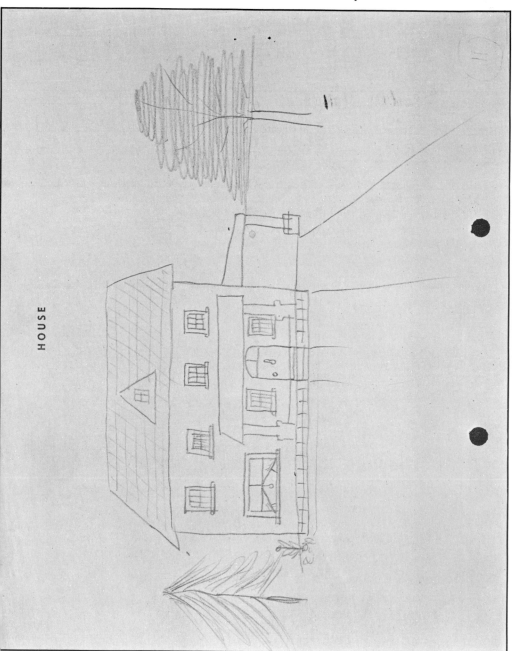

Figure 10

TREE

Figure 10

PERSON

Figure 10

cupation, P2]. (2) The ornamental clothing details are emphasized [narcissistic self-contemplation with compensatory self-adornment, P1]. (3) The nose, the cigar, and the tie, all believed to be phallic substitute objects, are emphasized [sexual maladjustment, P2].

II.   Proportion

Tree: The Tree is rather large compared to size of the page [S feels constricted by and in his environment, P2].

III.   Perspective

House: The House is placed toward the upper left corner [immature reaction to home, P1].

Tree: (1) The Tree is placed somewhat "up" on the page [mild feelings of striving, P1]. (2) It leans toward the right [the S attempts to suppress the past, with concomitant mild over-evaluation of the future as a satisfaction source, P1; the S feels unable to obtain emotional satisfaction in his environment, P2].

Person: (1) The Person is almost centered on the page [rigidity and basic insecurity in psycho-social situations, P2]. (2) The Person's movement is a startle reaction at the sight of passing girls, so Mr. N later explained [sexual maladjustment, P2].

IV.   Comments

A.   Drawing Phase.
        Tree: After producing the branches, Mr. N. remarked, "I'm more interested in dead trees than I am in live ones; is that O.K.?" [P2. He recognizes the morbidity of his interest, which may also indicate mild self-destructive tendencies].

        Person: Before drawing his Person, he asked, "The whole Person? Should it be a likeness of a living person or the drawing is the point? I have a special character I like to fool with." He then remarked that he had drawn this Person many times before, but never below the waist [indecisiveness and sexual conflict, P2. The disturbing pelvis area had been avoided heretofore].

B.   Post-Drawing.
        Tree: (1) Mr. N. stated that his Tree appeared to be more femi-

nine than masculine, made him think of his mother dead, in effect, since she deserted her family when Mr. N. was 9 years old ⌈need for maternal succorance, P$\bar{1}$⌉. (2) Mr. N. first stated that his Tree was dead ⌈strong feelings of inadequacy, with depression, P$\bar{2}$⌉; but later, he amended this to say that the Tree was living, but was neither healthy nor strong ⌈he is able to view the future as not completely bad, P$\bar{1}$⌋.

Person: In response to, "How does he feel?" Mr. N. said, "He should feel good, for he's supposed to be the slap-happy type," ⌈rejection of present state, P$\bar{2}$⌉.

V. Content

House: In this House he and his brother spent an unhappy time in their early childhood after their mother had deserted them, and their father had left to seek work ⌈the negative valence is strong, P$\bar{2}$⌉.

Tree: The Tree was in the yard of a house in which Mr. N. had had pleasant experiences ⌈a wish to return to a dependent, responsibility-free childhood role, P$\bar{1}$⌉.

Person: (1) The caricature is " 'Oscar', a drug store cowboy, who is a dope" ⌈ego-inflation by devaluation of another figure, P$\bar{1}$⌉. (2)   Oscar stands watching the girls go by, "It's all in his head" ⌈sexual inadequacy, with voyeuristic components, P$\bar{2}$⌉. (3) Oscar is, "Daydreaming like me - I'd be standing on the corner wondering how my wife was; what was going on at home" ⌈anxiety concerning his marital relationships, P1; phantasy as a source of satisfaction, P$\bar{1}$⌉.

Summary

Quantitative: The H—T—P Raw G I.Q. is 107, the Net Weighted Score I.Q. is 123; the former represents Mr. N's present functional level, the latter is a potential which he may ultimately realize ⌈his Wechsler-Bellevue I.Q. is 12$\bar{1}$⌉. The excessive number of detail items used suggests strong overt concern with the superficial aspects of everyday living and with what others think of him. The unusually high number of factors used for the House indicates that presumably his greatest source of difficulty is his present unsatisfactory marital adjustment.

Qualitative: The S exhibits: (1) severe sexual maladjustment producing painful anxiety; (2) a tendency to avoid interpersonal relationships whenever possible; to act in a rigid, indecisive manner in unavoidable relationships; (3) major needs for security, affection, masculinity, achievement, and autonomy; (4) a feeling that his environment is cold, constrictive, and non-satisfying; that he is inadequate to cope with it; (5) attempts to suppress the past with concomitant over-evaluation of the future as the source of satisfaction; (6) a tendency to seek satisfaction in phantasy.

Impression: Psychoneurosis, mixed type; present intellectual function average; potential function above average to superior. The prognosis for improvement is reasonably good. Psychiatric treatment is strongly recommended.

Case 2. M. H.
History

Mrs. M. H. was born 35 years ago in a rural county of Virginia, the fourth of seven children. Her economic and social background was lower middle class. The family history was negative for mental disease and deficiency.

She completed high school, without failing a course and in the average period of time, then entered a nurses' training course in a Metropolitan Hospital. She stopped after four months of probationary work to marry a cab driver who had been married and divorced once before. After marriage she worked as a sales clerk in several drug stores.

Her marital life was stormy. To begin with, she renounced her family's religion (Primitive Baptist) to join her husband's church (Roman Catholic). Her husband, described by her as a sort of Norse God in appearance, was flagrantly and frequently unfaithful. She wanted children; he did not. She had two miscarriages and to her great disappointment never gave birth to a living child. Three years ago she divorced her husband on the grounds of adultery. Since then, whenever he comes to see her, which is frequently, she becomes very much upset because she still is strongly attracted to him.

Three days before the H–T–P was administered, her husband visited her and urged her to run off with him; this visit came just when Mrs. H. had almost decided to marry someone else. That night she took an overdose of phenobarbital, but under circumstances which made it almost certain that she would be discovered before death could occur.

A psychological examination was requested by her psychiatrist who wished to have a report on her personality structure and dynamics.

See Figure 11.

QUALITATIVE ANALYSIS
I. Details

House: (1) The chimney, an essential detail, although drawn in several

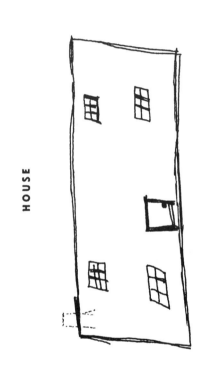

HOUSE

Figure 11

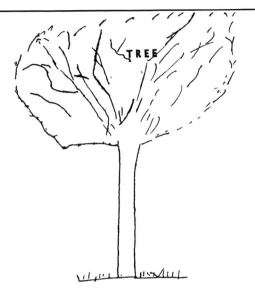

TREE

Figure 11

PERSON

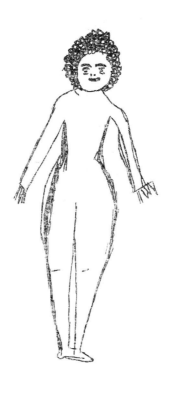

Figure 11

Case 2. M.H.

Quantitative Scoring

Name: *Mrs. M.H.*   Date: *1946*   Examiner: *JNB*

Sex: *Female*   Age: *32*   Occupation: *Psych. Aide*   Marital Status: *Divorced*

HOUSE	TREE	PERSON	RECAPITULATION		
Details	Details	Details	Raw:	D __ 14 A __ 25 S __ 2	
100 (2)__D2 102 ____ D2 107 (2) __ A2 113 (2) __ A2	203 (4)___A3 204 (5)___ A3 205 (5) __ A3 206 (5) __ A3 207 (1)__ D1 208 (1)__ S1	300 II(b)_A3 301 (4) __A1 305 (2) __ A2 306 (3) __ A1 307 (4) __ A1 308 (2) __ A1 311 (4) __ D2 314 (1) __ S1 315 (4) __ A1 316 (1) __ D2		Score I. Q. % Raw G:_____ 66_____ 81 Net Weighted:_____ 31_____ 82 Weighted: Good: 55_____ 86 Flaw: 24_____ 75	
			Details:	$\frac{15}{5}$	D.Av to Av. D. Av.
Proportion	Proportion	Proportion			
119 II (b)_A2	209 II__ A2 211 I __ A2 212 (3)__ A1	318 (2)___A1 319 (2)__ A1 321 (2)__ A2 323 II (b) A1 323 III (c) A2 323 IV (b) D1	Proportion:	$\frac{9}{1}$	D.Av to Av. Av.
			Perspective:	$\frac{3}{8}$	Imb. to Mor. Imb.
			House:	$\frac{3}{3}$	Imb. Bord.
Perspective	Perspective	Perspective			
129 III__D1	215 (3)__ A3 216 I __ D2 216 II __D1 216 V (a)_D1 217_____D1	324 (4)___A3 326 (1)(b) A1 327 (2)__D1 329 II (a) D1 333 _____ D1	Tree:	$\frac{9}{5}$	Sup. Imb.
			Person:	$\frac{15}{6}$	D. Av. D.Av. to Av.

Figure 11

positions, finally was erased ⎡sexual conflict, P2⎤. (2) There is pathoformic reinforcement of the containing lines ⎡she finds it difficult to maintain control in intrafamilial situations, P1⎤.

Person: (1) Although the Person is presented full-face and nude, no sexual characteristics are shown ⎡sexual conflict and feeling of helpless exposure, P2⎤. The detail sequence is frankly pathological with the legs and feet drawn first, then the trunk; and the facial characteristics last of all ⎡strong body conflict; marked reluctance to identify, P3⎤. (3) There is marked overemphasis of the trunk, thigh and leg lines ⎡she is acutely aware of her sensual drives which she restrains with difficulty and which produce strong guilt feelings, P2⎤.

II.   Proportion

House: There is an unusual proportional disparity between the vertical and horizontal measurements in favor of the latter ⎡"home" has great temporal meaning in the psychological field; "home" is a source of elemental satisfaction, P2⎤.

III.   Perspective

House: Facade presentation ⎡a desire to suppress expression of true feeling, P1⎤.

Tree: (1) The Tree is paper-chopped at the right top ⎡she has a tendency to seek future satisfaction in phantasy, P2⎤. (2) The use of implication comes close to being contaminated ⎡this indicates an inability to plan logically and symbolizes her feeling of disorganization P1⎤ .

Person: (1) The feet are in an unusual positional relationship ⎡she feels that she must exert a conscious effort to "hold herself down, P2⎤ .

General: All three wholes are (1) "centered" on the page from a lateral standpoint ⎡generalized rigidity and tension, P1⎤; (2) above the center on the vertical axis ⎡feelings of futile striving, P2⎤.

IV.   Time

House: (1) The time consumption of 6':35" is pathoformic ⎡"home" is an area of conflict, P1-P2⎤. (2) There was a pathological intra-whole pause for the chimney ⎡sexual conflict, P2⎤.

Person: (1) The time consumption of 6':48" is pathoformic ⎡intra-personal and inter-personal conflict, P1-P2̄⌉, (2) There was an intra-whole pause prior to drawing the facial characteristics ⌈reluctance to produce a self-portrait, P1̄⌉.

V.   Line Quality

General: Tne line quality vacillated markedly from time to time in each whole ⌈generalized indecision and ambivalence, P2̄⌉.

VI.   Criticality

House: The erasure for the chimney was strongly pathological ⌈severe conflict is aroused by the male sex symbol, P3̄⌉ .

General: For each whole there was occasional erasure, but little was corrective ⌈her flaw recognition bespeaks a fair basic intellectual capacity, but her inability to improve indicates a presently depressed function, P2̄⌉.

VII.   Attitude

General: A progressive tendency toward abandonism was exhibited ⌈pathoformic fatigability and increasing negativism, P1̄⌉.

VIII.   Drive

General: Quick withdrawal from the task situation followed the completion of each whole ⌈pathoformic aprosexia, P1̄⌉ .

IX.   Comments

A.   Drawing Phase
   House: (1) Before drawing the chimney she remarked that the House looked like a jail ⌈affection for her husband binds her, P1̄⌉. (2) Immediately after rejecting the chimney, she said that the House did not look right, looked more like a barn than a house ⌈barns lack warmth; her domestic role in many respects resembled that of a domestic animal, P1̄⌉.
   Tree: Before drawing the branch structure, she commented upon the Tree's unfruitfulness ⌈her pseudo-sterility has produced strong feelings of inadequacy, P1̄⌉.
   Person: While drawing the facial characteristics she commented, "She looks like she is dead" ⌈elsewhere she stated that she would almost rather be dead than lose her husband, but that if she were to return to him, she might as well be dead, P2̄⌉.

B.   P–D–I

Person: (1) She described the Person as coming out of the tub and waiting to put on clothes of which she did not have an adequate supply ⌈exposed, dependent, poor, P1--further interrogation revealed that Mrs. H. had engaged in ritualistic bathing, P2̄⌉ .

General: (1) Mrs. H. laughed occasionally while each whole was being discussed, but her laughter was mirthless ⌈tension-relieving attempts, P1̄⌉ . (2) Whenever sexual matters were discussed, she became restless and gave many overt signs of anxiety ⌈sexual conflict, P2̄⌉ . (3) Her grasp of reality was extremely poor ⌈her intellectual function was depressed by emotional factors, P2̄⌉ .

C.   Associations

General: There was strong perseveration upon the thema of herself, her present situation, her husband, her feelings of frustration at her inability to keep her husband and produce a child ⌈introspection is marked, P2̄⌉. A rather serious depression of mood pertained throughout ⌈although the suicidal attempt presumably was not genuine, she was definitely depressed, P2̄⌉.

X.   Concepts

House: The organization is poor; the House seems about to topple over ⌈clearly symbolizing her feeling of being overwhelmed by domestic problems, P2̄⌉.

Tree: First it was a deciduous shade Tree in the backyard of her paternal home ⌈longing to resume childhood status, P1̄⌉; then an evergreen in the forest ⌈abandoned, she rejects femininity, P2̄⌉.

Person: The identity was rigidly restricted to herself, ⌈P̄1̄⌉.

Summary

Quanitative: Mrs. H's H–T–P I.Q. scores are below what would be expected of a high school graduate, even of a rural high school. The disparity between the good and the flaw weighted scores, the disproportionate number of D2s, and the great scatter from whole to whole indicate the presence of a major disturbance. The sharp depression of the Perspective scores with simultaneous maintenance of relatively good Proportion and Details scores indicate that the disturbance probably is functional. The scores for the House suggest that her greatest sensitivity is in the intra-familial area, and most specifically in the marital area. The Tree scores seems to point to strong intra-personal conflicts.

Qualitative: Mrs. H. exhibits: (1) sexual maladjustment with a strong need for sexual satisfaction and concomitant strong feelings of guilt; (2) anxiety and depression; (3) almost overwhelming feelings of frustration at what she feels is futile striving for satisfaction; (4) a tendency to withdraw from reality; (5) obsessive-compulsive behavior; (6) strong needs for security and stability.

Impression: Psychoneurosis, reactive depression. Basic intellectual level, average; present functional level, low dull average.

Case 3. T. K.
History

T. K. is a 25-year-old man, the last born of five children, and the only boy. His youngest sister is 10 years his senior. His father and mother were poorly adjusted in their marital relationship, each was a dominant individual. The father, autocratic, rigid, and meticulous, apparently never made serious attempts to establish an affectional relationship with his son. The mother, who sought compensation for her marital dissatisfaction in an extremely active social life, alternately was over-protective and over-demanding.

T. K. suffered from nocturnal enuresis until he was 11 or 12 years of age. All his life, he has reacted to unpleasant situations with severe nausea.

T. K. was never a good student, though he is of above average intelligence; but he completed one year of college before finding academic work too demanding.

In his early adolescence, T. K. was discovered by his mother while he was masturbating with another boy. His first heterosexual experience was at 14 years of age when he went to a house of prostitution with other high school boys. His sexual relations with his wife (a person as stable as he is unstable, whom he married "on the rebound" two years ago) have never been satisfactory to him. He states that now, as always, he finds it impossible to experience satisfying coitus with a woman unless she is considerable older than he.

He was employed only a few months before enlisting in the Army. Although he was hospitalized several times for "nervous stomach" while he was in the service, he seems to have made a better adjustment to Army life than ever before or since, despite considerable rigorous combat duty. Shortly after his discharge from the Army, he was employed by a relative in a position which demanded more executive ability than he possessed.

Recently, he developed many obsessive fears, anxieties, and so-

matic complaints for which no physical basis was found.
See Figure 12.

QUALITATIVE ANALYSIS
I.   Details *

House: (1) There is marked emphasis on the containing lines [self-control is difficult, P2]. (2) The detail sequence is pathological: (a) the triangular roof over the right endwall was the seventh item drawn, but the wall below it was not drawn until almost all the main portion of House had been completed; (b) the last item drawn was the dilapidated steps to the far right [fear of the future, P2]. The progressive deterioration of the detail quality is noteworthy [increasing emotionality, presumably due to associations aroused by the House, brought a striking depression of functional efficiency, P2].

Tree: (1) The trunk has no baseline [T. K. shuns reality contact, P1]. (2) There was frequent reinforcement of the branches [generalized anxiety, P2].

Person: *(1)* The detail sequence was pathological: (a) he drew the eyebrows, but not the eyes until three detail items later [he is very sensitive about his mild strabismus, P2]. (b) the ears were the 26th item drawn [he is very reluctant to accept criticism, P2]. (2) There was excessive general reinforcement [marked indecision, P2]. (3) The left arm and hand occasioned difficulty [sexual guilt, P1]; the feet gave still more difficulty [he feels responsibility-bound, P2].

(Note: A further explanation of these detail difficulties is provided by T. K.'s P–D–I comments, q.v.)

III.   Perspective

House: (1) The House is paper-chopped at both sides [the temporal aspects of "home" clash sharply, P3]. (2) There is deep shading of the foundation to the right [he is anxious about the future stability of his present home, P2]. (3) The quality of the spatial relationships deteriorates to the back and to the right. [T. K. appears less adequate the farther he goes behind his facade and the greater the future, the unknown, is emphasized, P2].

Tree: (1) T. K. began to draw a deciduous Tree in meticulous fashion, but erased it quickly when he was told [after he had asked] that he could draw another type of Tree. He then drew a rigid, spike-like Tree using the

Figure 12

Figure 12

PERSON

Figure 12

Case 3. T. K.

Quantitative Scoring

Name: *T. K.*   Date: *1948*   Examiner: *JNB*

Sex: *Male*   Age: *25*   Occupation: *Executive*   Marital Status: *Married*

HOUSE	TREE	PERSON	RECAPITULATION
			D——10
Details	Details	Details	Raw: A——29
			S——10
100(6)——S1	201————S1	300 II(b)-A3	
101————S1	203 (1)——D1	301 (5)——A2	
103———— S1	204 (5)——A3	306 (3)——A2	
104 (3)——A3	205 (5)——A3	307 (4)——A1	Score I. Q.
106 (2)——S1	206 (5)——A3	308 (2)——A1	
107 (2)——A2		310 (3)——A3	% Raw G:————————79————————96
111 (2)—— S2		311 (5)——A2	Net Weighted:———— 96————————117
113 (2)—— A2		312 ———— A3	Weighted: Good: 108————————121
115———— S2		315 (4)——A1	Flaw: 12————————95
		316 (4)——A3	
			Details: 23/1 Ab. Av. / Ab. Av. to Sup.
Proportion	Proportion	Proportion	
119 III(b)A2	209 II———A2	318 (3)——S1	
	211 I———A2	319 (3)——A2	Proportion· 10/0 Superior / Superior
	212 (3)——A1	320 (2)——A2	
		323 II(b)-A1	
		323 III(c)A2	Perspective: 6/9 Average / Imbecile
		323 IV(d)A3	
Perspective	Perspective	Perspective	House: 11/7 Superior / Imbecile
127 (2)——S1	215 (3)——A3	324 (4)—— A3	
131 II——D1	216 V(c)-A3	326 (1)(d)S1	Tree: 9/1 Superior / Superior
D1, D1, D1		329 II(c)-A3	
131 III——D1		333–D1, D1	
132 I—— D1			Person: 19/2 Average / Ab. Av.
134 I——D2			

Figure 12

unshaded areas to indicate the branch structure: he then abandoned this approach and adopted his final plan ⌈marked general indecisiveness; sexual role conflict, P2⌉.

General: Each of the three wholes is slightly "down" on the page ⌈mild depression, P1⌉.

IV.   Time

House: The time consumption was 11' : 57". This was pathological ⌈T. K. exhibits over-concern about home, P2⌉.

V.   Line Quality

House: The motor control is surprisingly poor ⌈emotional factors presumably interfered, for he has no organic difficulty, P2⌉..

Tree: (1) There is deep shading of the trunk ⌈he feels basically inadequate, P1⌉. (2) The lines of the upper portion of the trunk and the branch structure are relatively faint ⌈indecision and mild free-floating anxiety, P1⌉.

General: There is marked vacillation throughout the three wholes ⌈many conflicts are aroused by the stimuli, P2⌉.

VI.   Criticality

House: (1) No less than five transparencies are shown: each porch pillar and porch roof⌈emotion produced a sharp diminution of intellectual efficiency, P2⌉. (2) Mr. K. cannot produce his House within the page's lateral margins ⌈an almost crippling temporal spread appears, P3⌉.

Tree: He made half-hearted erasures of his first two attempts to produce a Tree ⌈he stated later that he tends to follow the line of least resistance, P2⌉.

Person: The rather good attempt to show the hands by implication ⌈placing them in the pockets⌉is contaminated by the transparency of the left arm at the pocket's edge ⌈guilt over auto-erotic activities--see P−D−I comments, second association, for other explanation, P1⌉.

VII.   Attitude

General: Each of the three wholes produced defeatistic, then frankly abandonistic tendencies [T. K. is badly maladjusted, P2̄].

IX.   Comments

A.   Drawing Phase

House: T. K. announced quickly that he was drawing his own house in the country; then from time to time he made remarks that indicated growing feelings of frustration and impotence [he does not find challenge stimulating, P1̄].

Person: (1) His first comment made while he was drawing the periphery of the head was, "The cowboy is a person" [T. K. is snobbish; later spoke disparagingly of his wife's family's lack of social standing, P2̄]. (2) Shortly after beginning to draw the arms he remarked, "It must be a tendency to make a head and shoulders, because every time I drew one of these in school, that's as far as I got--head and shoulders" [sexual conflict--avoidance of the body, pelvis, etc.; P2]. (3) His last comment was, "It's a pretty good man, if I could put on the feet" [emphasizing his feeling of restricted mobility, P1̄].

B.   P–D–I

House: When he was asked whom he would like to have live with him in his House, he replied with deep emotion, "I'd rather not have anybody!" [He has never formed a lasting, mutually-sharing, affectional relationship, P2̄].

Tree: (1) In answer to T3 he said, "I'd say the Tree was 12 or 15 years old, though the trunk would look older" [he, too, looks older but acts like a 12- to 15-year-old, P1̄]. (2) In reply to T6, he said, "I believe it's a woman...You might say they (Trees) are tender, beautiful--I believe particularly all evergreens I'd think of as being female—I believe it's the long hair" ["long hair" meant *mother;* unresolved mother-fixation, P2̄].

Person: (1) When the examiner queried him directly concerning what *feet* might mean to him, M. K. countered, "Go home you mean? I *thought about my own*" [he returns to the parental home whenever opportunity allows, P1̄]. Then he digressed to discuss his marriage which he termed a "rebound" affair, vividly describing his anger when his fiancee jilted him. He remarked that he felt that his present home was a happy one, but added wryly that this feeling was without *foundation* (see Details!). (2) To P10, he replied with strong emotion, "I can see the same face," [The "face" was his father's in a coffin, P2̄]. (3) When he was questioned concerning his spontaneous comment about his Person's feet, he explained that recently he had been unable to attend a funeral after he had heard someone remark that the feet had had to be cut off the corpse to get it into the coffin; since then he has been unable to rid himself of this thought [obsessive thinking, P2]. The weather about the House was said to be spring-like, warm, sunshiny ["home" is a place of warmth]; the sun was shining about the Tree, but, "The Tree makes you think of snow" [fear of the future, loss of present center-of-stage-role in which he receives adulation from his wife and his doting sisters, P1]. The weather was cloudy in the picture of the Person [inter-personal relationships are difficult; he is unable to regard his business superiors as other than father-substitutes and this has been a serious handicap, P2].

C.   *Associations*
     Person: (1) His Person first reminded him of a brother-in-law whom he fears very much, [pseudo-brother rivalry, P2]. (2) Later he said, "I want to say Daddy- he had a deformed left arm" [unresolved Oedipus, P2]. Then he entered into a long spontaneous discussion arguing that his father was not his ideal as his sister insisted [attempt to assert independence, P1], that he wished that his father were alive, [guilt, P1] so that his father could provide him with financial assistance which would enable T. K. to trade cars more frequently [dependence, P1].

X.   *Concepts*

House: This is a recognizable reproduction of his own home [not the parental home]. T. K. complains bitterly and at length about its inadequacies, disparaging it by comparison with his paternal home [his longing to return to the irresponsible role of a child is patent, P2].

Tree: At one time the Tree is in the yard of his parents' home [past]. at still another time it is a Tree that he would move to his own yard [the temporal vacillation is marked, P2].

Person: The multiplicity of identities of the Person is pathological. The Person is (1) a stereotype from childhood [easy to draw]; (2) Tom Mix [a hero-figure; publicly prominent]; (3) a brother-in-law rival for a sister's affection]; (4) his Father [rival for his mother's affection]; (5) "It could be myself" [as a cowboy he could rid himself of responsibility, act out certain childhood phantasies, P2].

Summary

At examination T. K. exhibited many of the common and overt symptoms of stress such as restlessness, onychophagy, and the like. Obviously he had screwed up his courage to come to the examiner; he also obviously regretted having done this. T. K. spent much time attempting to convince the examiner that there was nothing wrong with him.

Quantitative: There is a great disparity between: (1) the Net Weighted Score I. Q. and the Per Cent Raw G I.Q. and between the Weighted Good I. Q. and the Weighted Flaw I. Q. which seems to indicate the depressing effect of his disturbance on his intellectual efficiency. Potentially, he is of above average to superior intelligence; but at this time he functions at a much lower level. Analysis of the raw factors shows that all but one of the D-factors are D1s, and at least half of them are due to his marked indecision. The depression of I. Q. score, therefore, does not seem irreversible.

There is a marked depression of the Perspective scores with a retention of high level Proportion and Details scores; this suggests that his disturbance is relatively mild and to be regarded as functional.

Of the scores for the three wholes, the scores for the House and the Person are most affected, suggesting that he has strong conflicts in the areas of home and inter-personal relationships, both specific and general.

Qualitative: The S exhibits: (1) an unresolved Oedipus Complex [with crippling after-effects] ; (2) an inability to establish fully responsible, sharing, affectional relationships; (3) over-concern about the psychological past and the future which has a deleterious effect on his functional efficiency in the psychological present; (4) generalized anxiety, indecisiveness, specific fears, obsessions, and somatic complaints all of which tend to restrict his activities greatly.

Impression: Psychoneurosis, mixed type,; basic intelligence, above average to superior; present functional level, average. Mr. K. essentially is an immature and inadequate individual. Psychiatric treatment is recommended but the patient's lack of desire to change may prove to be a serious obstacle to therapy.*

Case 4. S. Y.

Mr. S. Y. is a 28-year-old, unmarried white male; the second of two children. His mother separated from his father when S. Y. was 2 years old. However, the mother soon remarried, and happily.

S. Y. completed high school in the usual amount of time; followed this with 18 months in business college, where he performed well.

---

* In fact it did not. Mr. K. responded well to treatment and at present is doing well maritally, economically, and socially, and has matured in highly satisfactory fashion.

Until he entered the Army in 1941, he was said to have been quiet and friendly, mixing freely with men and women. However, shortly after his induction, he developed gastro-intestinal symptoms which led to his hospitalization and discharge. After he left the Army, he improved and functioned well for about two years. In 1946, he became seclusive, tense, nervous, and irritable. He refused to mix with other people; insisted on staying home, reading and listening to the radio. He slept poorly. Before long he complained that people were watching him and laughing at him. In February, 1946, he was insitutionalized after having been arrested on a charge of indecent exposure.

At examination he was found to be mildly depressed and paranoidal. He attributed most of his difficulty to a gonadal weakness. He exhibited a strong castration fear. He was convinced that a change was occurring in the shape of his face and head which made even the most casual observer recognize his sexual weakness. Much of his time in the hospital was spent gazing into a mirror.

The diagnosis was schizophrenia, mixed type.

After psychotherapy proved ineffective, 27 insulin shocks were administered followed by 13 grand mal electro-shocks, which produced at first a state of exaltation and excitement, but was soon followed by sufficient improvement to justify his discharge.

In February, 1948, he regressed markedly, exhibited symptomatology similar to that which had led to his hospitalization in 1946.

See Figure 13.

QUALITATIVE ANALYSIS
I.   Details

House: There is a pathological absence of essential details. Tnere are: (a) no doors and (b) no windows below the attic level [crippling reluctance to contact reality, P3]. (2) The detail sequence is pathoformic: the attic windows were the last items drawn [the attempt was to conceal the fact that phantasy is a satisfaction source, P1].

Tree: (1) The Tree was produced working from the top downward [this is a freer, but still a reluctant approach to reality, P1] with each detail on the left being followed immediately by its counterpart on the right [a great need for balance--such an emphasis on symmetry often is seen in the drawings of schizoid and obsessive-compulsive Ss--ambivalent temporal valence, P2]. (2) The one-dimensional roots were drawn spontaneously [a gross denial of reality in one of his intellectual level, P3]

Person: (1) Although the Person is shown full-face and nude, no genitalia are drawn [sexual conflict, feelings of impotence, P2]. (2) The ears

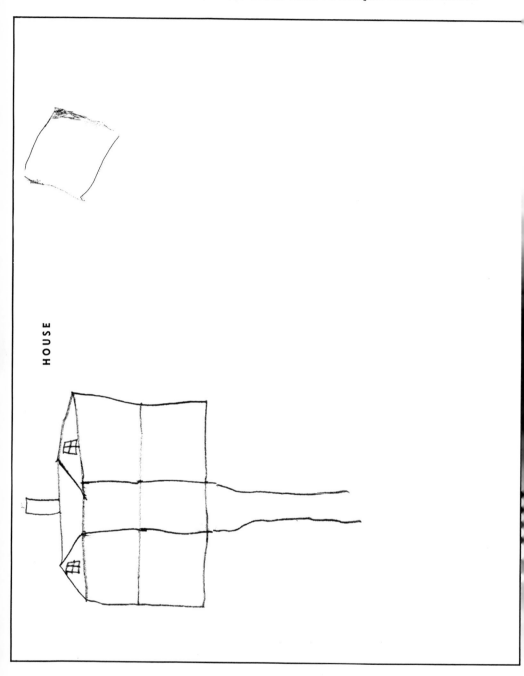

Figure 13

TREE

Figure 13

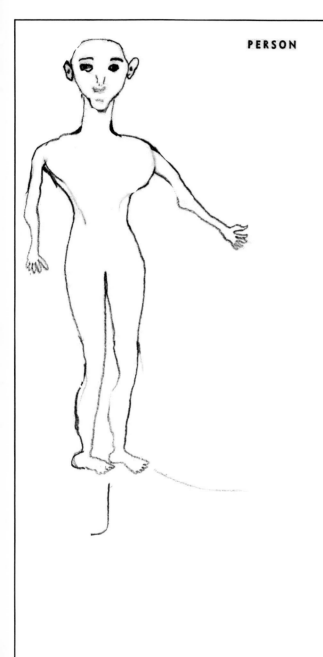

PERSON

Figure 13

Case 4. S. Y.

Quantitative Scoring

Name: *S. Y.*   Date: *1948*   Examiner: *S. L.*

Sex: *Male*   Age: *28*   Occupation: *None*   Marital Status: *Single*

HOUSE	TREE	PERSON	RECAPITULATION		
			Raw:	D.— 13 A— 24 S— 4	
Details	Details	Details			
106 (1)—D3	201——S1	300 II(b)-A3			
113 (2)—A2	203 (3)—A2	301 (4)—A1			
114—— S1	204 (2)—D1	303 (1)—S1		Score	I. Q.
	205 (2)—A1	306 (3)—A1			
	206 (1)—D1	307 (4)—A1	% Raw G: ———— 68 ———— 83		
		308 (2)—A1	Net Weighted: ——36—— 86		
		310 (3)—A3	Weighted: $\frac{\text{Good:}}{\text{Flaw:}}$ $\frac{59}{23}$ $\frac{90}{76}$		
		311 (5)—A2			
		312 ——— A3			
		315 (4)—A1			
		316 (1)—D2			
			Details:	$\frac{15}{4}$	D. Av. to Av. / Av.
Proportion	Proportion	Proportion			
119 II(a)-A1	209 II A2	318 (3)—S1	Proportion:	$\frac{10}{2}$	Av. / D. Av.
	211 I A2	319 (4)—A3			
	211 II(b) D1	320 (2)—A2	Perspective:	$\frac{3}{7}$	Imb. to Mor. / Imb.
	212 (3) A1	321 (2)—A2			
		323 II(b)-A1			
		323 III(c)A2			
		323 IV(b)D1	House:	$\frac{3}{3}$	Imb. / Bord.
Perspective	Perspective	Perspective	Tree:	$\frac{7}{6}$	Bord. / Imb.
123 I——D1	213——D2	324 (4)—A3			
127 (1)—D1	215 (1)—A1	326(1)(c)A2	Person:	$\frac{18}{4}$	Av. / Av.
	216 III—D1	329 II(a)-D1			
	216 V(a)-D1	332 I——D2			

Figure 13

were the 30th item drawn ⌈a denial of receptors of oral criticism--also possible hallucinatory scources, P2̄⌉. (3) There is over-emphasis of the eyes
⌈suspicious watchfulness, P2̄⌉ and of the head and neck ⌈graphic expression of his delusion, P3̄⌉.

II. Proportion

House: (1) This is not the malproportion of the "double perspective" of
mental deficiency, for here the size emphasis is placed on the endwalls
and not on the center wall ⌈the center symbolizes the self; the protective
endwalls symbolize the personality defences: this production also strongly
emphasizes the schizophrenic's temporal confusion, P2̄⌉. (2) The chimney
is over-emphasized ⌈sexual conflict and castration fear, P2̄⌉.

Tree: (1) All branches are one-dimensional ⌈satisfaction sources within
the environment are slight, P2̄⌉. (2) Tne roots are one-dimensional ⌈ele-
mental satisfaction sources are inadequate, too, P2̄⌉.

Person: The chin and the shoulders are overly masculine; the waistline
and the body curves overly feminine ⌈confused sexual role, P2̄⌉.

III. Perspective

House: The House, which was started in conventional three-dimensional
fashion, was carried through as a blueprint presentation, then completed
as 3-dimensional, ⌈P3̄⌉. This type of depiction vacillation has never yet
been seen in cases in which there was no organic deterioration.

Tree: The root structure is poorly organized ⌈basic instability and inadequacy, P2̄⌉.

Person: He had difficulty arriving at a final position for the left arm
⌈S. Y. is sinistral. The arm position may be hostile or friendly, P2̄⌉.

General: (1) All three wholes are in the upper left-hand corner of the
page ⌈generalized, well-developed regression, P2̄⌉. (2) Noteworthy is the
progressive--though not great--improvement from House to Person in quality, organization, etc. ⌈The House was an unfamiliar task for which he had
few cues; the Person was an easy task for this highly body-conscious S,
P1̄⌉.

IV.   Time

General: The time consumption was slightly excessive for all three wholes [S. Y. was reluctant throughout to commit himself, P1̅].

V.   *Line Quality*

General: Marked vacillation was seen throughout the three wholes [wide feeling tone fluctuation; generalized tension, P2̅].

VI.   *Criticality*

General: He was unable to complete the House correctly. He failed to recognize the incongruity of the ground transparency for his Tree [his present disorder has greatly diminished his intellectual efficiency, P3̅].

VII.   *Attitude*

General: Reluctant acceptance throughout [P1̅].

IX.   *Comments*

A: Drawing Phase
   House: After drawing the roof, the walls, and the chimney, he remarked, "I can get the outside, but how do you get the inside?" [profound feelings of impotence and reality confusion, P3̅].

   Tree: He complained that he knew how a Tree looked, but he simply could not reproduce one [organic impotence, P2̅].

   Person: After drawing the shoulders, he paused a moment and remarked, "Now I don't know whether to make a man or a woman" [confused sexual role, P2̅].

B.   Post-Drawing
   House: (1) He stated he preferred to live by himself [witndrawal, P1̅]. (2) His reply to H11 was, "There is no persecution angle or anything like that" [affirming the strongly suspected presence of deep feelings of persecution, P2̅].

   Tree: (1) When he was asked whether the Tree made him think man or a woman, he replied, "A person? It could be any of the three" [masculine, feminine or neuter!--confused sexual role plus probable castration fear, P3̅]. (2) When he was asked whether or not the Tree was healthy and strong, he said, "It could be good or rotten--*I'm no tree*--naturally this points to me ⌈extreme self-reference, P3⌉. (3) He said that the Tree had died recently at the top ⌈symbolizing his present illness, P11⌉.

Person: (1) In reply to P1, he stated, "A man, a woman, a girl, or a boy" ⌈confused sexual role, P3⌉. (2) In answer to P6, he commented, "He's facing this way, and might be wanting to go that way. He could be stretching his hand out to open the door to go outside, He might be hesitating whether to go outside or remain, he might be undecided, in a state of indecision" ⌈P2-a pathetic but clear portrait of himself⌉. (3) When he was asked at what the Person might be looking, he replied, "He might be casting his eye back inside himself" ⌈denial of objective reality, plus narcissistic self-contemplation, P3⌉ In reply to P7, he stated, "Just a drawing, no thought process" ⌈organic concreteness, P1⌉.

C.   *Associations*

House: In partial answer to H9, he replied, "I don't know whether it makes me feel pleasant or unpleasant" ⌈everything seems strange, P2⌉.

General: (1) The feeling tone essentially was bland, things might be good, might be bad; might be pleasant, might be unpleasant; might be happy, might be unhappy ⌈the divorce of affect and cognition seems to be about complete, P3⌉. (2) Several of his associations he immediately termed unreasonable,   but he could offer no improvement ⌈organic impotence, P2⌉.

X.   *Concepts*

House: Concerning his House, he said, "When I was drawing, I had a vague impression of my home, maybe I was kidding myself" ⌈he is not really sure of anything, P2⌉.

Tree: The Tree is an oak, located any place in the world ⌈again he cannot decide, P2⌉.

Person: The Person is himself, no one else ⌈he is certain of this--he is too self-engrossed to conceive of any other identity, P2⌉.

Summary

Quantitative: His Time Appreciation Test age-corrected I. Q. was 115. His Rorschach showed that he had a potential of high average. The H—T—P I. Q. scores are definitely lower than would be expected for one of his educational achievement. They suggest a marked depression of intellectual efficiency of long standing. The disparity between the Good scores and the Flaw scores implies a recent further diminution in function. The great depression of the Perspective scores indicates the presence of a serious functional disturbance.

The House strongly points to the presence of an organic component; and the Tree offers some support to this assumption. Since the Person is much superior to the House or Tree, a "recovery" capacity is implied which is certainly not suggested by the House. And such a "recovery" capacity would not be present if the organic component were great. The assumption, therefore, is that Mr. Y has a functional disturbance of major proportions, complicated by mild organic deterioration.

Qualitative: The organic signs are the: (1) marked disorganization of the House with the two-plane effect; (2) great scatter of the quality of the factors comprising the scores for the Tree; (3) many verbal expressions of impotence.

The schizoid signs are (1) the very faulty reality grasp; (2) the somatic delusions; (3) a strong tendency toward withdrawal from reality with emphasis upon phantasy as a satisfaction source; (4) the many expressions of blandness of affect (contrasting sharply with the strong anxiety expressed in the drawings); (5) his strong sexual conflict; (6) his intra-personal disorganization; and (7) his paranoid hyper-sensitivity.

Impression: Schizophrenia, mixed type, with mild organic deterioration [probably the result of shock therapy] . Hospitalization is recommended. The patient's marked regression after shock therapy implies that the prognosis is very poor.

Case 5.   S. E.

History

Miss S. E. is 19 years old. She comes from a home of relatively high eduational, economic, and social standing. She is the oldest of four children; the others are said to be "normal." Miss E. is reported to have had a birth injury which left her with a mild spasticity which affects all extremities but is most pronounced on the left side. When she was eight years old, it was evident that she was not of average intelligence; and when she showed signs of strong sibling rivalry, she was sent to a private training school. Her performance on psychological tests at this school indicated that she was to be regarded as a mental defective of the moron level. When she was 15 years old, she became so unmanageable that she was returned home. In 1947, since she no longer could be controlled at home, she was sent to the Colony.

Immediately after her admission, she went into an acute psychotic episode, refused to respond to verbal interrogation of any sort, and rejected all formal psychological examination except the drawing phase of the H—T—P. Her behavior during the first year of institutionalization was that of a "typical" catatonic schizophrenic: she was assaultive and highly negativistic at times, and often had to be secluded for the protection of of herself and others.

This case is presented because: (1) it indicates the possibility of deriving useful diagnostic information from a very disturbed, highly negativistic person; (2) her drawings in quality closely resemble those of the typical "back ward" schizophrenic.

See Figure 14.

QUALITATIVE ANALYSIS
I.   Details

House: (1) The chimney is missing [sexual maladjustment and/or strong feeling of hostility toward family, P2]. (2) The window lacks panes [hostility, P1].

Person: Many essential details are lacking; facial characteristics, trunk, etc. [denial of sensory modes of contact, and possibly self-destructive tendencies, P3].

General: (1) The last item drawn for each whole was a "basic contact item." for the House, the door; for the Tree, the baseline of the trunk; for the Person, the feet [a generalized marked reluctance to make contact with reality, P2]. (2) There is a progressive diminution of reality contact with greater and greater hostility expressed [the negativism increases in strength almost to frank rejection, P3].

II.   Proportion

General: Each whole is tiny in comparison to the form page size [very strong feelings of inadequacy; very strong withdrawal tendencies, P3].

House: The House appears to be about to collapse [her "home" situation is lost--hostile reaction formation, rejection of home, P3].

Tree: White space is used to indicate details by implication [hostility, P1].

Person: (1) There is absolute symmetry of the few details shown [insecurity, P2]. (2) The feet point in opposite directions [ambivalent immobil-

HOUSE

Figure 14

TREE

Figure 14

PERSON

Figure 14

Case 5. S. E.

Quantitative Scoring

Name: *S. E.* Date: *1947* Examiner: *S. L.*

Sex: *Female* Age: *19* Occupation: *None* Marital Status: *Single*

HOUSE	TREE	PERSON	RECAPITULATION		
				D— 21	
Details	Details	Details	Raw:	A — 9	
				S — 0	
100 (3)—A1	203 (3)—A2	300 I (a)_D3			
102____D2	204 (4)__A2	301 (1)__D3			
108____D1	205 (4)__A2	302 (1)__D3			
113 (2)__A2	206 (3)__A2	304 (1)_D1		Score	I. Q.
		305 (1)_D2			
		306 (1)—D2	% Raw G:	30 ———43	
		307 (1)_D3	Net Weighted:	(−45) ——— 35	
		308 (1)—D1	Weighted: Good:	16 ———34	
		309 (3)_D2	Flaw:	61 ———34	
		311 (1)_D3			
		313 (3)_D2			
		315 (2)_D2			
		316 (1)—D2	Details:	$\frac{6}{15}$	Imb. / Imb.
Proportion	Proportion	Proportion	Proportion:	$\frac{3}{2}$	Imb. / D. Av.
119 II(a)-A1	209 II__A2	319 (1)—D1			
	211 I___ A2		Perspective:	$\frac{0}{4}$	Imb. / Av.
	212 (1)__D2				
Perspective	Perspective	Perspective			
No Score	216 V(a)_D1	325 (1)_D2	House:	$\frac{3}{2}$	Imb. / Ab. Av.
		329 II(a)_D1			
		332 I___ D2	Tree:	$\frac{6}{2}$	Mor. to Bord. / D. Av. to Av.
			Person:	$\frac{0}{17}$	Imb. / Imb.

Figure 14

ity, P$\overline{2}$]. (3) The arms are stretched out receptively [need for affection, protection, etc., P$\overline{2}$].

General: (1) All three wholes are located in the extreme upper left corner of the page [marked regression, P$\overline{3}$]. (2) All three wholes appear to be far distant from the observer [she is almost inaccessible, P$\overline{3}$].

IV.   Time

General: The time consumption for the House, 1':30", and for the Tree, 49" was excessive [P$\overline{2}$]; that for the Person, 9':46", was highly pathological [P$\overline{3}$]. Her ever-increasing negativism was accentuated greatly by the Person.

V.   Line Quality

House: Motor control for the House was poor [apparently caused by the extreme emotionality aroused by association with her home, P$\overline{2}$].

IX.   Comments

General: Not only did she refrain from making spontaneous comments during the drawing phase, but she flatly refused to respond to the P—D—I [functional mutism, in effect, P$\overline{3}$].

X.   Concepts

General: Since she would not respond to questioning, her drawings can only be appraised as self-portraits: as such, they reveal an acutely inaccessible, hostile, negativistic individual, who feels wholly inadequate to cope with her environment, [P$\overline{3}$].

Summary

Quantitative: The H—T—P scores at first glance might seem to indicate that her intelligence level is that of an imbecile. However, Miss E. used only 30 factors in producing her House, Tree, and Person, whereas the average well-adjusted imbecile presents about 38. The relatively high calibre of the flaw scores for Proportion and Perspective tends to rule out simple mental deficiency. The scatter of the raw factor quality ranges from imbecile to average, strongly indicating the presence of a major personality disorder. In short, it is to be assumed that Miss E's expression is being seriously interfered with and her scores do not necessarily represent her basic intelligence level. This supposition is supported by the fact that the House and the Tree are qualitatively well above the imbecile level. The depression of the scores for Perspective, Proportion, and Details suggests that she is acutely disturbed. Her drawings reveal an organizational ability which indicates that the major operating factor is functional, though a minor organic component also may be present. It is suspected that when Miss E. is not acutely disturbed, her intellectual potential is borderline ⌊based on her level of concept formation⌋.

Qualitative: Miss E. exhibits: (1) great negativism; (2) functional mutism; (3) intense hostility ⌊some directed at herself⌋; (4) paranoid hypersensitivity; (5) schizophrenic denial of and withdrawal from reality.

Impression: Schizophrenia, catatonic type, with possible high grade mental deficiency of the exogeneous ⌊natal trauma⌋ type.

Case 6. S. G.

History

This 40-year-old, white, unmarried male is the fourth of seven children; the others are said to be "normal". A native Virginian, he had entered the Colony for the second time prior to administration of this H–T–P. Between his two colonizations, he had twice received treatment for alcoholism at the Western State Hospital. His environment, both socially and economically,   was superior. However, his over-indulgent and protective mother thwarted all the efforts of his father to prepare S. G. for an adequate adult role.

He graduated from high school in the usual period of time and attended the University of Virginia for several semesters. He never has, even remotely, been self-supporting. He says, "I was born a gentleman-- only a fool would work."

Since he was 6 years of age, when presumably he had an encephalitis, he has become progressively more and more asocial. He reacted violently to the death of his mother 16 years ago, and after he had threatened to kill his father, he was institutionalized.

In recent years he has been consistently alcoholic outside of an institution. Organic deterioration seems to have taken place.

See Figure 15.

QUALITATIVE ANALYSIS

I.   Details

House: (1) The windows lack panes ⌊indicative of hostility and possible

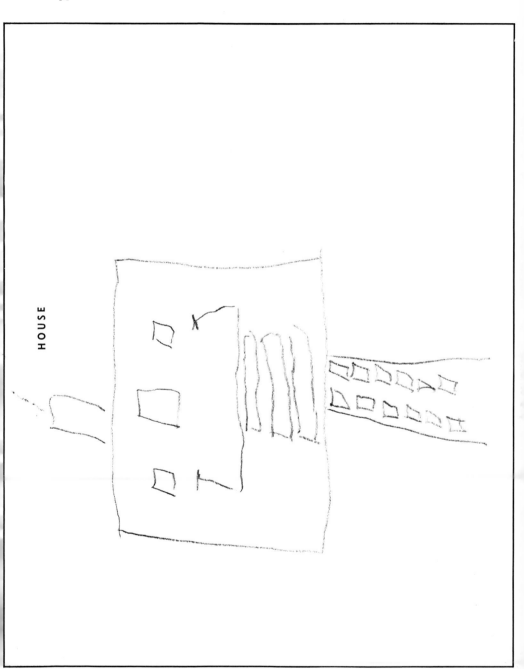

Figure 15

TREE

Elberta

Figure 15

PERSON

Figure 15

Case 6. S. G.

Quantitative Scoring

Name: *S. G.*   Date: *1947*   Examiner: *JNB*

Sex: *Male*   Age: *40*   Occupation: *None*   Marital Status: *Single*

HOUSE	TREE	PERSON	RECAPITULATION		
Details	Details	Details	Raw:	D— 26 A—12 S—2	
100 (2)—D2	200——— D2	300 II(a)_A1			
108——— D1	203 (1)—D1	301 (3)—D1			
112 (1)—D1	204 (2)—D1	305 (2)—A2		Score	I. Q.
113 (2)—A2	205 (2)—A1	306 (1)—D2			
114——— S1	206 (4)—A2	307 (2)—D2	% Raw G:	35 ———46	
		308 (1)—D1	Net Weighted:	(−23) ———46	
		309 (3)—D2	Weighted:	Good: 31———58	
		311 (3)—D1		Flaw: 54———42	
		313 (3)— D2			
		316 (1)—D2			
Proportion	Proportion	Proportion	Details:	6/14	Imb./Imb.
119 II(b)_A2	212 (3)—A1	318 (1)—D1	Proportion:	4/4	Imb./Imb.
		319 (4)—A3			
		323 I(a)_D2			
		323 II(c)_A2	Perspective:	4/8	Mor./Imb.
		323 III(a)D2			
		323 IV(a)D2			
Perspective	Perspective	Perspective	House:	4/8	Mor./Imb.
125 II(a)_D2	215 (1)— A1	326(1)(a)D1			
129 III— D1	216 V(a)_D1	327 (1)— D2	Tree:	4/4	Mor./Mor.
131 III— D1		329 II(c)_A3			
132 II— D1		331——— S1	Person:	6/14	Imb./Imb.
133——— D3					
134 IV— A3					

Figure 15

oral and/or anal eroticism, P$\overline{2}$]. (2) The door and the steps were the last items drawn [S. G. determines the terms on which he will make contact, P$\overline{1}$].

Tree: (1) There is a deeply shaded area on top of the left lower branch [on being questioned, he said that this symbolized the death of his mother, P$\overline{2}$].

Person: (1) The mouth and the arms were the last items drawn [the hostility-expressing modes were suppressed until last, P$\overline{1}$]. The Person is a "stick man" [the S aggresses against the examiner and mankind in general, P$\overline{2}$].

II.   Proportion

House: The door and the windows are too small relative to the wall in which they appear [inaccessibility and lack of interest in others, P$\overline{2}$].

Tree: The Tree is small in comparison to the page's size [this symbolizes his feeling of inadequacy, P$\overline{2}$].

Person: The malproportion throughout the Person is general, obvious, and great [savage caricaturing of a fellowman, and through him, of people in general, P$\overline{3}$].

III.   Perspective

General: The disorganization of the spatial relationship of the details illustrates the "segmentalism" of detail presentation which is almost never found in the absence of an organic disturbance. There are, for example, for the *House:* (1) the door placed far above the steps; (2) the door placed slightly above the windows; (3) the roof which is said to be *covering* the door is shown *below* the door; (4) the chimney suspended above the roof, P3; for the *Tree:* branches which are never attached to the trunk, and not always attached to each other, P3; for the *Person:* arms which are not attached to the trunk, P3.
　　　　　The House and the Tree are in the upper left corner of the page [regression of concept and basic insecurity, P$\overline{2}$]--one suspects that the Person would have been placed there, too, but for the fact that the Person as it does with many psychopaths, produced a hostile, aggressive reaction which permitted or engendered a different type of placement, P1.

V.   Line Quality

General: Poor motor control and excessive force were exhibited in each of three wholes ⎡evidence suggestive of the presence of organic damage, P$\overline{2}$⎤.

VI. Criticality

General: The marked diminution of the critical faculty is pathognomonic of organic disturbance, since S. G. obviously is not psychotic, ⎡P$\overline{3}$⎤.

VII. Attitude

General: He expressed freely and frankly his wholehearted distaste for the entire task ⎡as stated elsewhere, "work" is abhorrent to him, P$\overline{2}$⎤.

IX. Comments

A. Drawing Phase
House: The few comments that he made while he was drawing indicated a recognition of his inadequacy, with some feeling of frustration at his inability to perform better ⎡organic impotence, P$\overline{2}$⎤.

Person: While he was drawing the Person, he launched into a lengthy, irrelevant, but well worded account of his trip to the New York World's Fair ⎡the marked disparity between the concept quality of his verbal comments and his drawings, favoring the verbal, suggests the presence of a major organic component, P$\overline{2}$⎤.

B. Post—Drawing
House: Mr. G's comments revealed an inferior grasp of reality ⎡intellectual deterioration, P$\overline{2}$⎤.

Tree: (1) He described his Tree as a delicate Tree needing much personal care and attention ⎡he feels that he deserves kind and painstaking care by others; that a parasitic existence is his right, P$\overline{2}$⎤. (2) In answer to T7, and in justification of his statement that the Tree looked more like a woman than a man, he said, "The hair on top of the head or along under the arms and other places" ⎡from one of his prior intelegince level and cultural background such a statement strongly suggests intellectual deterioration and psychosexual confusion, P$\overline{2}$⎤. (3) The weather about the Tree was said to be bitter cold; a wind of gale proportions was blowing and probably would damage the Tree ⎡the environment is cold, hostile, oppressive, P$\overline{2}$⎤. (4) While he was being questioned in the P—D—I, he wrote *Elberta* under his Tree ⎡he has a compulsive need to structure the situation, P$\overline{2}$⎤.

General: His P—D—I was seasoned with many spontaneous, irrelevant, and lengthy comments [The S constantly attempted to impress the examiner with his wide range of information, P2̅].

C. Associations

House: Mr. G's House reminded him, among other things, of his many drinking bouts [by degrading himself he expressed aggression toward his family, P2̅].

Person: His Person made him think, among other things, of a friend whom he had once fought and whose eyes he said he had blackened, after which it was easier to distinguish the friend from the friend's twin brother [S. G. wishes to convince someone outside his family that he is physically dangerous. In actuality he has had to be protected from the other patients, P2̅].

X.   Concepts

House: This is a small tenant house on his father's farm, a house to which he has gone many times to sober up [again he debases his family by self-degradation, P2̅].

Tree: This is a peach tree, despite the fact that his father has nearly 10,000 apple trees [a subtle expression of his freely verbalized feeling that he is not of the common herd, P1̅]. This also points up his confused psychosexuality, for the peach tree usually is regarded as definitely feminine [P2̅].

Person: The Person is a friend in delirium tremens, shouting for beer, while Mr. G. stands out of sight, also waiting for beer [the implication is that Mr. G. drinks like a gentleman. This also represents aggression against a man who is not in a hospital as Mr. G. is, P2̅].

Summary

Quantitative: At the time when S. G. attained I. Q. scores on the H—T—P in the high imbecile-low moron range, he still scored a Wechsler-Bellevue I. Q. of 94 [the Performance I. Q. was 66̅]. This disparity, since S. G. is not psychotic, strongly indicates that organic deterioration has taken place. The almost uniform depression of the scores for the disparate wholes and for Perspective, Proportion, and Details, respectively, also indicates a well-advanced mental deterioration of an organic nature.

Qualitative: S. G's H—T—P reveals the presence of the following characteristics which are typically found in the drawings of Ss with organic mental deterioration:　(1) disorganization for all three wholes [the proportional and positional relationship of the details is badly distorted]; (2) very inferior criticality; (3) poor motor control; (4) the classical, small, tortuous, one-dimensional Tree: (5) strong feelings of violence and destructiveness; (6) poor reality grasp.

In addition there are seen:　(1) sexual maladjustment; (2) strongly hostile feelings toward persons whom he holds in ill-concealed contempt [the free and frank verbal expression of which has frequently caused him difficulty]; (3) inability to form lasting, responsible, sharing, affectional relationships; (4) hostility towards his family, so strong, that he is willing to degrade himself if in so doing he can also degrade his relatives; (5) ideas of persecution; (6) delusions of grandeur.

Impression:　Psychopathic personality [post-infectional] with asocial trends; organic intellectual deterioration [chronic alcoholism].

Case 7. K. F.
History

K. F., a 50-year-old, white female, was born in a North Central State. Her family history reveals much pathology: a maternal first cousin had dementia praecox; a maternal aunt had a manic-depressive psychosis, depressed type.

She completed the 10th grade at the age of 16 years and then left school. Two years later she married; one child was born of this marriage. After 6 years, she divorced her husband, then remarried almost immediately. Her second marriage also ended in divorce, but only after 19 years. Her second husband was a chronic alcoholic.

Her childhood is said to have been uneventful. But at adolescence, she is reported as having been nervous, irritable and unstable, given to temper tantrums. She was making a poor social and school adjustment.

At 35 years of age, she had her first manic episode. In 1938, '40, '43 and '45 she was again hospitalized in a manic state. During her first several institutionalizations she was treated with metrazol and electroshock. During her last period of institutionalization, electro-shock, Reiter type, and carbon dioxide therapy stabilized her so that she could be placed in family care at the State's expense. She secured a license as a cosmetician, but has been unable to maintain steady employment because of her instability, characterized by over-talkativeness, fluctuating moods, and variable work output.

Her H—T—P drawings were made several months before her release to family care, at which time she appeared to be greatly improved clinically. See Figure 16.

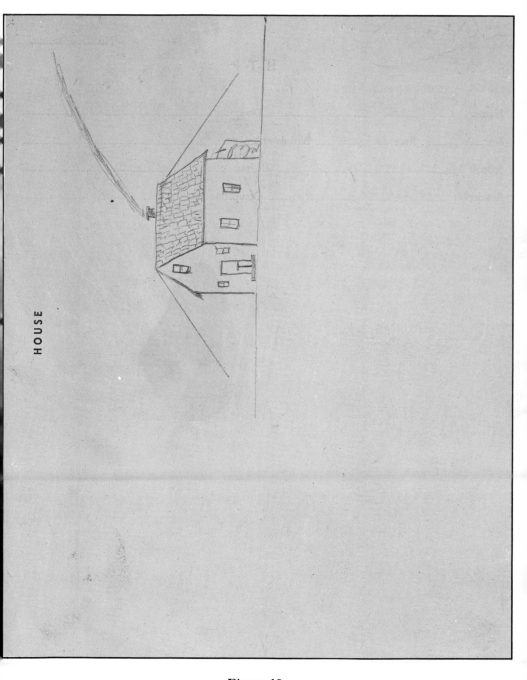

Figure 16

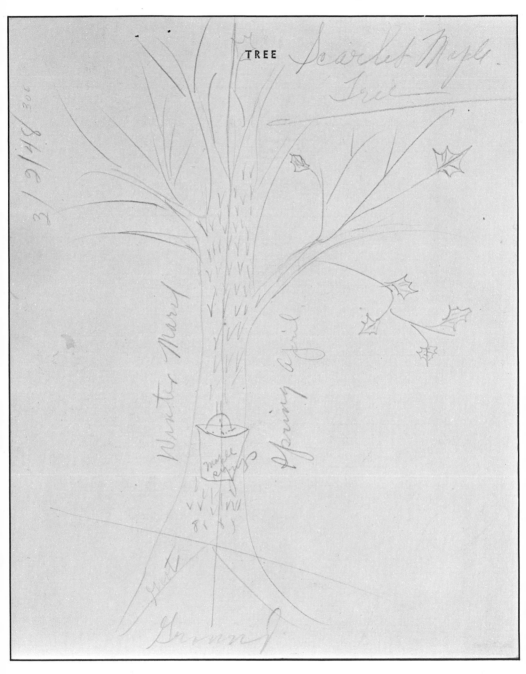

Figure 16

Figure 16

Case 7. K. F.

Quantitative Scoring

Name: *K. F.*   Date: *1948*   Examiner: *K. W.*

Sex: *Female;*   Age: *50*   Occupation: *Cosmetician*   Marital Status: *Divorced*

HOUSE	TREE	PERSON	RECAPITULATION		
Details	Details	Details	Raw:	D—5 A—30 S—8	
100 (6)_ S1	201____ S1	300 II(b)_A3			
101____ S1	203 (4)_A3	301 (6)_ S1			
103____ S1	204 (3)_ A2	303 (2)_ A1		Score	I. Q.
104 (3)_ A3	205 (3)_ A3	305'(2)_ A2			
106 (2)_ S1	206 (2)_ A2	306 (3)_ A1	% Raw G:————88————110		
107 (2)—A2		307 (4)—A1	Net Weighted:————90————114		
112 (2)_ S1		308 (2)—A1	Weighted: Good: 97 ——— 115		
113 (2)_ A2		310 (3)—A3	Flaw: 7 ——— 110		
		311 (6)—A3			
		315 (4)—A1			
		316 (4)— A3			
Proportion	Proportion	Proportion	Details:	24 / 0	Ab. Av. to Sup. Sup.
119 II(b)_A2	209 II ___ A2	318 (3)_ S1			
	211 I ___ A2	319 (3)_ A2	Proportion:	8 / 1	D. Av. Av.
	212 (3)_ A1	323 II(c)_A2			
		323 III(c)A2	Perspective:	6 / 4	Av. Av.
		323 IV(b)D1			
Perspective	Perspective	Perspective	House:	9 / 0	Av. to Ab. Av. Sup.
No Score	213 (1)_D2	324 (4)_ A3			
	215 (3)_A3	326(2)(b)A1	Tree:	10 / 3	Sup. D. Av.
	216 II__ D1	329 II(c)_A3			
	216 V__ A3	330 (2)_ A3	Person:	19 / 2	Av. Ab. Av.
	217 (1)_ D1	333____ D1			

Figure 16

QUALITATIVE ANALYSIS
I. Details

House: (1) The mountain in the background is an irrelevant distant "tie-in" detail [a need for security; maternal protection, P1]. (2) There is pathoformic reinforcement of containing lines [a feeling of striving to maintain integrity, P1]. (3) The shed to the right was the last item drawn [her future role is seen as inferior, P2]. (4) There is mild emphasis on the smoke leaving the chimney [a need for a warm home and anxiety attached to the home, P1].

Tree: (1) The syrup bucket, the tap, and the sap dripping from the Tree are irrelevant nearby ornamental details [the sexual symbolism is obvious, P1]. (2) There is a vertical dividing line] this symbolizes the bisexual and "bi-moodal" splitting of her personality, P3].

Person: (1) The features are alternately masculine and feminine [confused sexual role, P2]. (2) The decorative aspects of the costume are over-stressed [narcissistic self-adornment, P2]. (3) The body, hands, and feet are markedly feminine [an attempt to deny the figure as a portrait of her estranged husband and the bisexual aspects suggested by the facial characteristics, P2]. (4) The feet are deeply shaded [anxiety about her ability to attain and maintain autonomy, P2].

II. Proportion

House: (1) The whole is small in comparison with the page's size [inadequacy in the home situation, P1]. (2) The groundline is unusually long [basic insecurity, P1].

Tree: (1) The whole is pathologically large [feeling of environmental constriction, P2]. (2) The roots are small in comparison to the trunk [basic instability indicated, with the future seen as doubtful, P2].

Person: The hands and feet are tiny [an attempt to demonstrate a basic femininity, P2].

III. Perspective

House: (1) The whole is placed in the upper right corner, a most unusual placement [a desire to suppress an unpleasant past with concomitant over-evaluation of the future; a need to exercise strong intellectual control and reject emotional responses, P2] (2) The House is distant and slightly above the observer [goal attainment unlikely, P1].

Tree: (1) The Tree is mildly paper-chopped at the top ⌈this suggests an overly aggressive attempt to secure satisfaction, P2̄⌉. (2) The whole is slightly "up" on the page ⌈striving, P1̄⌉. (3) The groundline slopes sharply down to the right ⌈the future is seen as perilous; regression is feared, P2̄⌉.

Person: The Person is "absolutely framed" ⌈rigidity in interpersonal relationships, P2̄⌉.

VI.   *Criticality*

Tree: The roots are shown below the groundline ⌈a gross reality flaw in one of her intellectual level, P3̄⌉.

IX.   *Comments*

A. Drawing Phase
          Tree: After drawing the vertical dividing line, she stated, "This side of the Tree is spring, this side is winter. This is my Tree, I'm just half and half" ⌈her reality-grasp is gravely impaired, P3̄⌉.
          Person: (1) After drawing the hair on the head, she remarked, "My husband has very blond hair hanging down in his eyes. I must have got it mixed up" ⌈strong attachment to the husband persists, P1̄⌉. (2) After drawing the lower lines of the skirt, she laughed and remarked, "This is a hermaphrodite. I've got the features of a man" ⌈confused sexuality, P2 plus⌉. (3) She followed this with, "Shall we put an Easter bonnet on her? This must be when I had my short hair" ⌈denying the initial identification and accepting self-portraiture, P1̄⌉.

          General: She wrote comments on all three drawings ⌈she has a highly pathological need to define situations precisely, P3̄⌉. In this case the S wrote her answers to the P–D–I questions on a P–D–I form which makes all the more pathological her contradictory responses to successive questions.

B.   P–D–I
          House: (1) To the question, "What is the weather like in this picture?" she wrote, "Clear sky with a few *shattered* fleece clouds ⌈an expression, through parapraxis, of the effect of her shock treatment? P2̄⌉. (2) To the question, "As you look at that House, do you get the impression that it is above you, below you, or about on a level with you?" she stated, "About me." ⌈ideas of self-reference are very strong, P2̄⌉.

          Tree: (1) Her Tree is, "Pine, scarlet maple, white maple" ⌈sexual role confusion and over-expansive concept, to put it mildly, P3̄⌉. (2) In reply to T6, she first said: "No sex," then wrote, "Woman", and stated that it was feminine, "Because a maple tree bears sap in the Spring", ⌈P2⌉. (3) In response to T23, she wrote: "God in Person, or a glimpse of of Heaven" ⌊such symbolic identification of a sap bucket is a P3 response⌋.

Person: When she was asked how she felt about her Person, she said, "Good, because it is I." ⌊Some elevation of mood is still present; the egocentricity is obvious, P2⌋.

General: Her reality grasp as indicated by her P—D—I responses concerning all three wholes is very poor ⌈P2 to P3⌉.

C.   Associations
General: Her associations for all three wholes revealed a wistful, intense longing to return to the happier, more stable days of her childhood, adolescence, and early adulthood, P1

X.   Concepts

House: She would like very much to own this House ⌊she'd have her mother live with her--two unsuccessful marriages are enough, P1⌋.

Tree: The Tree is of her age, located in yard of her psychiatrist's home ⌊subjective dependent relationship, P1⌋.

Person: The Person is herself, at the age of 25 years, in an Easter parade ⌊the "honeymoon" phase of her second marriage and prior to any frank mental breakdown, P1⌋.

General: (1) There was pathological multiplicity of "identity" for all three wholes, ⌈P2⌉. (2) The House was well-organized and the plan carefully executed until the contaminating shed was added; from then on, despite the relatively good proportional and spatial relationships of the details within the wholes, the wholes progressively became more bizarre conceptually, In the last two wholes she gave free symbolic expression of a major personality disturbance, ⌈P3⌉.

Summary

Quantitative: The H—T—P I. Q. scores suggest that Mrs. F. is functioning capably at the above average level. Analysis of the factors comprising these scores, however, reveals a relative depression of the Perspective scores and a slight diminution of score from House through Person, which leads one to suspect the presence of a minor ⌐not too serious⌐ emotional disturbance.

Qualitative: Even the most casual qualitative inspection, however, reveals that Mrs. F. is not functioning as efficiently as the quantitative scores imply. She did well up to the point at which she contaminated the House with the shed, but the content quality from then on ⌐although the drawings themselves were executed capably⌐ was too deviant for one to expect her to be able to make a long-lasting satisfactory adjustment outside a hospital.

To sum up, qualitative analysis shows: (1) a pathologically impaired grasp of reality; (2) a sexual role confusion expressed in uninhibited fashion; (3) feelings ⌐expressed symbolically and with poignant clarity⌐ of being dominated by intense emotionality, the tone of which varies sharply from time to time; (4) a highly pessimistic view of the future; (5) an "abnormal expansiveness of expression,"; (6) strong needs for security, affection, and independence; (7) mild organic mental deterioration; (8) strong feelings of self-reference.

Impression: Manic-depressive psychosis, hypomania: basic intelligence level, above average; present functional level, borderline to dull average.

Case 8.   C. D.

History

Mr. C. D. is a 23-year-old, white male, the second of four children. His mother is a dominant, aggressive woman; his father is submissive and retiring Mr. D's older brother is said to exhibit many schizoid characteristics.

C. D. graduated from college four years ago and now is a college instructor. He has always prided himself on his literary achievements, artistic ability, good taste, and splendid physique ⌐the last is wishful thinking⌐.

In the Army during World War II, he served in the Mediterranean Theatre of Operations, where he acquired a large collection of pornographic photographs. His first homosexual experience was in the Army Since then he has had more than 50 homosexual paramours; recently he was deeply attached to a well-known author.

He has had but one heterosexual experience prior to his marriage two years ago to a woman nearly 10 years his senior; a woman who is highly conventional, socially stereotyped, and affect-starved. After three months, Mr. D..ceased trying to make a satisfactory heterosexual adjustment. When these H−T−P drawings were made, he was seriously contemplating separation from his wife.

An outstanding characteristic is Mr. D's very strong sensual appetites; attempts to satisfy these appetites have dominated his life. At times he shows moments of very painful insight.

See Figure 17.

QUALITATIVE ANALYSIS
I.   Details

House: (1) There are large clouds in the background ⌈mild, generalized anxiety, P1⌋. (2) There is over-emphasis on the windows ⌈orifice fixation, P2⌋. (3) There is an unusual number of windows in his bedroom--the room over the porch—⌈exhibitionistic tendencies, P2⌋. (4) No door is seen. C D. said that the door was on the left of the porch ⌈he makes contacts on his own terms only, P2⌋.

Person: (1) The deeply shaded lines at hip level are said by the S to be "pockets" ⌈sexual conflict, P2⌋. (2) The feet are heavily shaded ⌈anxiety concerning mobility; he feels trapped as a husband, P2⌋. (3) The head was the last item drawn ⌈a reluctance to identify what he later called a self-portrait; definite body-consciousness; and an attempt to deny phantasy drives, P2⌋. (4) The hands are poorly drawn ⌈a feeling of inability to cope with the environment; also a possible source of guilt feeling, P2⌋.

II.   Proportion

House: The House is small in comparison to the form page ⌈inadequacy in "home" situations in general and rejection of his marital status in particular, P1⌋.

Tree: The branch structure is too large in proportion to the trunk ⌈his satisfaction-seeking attempts imperil his personality balance, P2⌋.

Person: C. D. first drew only a high head with hostile, glaring eyes and a large sensuous mouth ⌈a negativistic insistence upon doing as he pleases, P2⌋. When the examiner repeated the original instruction to draw the whole Person, the S erased the large head and drew the relatively tiny figure ⌈a feeling of inferiority in interpersonal relations in general presumably enhanced by his present marital maladjustment, P2⌋.

III.   Perspective

House: (1) The House is placed high on the page ⌈a feeling of striving for an apparently unattainable goal, P2⌋. (2) It is high above and distant from the observer ⌈he has a strong desire to withdraw, to remain in aloof

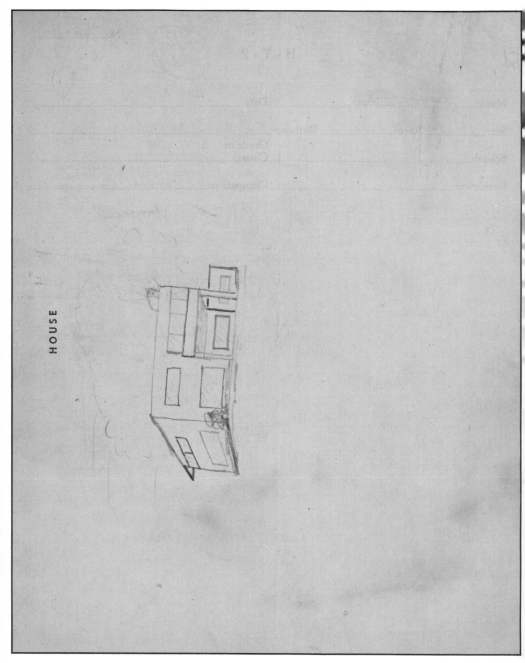

Figure 17

TREE

Figure 17

PERSON

Figure 17

Case 8. C. D.

Quantitative Scoring

Name: *C. D.*   Date: *1946*   Examiner: *S. L.*

Sex: *Male*   Age: *23*   Occupation: *Teacher*   Marital Status: *Married*

HOUSE	TREE	PERSON	RECAPITULATION		

Details	Details	Details			
100 (5)_ A3	201 ____ S1	300 II(a)_A1	Raw:	D —— 9 A —— 23 S —— 5	
104 (3)_ A3	202 ——— S1	301 (4)_ A1			
107 (2)_ A2	203 (4)_ A3	306 (3)_ A1			
111 (2)_ S2	204 (5) —A3	307 (4)—A1		Score	I. Q.
113 (2) —A2	205 (5) —A3	308 (2) —A1			
115 ——— S2	206 (5) —A3	310 (2) —D1	% Raw G:———————76 ———— 93		
		311 (3)—D1	Net Weighted:———·62 ———— 99		
		315 (3)—D1	Weighted: $\frac{Good:}{Flaw:}$	$\frac{71}{9}$	$\frac{98}{103}$
		316 (4)_A3			

Proportion	Proportion	Proportion			
119 II(b)-A2	209 II— A2	318 (1)_ D1	Details:	$\frac{18}{3}$	Av. to Ab. Av. Av. to Ab. Av.
	212 (3)—A1	319 (2)—A1			
		323 II(a)_D1	Proportion:	$\frac{6}{2}$	Mor. D. Av.
		323 III(c)A2			
		323 IV(d)A3			
			Perspective:	$\frac{4}{4}$	Mor. Av.

Perspective	Perspective	Perspective			
127 (2)_ S1	215 (3)_ A3	324 (4)_ A3			
131 II—D1	216 V(a).D1	326(1)(c)A2	House:	$\frac{8}{1}$	Av. to Ab. Av. Sup.
		329 II(a)_D1			
		333- D1, D1	Tree:	$\frac{9}{1}$	Sup. Sup.
			Person:	$\frac{11}{7}$	Mor. to Bord. D. Av.

Figure 17

isolation, P$\overline{2}$]. (3) The House appears to be suspended in midair [over-evaluation of the abstract with a concomitant tendency to reject the more mundane aspects of life, P$\overline{2}$]. (4) The chimney leads to a fireplace in his bedroom, over the porch, [he finds most warmth in bedroom situations; but he needs artificial warmth in his present married life, P$\overline{2}$].

Tree: (1) The Tree seems to be in process of toppling over [the S is aware of his potential personality disorganization, P$\overline{2}$], (2) Over-emphasis is placed on the branch structure to the right [over-evaluation of the future and over-emphasis on the need for intellectual control of powerful emotional drives, P$\overline{2}$]. (3) The entire Tree is heavily shaded [generalized anxiety is present, P$\overline{2}$].

Person: The Person stands with one foot tentatively thrust forward as if to test the temperature of the water before plunging in, so to speak, [a burnt-child reaction to unhappy interpersonal relationships, P$\overline{2}$].

VI.   Criticality

House: The porch pillar to the left is transparent [emotionality definitely is depressing his intellectual efficiency, P$\overline{1}$].

Person: The trousers appear to be transparent and reveal shorts [sexual preoccupation with exhibitionistic tendencies, P$\overline{2}$].

VII,   Attitude

General: At the start there was amazed incredulity, at the end some negativism, [P$\overline{1}$].

IX.   Comments

A. Drawing Phase
        The S exhibited emotionality by sighing before drawing the Tree and the Person, [P$\overline{1}$].

B. P—D—I
        Note: When these drawings were obtained, the P—D—I was just being developed; hence there is little to report.

Person: (1) In answer to, "Is that a man or a woman?" he stated vehemently, "Obviously a man!" [he is not too cetain concerning his own masculinity, P$\overline{2}$]. (2) To the question, "Who is your Person?" he said, "Me---in sloppy clothes which is what I like---" [rejection of convention,

P1]. (3) He continued with, "Sloppy dressing indicates also sloppy mind" [this remark, though not logical, indicates that he may doubt that he is the near-genius he purports to be, P1].

C. *Association*

General: The S's associations for the House and the Tree were above average in quality and revealed a wide range of interests. His comment concerning the Person was, "Mostly makes me wish I could draw better than I do, particularly human figures---so I would feel more appreciative of people when they compliment me on my art" [this self-regard is excessive, P2 to P3].

X. *Concepts*

House: He calls this a "wish-fulfillment" House [rejection of convention is patent, P1].

Tree: He has seen this pine tree on a small island in the Mediterranean and had admired it for its refusal to succumb to the elements; the wind obviously is of at least gale force [in a sense, this symbolizes his refusal to bow to the social pressure exerted against his deviant sexual activities, P2].

Person: The Person was the S himself, could be no one else [hypersubjectivity, P2].

Author's Comment: His concepts are unconventional, strongly subjective, and have high positive valence for him. The quality of his organization and presentation of these concepts, however, declined noticeably and progressively as he became increasingly emotional and negativistic.

Summary

Quantitative: His H—T—P I. Q.s are in the average range. The marked contrast between the H—T—P I. Q. scores and the Wechsler-Bellevue I. Q. of 133 indicates that Mr. D's sharp diminution in intellectual efficiency is produced by his present emotional disturbance. However, it is doubtful that his H—T—P I. Q. ever would be as high as his Wechsler I. Q.

In this case, the weighted Flaw score is higher than the weighted Good Score. This relatively higher Flaw score represents his hypercritical attitude. His use of less than the average number of factors for his score level suggests a mildly negativistic reaction to the test situation.

The marked relative reduction of both the Perspective and the Proportion scores indicates that the S is rather seriously disturbed [the organization of the House with its difficult perspective presentation and the fact that no Flaw score is more serious than a D1, rule out convincingly any possible organic involvement]. The sharp depression of the scores for the Person, while the scores for the House and the Tree remain high, suggests that interpersonal relations are the most prolific source of conflict for him.

Qualitative: C. D. exhibits: (1) strong sexual role conflict and narcissistic, exhibitionistic, oral and anal erotic tendencies; (2) feelings of almost intolerable environmental pressure; (3) over-striving against the tendency to seek immediate emotional satisfaction; (4) strong generalized anxiety; (5) a tendency to view convention and his fellowmen with contempt; (6) strong needs for autonomy, achievement, creativity.

Impression: Psychopathic personality with pathological sexuality. His basic intelligence level is above average to superior.

Case 9.   E. A.

History

E. A., a 16-year-old, white female, was seen in a Colony Mental Hygiene Clinic to which she had been referred by the County Welfare Department. Her parents had separated when she was a small child. She and her mother, a mental defective, went to live in the home of the mother's mother, a dominant woman with whom E. A. identified strongly, and upon whom she depended for emotional support.

Miss A. started school at the age of 7 years, stopped at the age of 14 years, when she was still in the third grade.

She was placed in the care of the Welfare Department when it was discovered that she was having sexual relations with boys in the community. Her adjustment to her boarding home was neither happy nor satisfying. When she was examined she was tense, mildly depressed, and expressed a strong desire to return to her grandmother's home.

See Figure 18.

QUALITATIVE ANALYSIS

I.. Details

House: The material for chimney and the paneling for the door appeared to be merely a perseveration of her method of presenting panes in the windows which had been drawn immediately before [the S1 quantitative evaluation of this "material", therefore, is highly suspect].

Person: The body and the legs are inferior in quality to the rest of the

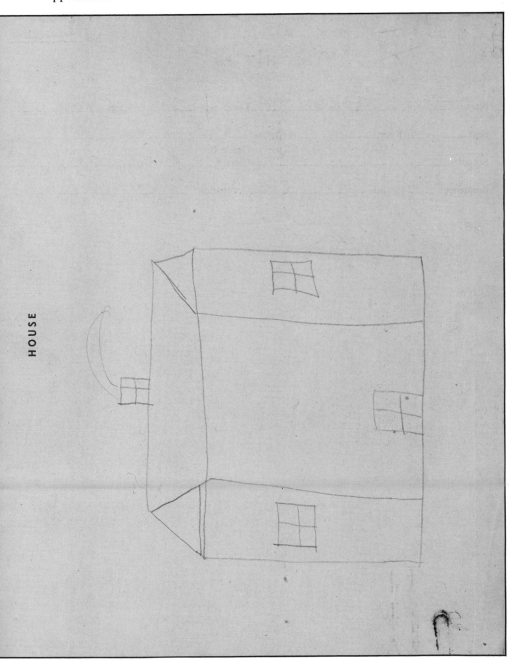

Figure 18

Figure 18

PERSON

Figure 18

Case 9. E. A.

Quantitative Scoring

Name: *E. A.*   Date: *1947*   Examiner: *S. L.*

Sex: *Female*   Age: *16*   Occupation: *None*   Marital Status: *Single*

HOUSE	TREE	PERSON	RECAPITULATION		
Details	Details	Details	Raw:	D— 18 A— 17 S— 2	
103 ____ S1	203 (3)_ A2	300 II(a)_A1			
106 (2)_ S1	204 (4)_ A2	301 (3)_ D1			
113 (2)_ A2	205 (4)_ A2	306 (3)_ A1			
	206 (3)_ A2	307 (3)_ D1		Score	I. Q.
		308 (1)_ D1			
		311 (5)_ A2	% Raw G:———— 51 ———— 64		
		315 (3)—D1	Net Weighted:——— 7 ——— 66		
		316 (1)—D2	Weighted: Good: 37——— 68 / Flaw: 30 ——— 66		
Proportion	Proportion	Proportion			
119 II(a).A1	209 II—_ A2	318 (1)_ D1	Details:	10 / 5	Bord. / D. Av.
	211 L___ A2	319 (1)_ D1			
	212 (3)_ A1	323 II(b).A1	Proportions:	5 / 4	Imb. to Mor. / Mor.
		323 III(a)D2			
		323 IV(a)D2			
Perspective	Perspective	Perspective	Perspective:	4 / 9	Mor. / Imb.
123 I—— D1	215 (3)— A3	324 (1)—D1			
127 (1)—D1	216 V(b).A1	325 (2)—D1			
130 III_ D1		326(1)(b)A1	House:	5 / 4	D. Av. / Mor. to Bord.
133 —— D3		327 (2)—D1			
134 IV_ A3		329 II(a)_D1	Tree:	9 / 0	Sup. / Sup.
		332 I—— D2			
			Person:	5 / 14	Imb. / Imb. to Mor.

Figure 18

Person ⌈guilty denial of sensual satisfaction sources, P1̄⌉.

Author's Comment: This relatively primitive detail presentation for all
three wholes is commonly seen in the H—T—P productions of the mentally
deficient.

II.   Proportion

House: (1) This is the largest of the three wholes ⌈nostalgia, P1̄⌉.
There is vertical elongation of the endwalls ⌈a proportional distortion
frequently made by mental deficients, P1̄⌉.

Tree: The size emphasis is on the lower portion of the branch structure
⌈she seeks satisfaction at the elemental, concrete level, P1̄⌉.

Person: From the standpoint of Proportion, the Person is the poorest
drawn of the three wholes ⌈fatigue plus mild depression, P2̄⌉.

III.   Perspective

House: The smoke's movement suggests that a rather strong wind is
blowing from left to right---the conventional direction ⌈she feels strong
environmental and emotional pressure, P2̄⌉. The placement relationship of
the windows and door is inferior ⌈this expresses graphically her adjustment difficulties, P2̄⌉.

Tree: (1) The Tree leans slightly to the right ⌈she attempts to repress
memories of the unpleasant past; tends to over-value the future as a satisfaction source; emotion satisfaction-seeking has been painful, too, P2̄⌉.
(2) The white space is used as implication ⌈mild hostility, P1̄⌉.

Person: The Person is drawn with the arms outspread receptively ⌈need
for affection, P1̄⌉.

General: The House, Tree, and Person are placed progressively more
to the left of the vertical center ⌈increasingly regressive tendencies are
expressed, P1̄⌉. The Person is the closest to the bottom of page ⌈psycho-
social relationships have been depressing and have been essentially
concrete, P1̄⌉.

IV.   Line Quality

Person: The line quality of the Person is inferior to that employed for
the House and the Tree ⌈emotionality aroused by associations with the

Person has reduced her intellectual control, P$\overline{2}$].

General: There is a lack of force throughout ⌈mild depression plus a generalized feeling of inadequacy, P$\overline{1}$].

IX.   Comments

A.   *Drawing Phase*
        General: Drawing phase comments were restricted almost entirely to verbal expressions of inadequacy which increased in number from the House through the Person ⌈the S shows the insightful and painful recognition of intellectual incapacity not infrequently exhibited by morons, P$\overline{1}$].

B.   *P—D—I*
        House: She would like to have her mother and grandmother live with her ⌈nostalgia, and a denial of a need for "man", P$\overline{2}$].

        Tree: Her Tree was killed several weeks ago by being hacked upon ⌈this symbolizes her feeling of being pushed about by people in her environment, P$\overline{2}$].

C.   *Associations*
        House: Home ⌈simple nostalgia; emotion was expressed clearly, P$\overline{1}$].

        Tree: (1) Christmas ⌈pleasure-starvation, P$\overline{1}$]; (2) being home ⌈nostalgia, P$\overline{1}$].

        Person: (1) A boy who ought to be in jail ⌈in effect, "He tempted me", P$\overline{2}$]. (2) She does not like the boy because he wears no clothes ⌈denial of temptation, and, in a sense, of reality also, P$\overline{2}$].

X.   Concepts

House: The House next door ⌈nostalgia---she could see it from her window at home, P$\overline{1}$].

Tree: A fir Tree in the yard of her present boarding home. It looks like a woman, because it is not very strong ⌈feeling of feminine inferiority, P$\overline{1}$]; it needs life ⌈she feels dead, in effect, P$\overline{2}$].

Person: A man about to hug a woman ⌈need for sexual satisfaction, perhaps with some envy of man's relatively free role in such situations, P$\overline{1}$].

Summary

Quantitative: There is an almost absolute uniformity of the H—T—P scores and the I. Q. score components. The Perspective, Proportion, and Details scores are typical of mental deficiency, At first glance the scores for the Tree might appear to represent an amazing potential. In appraising them, however, it must be remembered that the scores for the Tree are de- rived from raw scores; an appraisal of the raw scores in this instance reveals that their *weighted* value is dull average, not superior. This find- ing, plus the fact that the Tree is the easiest of the three wholes to draw, indicates that these scores need not be regarded as contradicting the validity of the assumption that E. A. is mentally deficient.

Qualitative: E. A. does not appear to be severely maladjusted. At this time she exhibits in relatively mild form: (1) sexual conflict, with feelings of guilt; (2) feelings of pressure from what she views as an essentially unfriendly environment; (3) nostalgia; (4) affect hunger; (5) feelings of generalized inadequacy and insecurity; (6) painful insight into her intel- lectual limitations.

Impression: Mental deficiency, familial, with a mild reactive depression. Her functional intelligence level is high moron; the potential level is borderline.

Case 10.   P. G.*
History

P. G., a 22-year-old, white male, was born in Virginia. He is the only child of his father's second marriage. He has four living half-siblings; one is dead. The youngest half-sibling is 14 years P. G.'s senior. Mr. G.'s environment was above average both economically and socially. His parents are happily adjusted despite the fact that his mother is nearly 20 years younger than his father. P. G. served three years in the Army Air Corps and at present is attending college. P. G. adjusts easily in social situations; essentially is friendly. He has attempted to compen- sate for feelings of inferiority plus self-consciousness because of his un- usual height [6 feet, 5 inches] by adopting an extraversive mask. He exhi- bits a mildly neurotic necessity to structure situations totally, even when telling simple jokes. He delights in the role of the iconoclast and defends unconventional theories stubbornly but capably. He tends to be attracted by the concrete and the tangible, to be repelled by the abstract and in- tangible. His mild egocentricity and relatively quick temper have caused him trouble at times.

See Figure 19.

---

* No relation to Case 6   (S. G.)

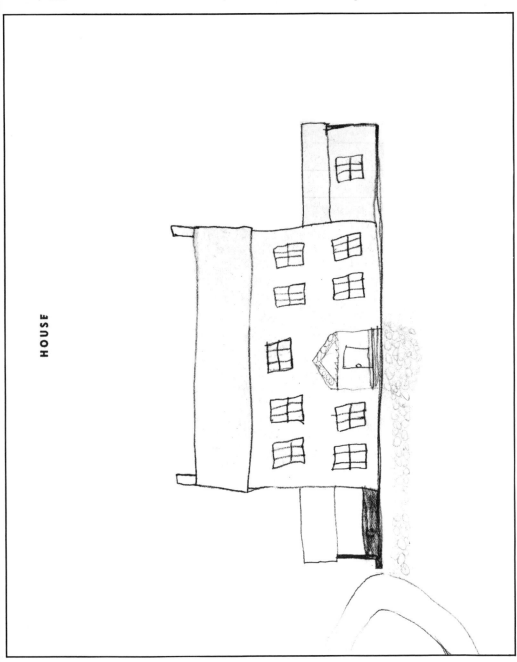

Figure 19

Figure 19

PERSON

Figure 19

Case 10. P. G.

Quantitative Scoring

Name: *P. G.*   Date: *1948*   Examiner: *M. C. H.*

Sex: *Male*   Age: *22*   Occupation: *Student* Marital Status: *Single*

HOUSE	TREE	PERSON	RECAPITULATION		

Details	Details	Details	Raw:	D—— 4 A—— 34 S—— 5	
100 (5) _ A3	201——— S1	300 II(b)- A3			
104 (3)_ A3	203 (4)_ A3	301 (5)_ A2		————————	
107 (2)_ A2	204 (5)— A3	303 (2)— A1			
111 (2)_ S2	205 (5)_ A3	304 (2)_ A3		Score	I.Q.
112 (1)—D1	206 (5) — A3	305 (2)—A2			
113 (2)—A2		306 (3)—A1	% Raw G:——————— 90 ——— 115		
114 ——— S1		307 (4)—A1	Net Weighted:——— 95 ——— 117		
		308 (2)—A1	Weighted: Good: 99——— 116		
		310 (3)_ A3	Flaw: 4——— 120		
		311 (6)—A3			
		312 —— A3			
		315 (4)— A1			
		316 (4)—A3	Details: 24/1	Ab. Av. / Ab. Av. to Sup.	

Proportion	Proportion	Proportion	Proportion: 8/2	D. Av. / D. Av.	
119 II(b)-A2	209 II——A2	318 (3)— S1			
120 (4)_ D1	211 I—— A2	319 (3)_ A2	Perspective: 7/1	Sup. / Sup.	
	212 (3) —A1	323 II(b)-A1			
		323 III(b)D1			
		323 IV(d)A3			

Perspective	Perspective	Perspective	House: 8/3	Av. / Av.	
130 III—D1	215 (3)— A3	324 (4)— A3	Tree: 10/0	Sup. / Sup.	
134 IV— A3	216 V(b)-A1	326 (2)(d)S1			
		329 II(c)-A3			
		330 (2)—A3	Person: 21/1	Ab. Av. / Ab. Av.	

Figure 19

QUALITATIVE ANALYSIS
I.   Details

House: (1) The baseline was drawn first, later reinforced several times [insecurity---this House is not yet his, P1]. (2) The 1-dimensional steps are of inferior quality [the S is not easily approached, P2]. (3) The porch to the left, which faces the road leading to the paternal home, is deeply shaded [anxiety is aroused by a desire to return to his former childhood role, P2]. (4) After drawing the wing to the right which he plans to build into a bedroom for himself and his bride, he drew the road and the rock walkway from the door to the road [this appears to symbolize the ambivalent temporal attitude of many prospective bridegrooms, P1].

Tree: The groundline was drawn first [insecurity---but not great, for it is not deeply shaded, P1].

Person: (1) There is overemphasis on the body [it is not surprising to find heightened body-consciousness in a prospective bridegroom, P1]. (2) The arm and hand were drawn last [he postponed the extended hand of friendship until the last possible moment, P1]. (3) The hand is deeply shaded [in effect this says, "Accept me as I am, with hand soiled in honest toil, or not at all"; at times, he rebels strongly against convention, P2].

General: The House and the Tree were drawn in a highly methodical, precise fashion; bottom to top, left to right [the S works most happily when he is systematic, P1]. The detail sequence for the Person was less orderly than for the House and the Tree [the S found self-portraiture to be disturbing, P1].

II.   Proportion

House: The door is slightly smaller than average [reticence, P1].

Tree: The branch structure is somewhat large in proportion to the trunk [mild overstriving, P1].

Person: The arm is somewhat too long [self consciousness, P1--he would rather manipulate 3-dimensional, objective things than deal with symbols and abstractions].

III.   Perspective

House: (1) The House is framed [mild rigidity, P1] and a little below center vertically ⌈mild depression, P1---when this House was drawn, he did not know whether he could obtain this House or not⌋. (2) The bathroom window is placed in a somewhat unusual fashion above the other four windows in the same story ⌈excessive modesty, P1⌋.

Tree: The shading used for implication is well executed ⌈examiner's comment⌋. The shading occasionally overlaps the peripheral line ⌈mild inhibitory difficulty and mild generalized anxiety, P1⌋. (3) The Tree is above center on the vertical axis ⌈mild striving, P1⌋.

Person: (1) This Person is in absolute profile, but of the "reversed" type ⌈hostility in interpersonal relationships in general is expressed by the absolute profile presentation, but the reversal of profile---patient is a dextral--indicates conscious efforts to control this hostility, P1 to P2⌋. (2) The Person is rigid, but he is leaning slightly forward with hand outstretched ⌈expressing again the S's conflict in interpersonal relationships with specific attempts to be more friendly, P1⌋.

IV.   Time

House: (1) The time consumption for the House, 10':30", is a bit excessive ⌈this reflects the strong positive valence which this home has for him, P1⌋. (2) There was an intra-whole latency of 2 minutes before he drew the road and walkway ⌈he could not deny the strong "pull" of the less demanding past, P2⌋.

Person: (1) During an initial latency of 85 seconds, so Mr. G. said later, he repressed his original impulse to draw Schmoe, the cartoon character which is never drawn in full ⌈his basic insecurity is made apparent by his need to devalue others, P1-P2⌋. (2) His total time consumption 16':30", was definitely excessive ⌈in part it may be attributed to over-acute self-consciousness, P2⌋.

V.   Line Quality

Examiner's Comment :   The line quality throughout is rather good; his control is not constrictive; the lines are fluid.

VI.   Criticality

Person: When he was asked why his Person's hand was drawn as black, he remarked that the hand was shaded to cover certain mistakes that he had made, that he felt that it was better to do this than to erase ⌈the pathoformicity of his initial inability to admit a mistake is lessened slightly by the subsequent verbalization, P1 to P$\overline{2}$].

VII.   Attitude

Examiner's Comment·   Throughout the examination, Mr. G. tried to appear to be cynically amused; ultimately he found the task mildly disturbing.

IX.   Comments

A.   *Drawing Phase*
Person: Mr. G's comments made while he was drawing the Person, revealed his sensitivity about his rather great height and showed his tendency to act the iconoclast, [P1 to P$\overline{2}$].

B.   *Post-Drawing*
Tree: (1) He saw himself faced by the old, large, strong Tree, the only one of its kind in the group [father figure, P$\overline{1}$], with the sun shining on his [the S's] back [he sees himself as the object of concern of both parents, P$\overline{1}$]. (2) He remarked that inner branches tend to die when they do not get sunshine [this symbolizes the loss of childhood illusions and his need for affection, P $\overline{1}$].

Person: (1) His initial comments on the Person indicated that he felt that such questioning was nonsensical [resentment at being asked questions, his answers to which might be too revealing, P1 to P$\overline{2}$]. (2) In reply to P19, he said, "Nothing--he should be self-sufficient" [his needs for independence and autonomy are patent, P1 to P$\overline{2}$].

C.   *Associations*
Tree: For Mr. G., Trees are simply trees, nothing else, and they suggest nothing else [he distrusts abstraction, P$\overline{1}$].

Person: To P9, he answered, "A model in a store window [only a "dummy" dresses in such stylish fashion--convention rejection, P1 to P$\overline{2}$].

X.   Concepts

House: This House is an old structure on his father's farm; it has been owned by his father's family for many years and has much sentimental and prestige value for Mr. G. [here, in socially acceptable fashion, he can establish his home without having to adapt to new and strange surroundings, P$\overline{1}$].

Tree: The similarity between the characteristics here ascribed to the Tree, and elsewhere to Mr. G's father, is marked [the S seems to identify very closely with his father, P1].

Person: Mr. G. refused to attempt to identify the Person [though the drawing actually resembles him, P2].

Examiner's Comment: There is an excess of subjectivity which might represent a potential source of danger, but one suspects that it is in large measure the heightened self-awareness of a prospective bridegroom.

Summary

Quantitative: The H–T–P I. Q. scores are in keeping with Mr. G's demonstrated intelligence level of above average to superior. The uniformly high level of the scores rules out the presence of a serious maladjustment. The relatively superior Flaw over Good weighted score appears to reflect the S's hypercritical attitude. The relatively high A-score and the comparatively low S-score and D-score connote some rigidity and concretivity. The lower level of the scores for the House in relation to the scores for the Tree and the Person appears to be accounted for by the fact that (1) the House as the first in a series of new tasks was the most difficult to draw [in turn, this connotes some inflexibility of adaptiveness]; (2) the House is the whole of greatest positive valence to him [emotions aroused by associating with it presumably interfered with its production]. There is a mild depression of the Proportion score; however, it is slight and produced by D1s only; it may be interpreted, in part, as reflecting Mr. G's slightly disturbed sense of values.

Qualitative: Mr. G. exhibits :   (1) the heightened body-consciousness and ambivalent "temporality" of the prospective bridegroom; (2) an immature, rigid view of and reaction to convention; (3) mild insecurity in interpersonal relationships to which he reacts by: (a) developing a pseudo-extroversive behavior pattern; (b) a tendency to be hypercritical; (4) a tendency to distrust the unfamiliar, the abstract, the complicated, and the sophisticated.

Impression: Above average to superior intelligence; no serious personality maladjustment.

Appendix B   Schematic Outline for the Analysis of the H-T-P [*]

By
George Mursell, Ph.D.
Rainer School
Buckley, Washington

Even the most skilled and experienced psychologist may find it impossible to keep in mind all the material necessary for a complete analysis of an H—T—P protocol. Haphazard referral to the source books of Buck, Hammer, *et al* would soon wear out the pages of their books, the patience of the clinician, and most important of all would lead the examiner to overlook many essential elements of the analysis. The following schematic outline, therefore, is provided to assist the clinician in his evaluation of the total personality picture of his client, both from drawings and P—D—Is.

I.   *Details* (parts of the whole)

     A.   *Type and Quantity* (*Relevant*--Essential and Non-essential; *Irrelevant*--Nearby and Distant; *Bizarre*).

     B.   *Presentation Method* (1-dimensional; 2-dimensional; Full-shading; Partial-shading; Positionally).

     C.   *Detail Sequence.*

     D.   *Emphasis:*

         1.   *Positive*

            (a)   emotional expression.

            (b)   deviant sequence.

---

[*]   Modified to conform to the text of this edition of the manual. (J. N. B.)

               (c) excessive erasure, reinforcement, time use.

               (d) presentation in deviant fashion.

               (e) perseveration.

               (f) verbal comment.

               (g) traumatic detailing.

    2. *Negative*

               (a) omitting essential detail.

               (b) incomplete presentation.

               (c) evasive comment or refusal to comment.

  E. *Consistency*

II. *Proportion* (size relationship)

  A. *Whole to Drawing Form Page*

    1. Whole constriction.

    2. Space constriction.

  B. *Intra-Whole* (segment to whole, segment to segment).

  C. *Consistency.*

III. *Perspective* (spatial relationships)

  A. *Whole to Page Relationships*

    1. Horizontal Axis.

    2. Vertical Axis.

    3. Drawing Form Page Quadrants.

    4. Drawing Form Page Margins.

               (a) Paper-chopping.

               (b) Paper-topping.

               (c) Paper-siding.

               (d) Paper-basing.

  B. *Whole to Viewer Relationship*

    1. Apparent Plane--Drawn Whole to Viewer.

               (a) Bird's-Eye View.

               (b) Worm's-Eve View.

    2. Apparent Physical Distance--Drawn Whole From Viewer

    3. Position of the Drawn Whole *vis-a-vis* the Viewer.

               (a) Full-face (facade, depth indicated, reversed).

               (b) Profile (partial, complete, reversed).

               (c) Deviations from Reality (perspective loss, double-perspective, triple-perspective, two-plane effect, blueprint, bizarre presentation).

      C.   *Intra-Whole*

      D.   *Transparency*

      E.   *Movement*

      F.   *Consistency*

IV.   *Time Consumption*

      A.   *Time Consumed Versus Quality of Drawing*

      B.   *Initial Latency*

      C.   *Intra-Whole Pause*

      D.   *Comment Pause*

      E.   *Consistency* (from whole to whole, or series to series).

V.   *Line Quality*

      A.   *Motor Control*

      B.   *Force Used* (general and/or specific).

      C.   *Type* (sketchy or interrupted, rigidly straight, curving).

      D.   *Consistency*

VI.   *Criticality*

      A.   *Verbal*

      B.   *Active* (abandonment, erasure without redrawing, erasure with redrawing).

      C.   *Consistency*

VII.   *Attitude Towards the Task*

      A.   *Whole Task* (willing acceptance, indifference, negativism, rejection).

      B.   *Specific Wholes* (note any variation in attitude from whole to whole).

VIII.   *Drive*

      A.   *Amount* (psychomotor increase, decrease, or fluctuation).

      B.   *Control* (ability to control emotional response to task).

      C.   *Consistency*

IX.   *Color*

      A.   *Choice* (swift, slow, vacillant).

      B.   *Application*

          1.   Method (black or brown used like pencil; shading).

          2.   Amount (number of colors, area of whole and page

shaded).

    3.   Control (shading neat or "spilled").

  C. *Conformity*

    1.   To convention (popular usage).

    2.   To reality.

  D. *Symbolism:* (interpret with greatest caution).

  E. *Consistency*

X.   *Comments*

  A. *Drawing Phase Comments*

    1.   Volume.

    2.   Relevance (superfluous, irrelevant, bizarre).

    3.   Range.

    4.   Subjectivity (self-reference).

    5.   Emotionality.

    6.   Point of occurrence (during drawing of any whole).

  B. *Post-Drawing Phase Comments*

    1.   Volume.

    2.   Relevance.

    3.   Pressure (*P* questions).

    4.   Reality (*R* questions).

    5.   Associations (*A* questions).

       (a) Number (wide individual difference possible).

       (b) Relevance.

       (c) Conventionality (note deviations).

       (d) Subjectivity.

       (e) Feeling Tone

    6.   "Life".

    7.   Movement.

    8.   Consistency.

XI. *Concepts*

  A. *Content*

    1.   *House* (as self-portrait)

       (a) S's psychosexual maturity and adjustment.

       (b) S's accessibility.

       (c) S's contact at level of reality.

       (d) S's intra-personal balance.

       (e) Degree of rigidity of S's personality.

       (f) Relative roles of psychological past and future in S's psychological field.

(g) Attitude towards family and/or S's interpretation of family's feeling towards him.

House (as other than self-portrait).

(a) Home as it is now.
(b) Home as S would like it to be.
(c) Unsatisfying home of the past.
(d) Satisfying home of the past.

2. *Tree* (as self-portrait)

(a) S's subconscious picture of himself in relation to his psychological field in general.
(b) S's subconscious picture of his development.
(c) S's psychosexual level.
(d) S's contact with reality.
(e) S's feeling of intra-personal balance.

Tree (as someone other than S)

(a) Usually Person most liked or disliked.

3. *Person* (as a self-portrait)

(a) S as he now is.
(b) S as he now feels.
(c) S as he would like to be.
(d) S's concept of his sexual role.
(e) S's attitude towards inter-personal relationships in general.
(f) S's attitude towards a specific inter-personal relationship.
(g) Certain specific fears, obsessive beliefs, etc.

Person (other than as a self-portrait)

(a) The person in the S's environment whom the S most likes.
(b) The person in the S's environment whom the S most dislikes.
(c) A person toward whom the S has ambivalent feelings.

B. *Conventionality*

1. Unusual concept.
2. Unconventional concept
3. Pathological concept.

C. *Subjectivity*

D. *Multiplicity*

E. *Valence*

      F.   *Organization*

      G.   *Consistency*

XII.   *Summary*

      A.   *Test Situation Observations*

          1.   Cooperativeness.

          2.   Stress Symptoms.

          3.   Physical disabilities.

          4.   Mannerisms.

          5.   Attention span.

          6.   Empathy.

          7.   Reaction time.

          8.   Orientation.

      B.   *Intelligence*

          1.   H−T−P derived II.Q.s.

          2.   Present H−T−P I. Q.−indicated functional level and basic intelligence level as measured by internal comparisons of H−T−P factors.

          3.   H−T−P I. Q.s versus structured I. Q.s

          4.   Artifacts affecting H−T−P I. Q.s

          5.   Evidence of concrete thinking.

      C.   *Affect*

          1.   Tone.

          2.   Intensity.

          3.   Appropriateness.

          4.   Control.

          5.   Consistency.

      D.   *Verbalizations*

          1.   Flow.

          2.   Spontaneity.

          3.   Modulation.

          4.   Idea content.

      E.   *Drive*

          1.   Level.

          2.   Control.

          3.   Consistency.

      F.   *Psychosexual*

          1.   Satisfaction levels and their relative dominance.

          2.   Conflicts and their probable sources.

      G.   *Inter-environmental*

    1. *Satisfaction sources*
       (a) reality-fantasy.
       (b) extratensive-intratensive.
       (c) extracathection-intracthection.
       (d) range
    2. *Goals*
       (a) attainability
       (b) intensity.
    3. *Temporal dominance*
    4. *Adaptability*
    5. *Accessibility*

H. *Inter-personal relationships*
    1. *Intra-familial*
       (a) affective tone.
       (b) intensity.
       (c) permanence.
       (d) flexibility.
       (e) identification.
       (f) felt-role within the family.
    2. *Extra-familial*
       (a) affective tone.
       (b) intensity.
       (c) permanence.
       (d) flexibility.
       (e) parental-substitute reaction.
       (f) felt-role within society.

I. *Intra-personal balance*

J. *Major needs*

K. *Major assets*

L. *Impression* (diagnosis)

M. *Prognosis* (make with greatest caution)

INDEX